LIGHTHOUSES
OF THE
FLORIDA
KEYS

LIGHTHOUSES OF THE FLORIDA KEYS

Love Dean

Pineapple Press, Inc.
Sarasota, Florida

Inquiries should be addressed to:
Pineapple Press, Inc.
P.O. Box 3899
Sarasota, Florida 34230

Library of Congress Cataloging-in-Publication Data

Dean, Love.
    Lighthouses of the Florida Keys / by Love Dean. — 1st ed.
       p.   cm.
    Includes bibliographical references and index.
    ISBN 1-56164-160-X (hardcover ; alk. paper). — ISBN 1-56164-165-0
    (pbk. : alk. paper)
       1. Lighthouses—Florida—Florida Keys.   2. Florida Keys (Fla.)—History
    I. Title.
    VK1024.F6D43 1998
    387.1'55'0975941—dc21   98-20541
                                                                              CIP

First Edition
10 9 8 7 6 5 4 3 2 1

Design and composition by E.T. Lowe Publishing Company, Nashville, Tennessee
Printed by Edward Brothers, Lillington, North Carolina

For Philip M. Winslow, M.D.

ACKNOWLEDGMENTS

It gives me great pleasure to thank all those who have helped me in the preparation of this most recent edition: Wright Langley, Jim Klupper, George Born, Dixie Lee Nims, and Nora Denslow. Once again I am indebted to the United States Coast Guard Aids to Navigation (ATON) personnel, Seventh Coast Guard District, Miami, for their gracious and generous help. Special recognition and thanks are due to Captain Walter S. Miller, Lt. Dave Series, Chief Richard "Beau" Lewis, Lt. Christopher Shivery, and Public Affairs Specialists Veronica Bandrowsky and Jeff Hall. I also want to thank Chief Charlie Pantelakos and Ray Potter, BM2, Aids to Navigation Team (ANT), Key West.

I am especially pleased to acknowledge the help given me by F. Ross Holland. This book would not have been possible without the efforts and support of June Cussen at Pineapple Press.

CONTENTS

Foreword by F. Ross Holland Jr.   11

Introduction   13

1. Cape Florida Lighthouse (1825)   33

2. Key West Lighthouse (1826)   49

3. Dry Tortugas   71

   Lighthouse on Garden Key (1826)

   Lighthouse on Loggerhead Key (1858)

4. Sand Key Lighthouse (1827)   103

5. Carysfort Reef Lighthouse (1852)   127

6. Northwest Passage Lighthouse (1855)   165

7. Sombrero Key Lighthouse (1858)   181

8. Alligator Reef Lighthouse (1873)   201

9. Fowey Rocks Lighthouse (1878)   221

10. American Shoal Lighthouse (1880)   237

11. Rebecca Shoal Lighthouse (1886)   255

Notes   269

Index   294

FOREWORD

The lighthouses and the marine environment of the Florida Keys have been significantly affected by events that have occurred since the 1982 publication of Love Dean's book *Reef Lights—Seaswept Lighthouses of the Florida Keys*. One of the most notable is the increasing interest throughout the United States in preserving our country's beautiful and historic lighthouses. In the Florida Keys, two early nineteenth-century lighthouse stations have been restored: Cape Florida and Key West. The Cape Florida tower is regarded as south Florida's oldest standing structure, and since its extensive renovation it again functions as an active navigational aid. Although no longer active, the Key West Lighthouse, following restoration, was opened to the public in early 1989, to launch the lighthouse bicentennial.

There are six iron pile lighthouses built on the offshore coral reefs. In 1989 a potentially disastrous fire broke out in one of them—the Sand Key Lighthouse off Key West. Afterward the U.S. Coast Guard determined the structure was still serviceable. Repairing the damaged sections and scaling and repainting the wrought-iron tower has proved to be a long and difficult task. The U.S. Coast Guard expects the lighthouse to be in service sometime in 1998.

The United States Postal Service selected another Reef Light, American Shoal, to be one of four lighthouses depicted on their lighthouse series issued on April 26, 1990. The lighthouse off Lower Matecumbe Key, Alligator Reef, is now in the process of being nominated to the National Register of Historic Places, and the Carysfort Reef

Lighthouse, the oldest functioning lighthouse of its kind, is being adapted for use as the country's first offshore marine research facility.

Dean documents these and other recent changes in the Keys without neglecting historic material. This revised and expanded version of her earlier book makes the issuance of this publication doubly worthwhile. The book covers a dozen lighthouses along the southern coast of Florida—the lighthouses that were placed to guard vessels against the threatening reefs and shoals of that area.

Before the coming of the lighthouses to this part of Florida, the area was extremely hazardous for the ship captain to navigate in and around; numerous ships, from the sixteenth to the twentieth centuries, dot the bottom of the sea off the Keys, attesting to the viciousness and capriciousness of the weather and sea and to the unseen obstacles lurking just below the ocean's surface. The wreckers in the area prospered from the misfortunes of ship captains.

Dean has gone to the basic sources, including the records of the National Archives, for her revisions and information on the lighthouses she discusses. This edition reflects not only an understanding and affection for this section of the Florida coastal area but also conveys the history of some spectacular lighthouses and the mission they served and continue to serve. Moreover, the book imparts an insight into the lives of the people who manned these aids to navigation through the years, and the joys, the loneliness, the sense of duty, and the danger that was part of their everyday lives.

One comes away from this book with an appreciation of the beauty of the area and a better grasp of its dangers, and why lighthouses were and still are so critically needed in the Florida Keys.

F. Ross Holland
Author of *America's Lighthouses* and
Great American Lighthouses

INTRODUCTION

Sailing southwest and westward along the Atlantic side of the Florida Keys at night is a precarious adventure. Smaller vessels hug the treacherous coral reefs lying offshore to avoid the strong current of the Gulf Stream flowing in the opposite direction. In daylight and in clear weather, the navigator's job is made easier because of the unusual clearness and the distinct color contrasts of the seawater. The water over the reefs is light green, mottled with pale ochre and dark brown. The deep Gulf Stream water is dark blue and creates a demarcation line along the stream's shallower western edge. Between the stream and the reefs, the water is aquamarine.

At night and in storms these brilliant color guides disappear. Blackness is all around. Before the building of lighthouses along the Florida Keys, no way existed for mariners to know how close they were sailing to the reefs at night. Many a sailor taking this coastal route must have expected at any moment to hear and feel the raking of the hull by the delicate yet jagged coral growth. It was only when a guiding light appeared that sailors could be assured of a safe course.

Little is known about the early history of guiding lights, but probably as soon as boats put out to sea some type of land signal was used, even if it was nothing more than a fire kindled upon a headland. The higher a signal is placed, the farther out to sea it can be seen. Thus, thousands of years ago, people built massive towers on which fires burned constantly. During the day, smoke was visible at sea, and at night the fire's glow could be easily identified.

The first lighthouse of which written record exists is the Pharos of

The Pharos Lighthouse of Alexandria, Egypt, as pictured in John Harris's Complete Collection of Voyages and Travels, *London, 1744. Completed about 280 B.C., some archaeologists theorize the structure may have been almost 600 feet high.* (RARE BOOK ROOM, PERKINS LIBRARY, DUKE UNIVERSITY)

Alexandria. Our word *pharology* derives from Pharos and means the scientific theory and treatment of signal lights and lighthouse construction. Pharos was the name of the long, narrow island that protected the harbor of Alexandria, Egypt, from windstorms and high seas. Egyptians began building a lighthouse on this island around 300 B.C. and completed it twenty years later. No one knows exactly what the tower on Pharos looked like or how tall it was; estimates on its height range from 330 to over 450 feet. The only manmade structure higher at that time was the Great Pyramid of Cheops. Historians believe that the Pharos was the tallest structure ever built until the construction in the twentieth century of steel-framed skyscrapers.

Although mystery still surrounds the Pharos of Alexandria, historians consider it one of the seven wonders of the ancient world. In the eighth century, an earthquake toppled the lantern. In the 1100s, another earthquake left only the lower story in place. An earthquake in the 1300s completely destroyed the lighthouse.[1]

Roman seafarers considered the Pharos an important navigational aid. As the Roman Empire expanded and commerce increased, the Romans constructed light towers at their important ports of trade. Historians have identified about thirty Roman lighthouses from the Black Sea to the Atlantic Ocean built before the empire collapsed in the sixth century.[2]

When commerce declined during the Dark Ages, no new major lighthouses were built. There is documentary evidence, though, that the medieval church maintained Ecclesiastical Lights, such as the one at Hooks Point, Waterford, Ireland. The monks who kept this light in the early thirteenth century had the right to collect tolls from the ships entering the port of Waterford.[3]

The English gave impetus to the development of navigational aids when in 1565 the government created a central authority called Trinity House. This authority built and maintained navigational aids throughout Britain.[4]

During the colonial period in America, each of the colonies took responsibility for its own lighthouses. In 1716 the first permanent lighthouse in the American colonies was built on Little Brewster Island in Boston Harbor by the Massachusetts Bay Colony. Vessels using the harbor were charged a tonnage tax to provide funds for maintaining

Massachussetts Bay Colony built the first lighthouse in the American colonies in 1716, on Little Brewster Island in Boston Harbor. It was blown up by the British in 1776. The second Boston lighthouse was erected in 1783, on the site of the original tower. In 1859 the tower was raised to its present height of eighty-nine feet. (NATIONAL ARCHIVES)

the light. As the need for navigational aids in other harbors increased, colonial governments or private groups built additional lighthouses. There was no central authority responsible for the establishment or maintenance of navigational aids until after the American Revolution and the creation of the federal government.[5]

In 1789 many people felt that lighthouse construction and maintenance should continue to be supported by dues imposed on domestic and foreign commerce, similar to the policies of Great Britain and other European countries. Congress, however, believed that the lights should be as free as air because they were established not only for the interests of commerce but for the sake of humanity. The ninth law passed by Congress, and the first one to make any provision for pub-

lic works, provided that "the necessary support, maintenance and repairs of all lighthouses, beacons, buoys . . . shall be defrayed out of the
Treasury of the United States." The secretary of the treasury directed
the details of lighthouse work. Alexander Hamilton, the first secretary, took personal responsibility until 1792, when he assigned those
duties to the commissioner of revenue.[6]

By the end of the eighteenth century, there were twenty-four lighthouses in the United States, all of them built to direct ships into harbors. The oil lamps used did not have reflectors, and each of the lights
showed the same signal (characteristic): a steady glow referred to as
"fixed." Before 1781 all lighthouses had fixed lights that were difficult
to identify at night. With the invention of the revolving light, lighthouses could show periods of light and dark (eclipse) rather than a
steady glow. Lampists could set the sequence of light and eclipse for
various intervals. Every lighthouse had its own characteristic, which
provided mariners with the means of identifying each light, its place,
and purpose.[7]

In the daytime mariners can identify lighthouses by the architectural design of the structures, and light towers by the way they are
painted with a special color combination or pattern, such as stripes or
bands. Most of the early lighthouses in the United States were either
conical towers of rubble stone masonry or wooden towers erected on
the keeper's dwelling and framed into the roof of the house. The sites
chosen were generally on land, on large rock outcroppings, or on solid
rock foundations in the sea.[8]

In the 1830s Alexander Mitchell designed a lighthouse in England
that would eventually influence the design of six of the lighthouses
built in the Florida Keys. It differed from conventional lighthouses in
both architectural design and in the manner of construction. Trinity
House decided that the Thames estuary needed a navigational aid, but
this entailed building the lighthouse on a sandy seabed. At the time, it
seemed impossible to erect a tower on such a site. Nevertheless,
Mitchell invented the screwpile lighthouse built of wrought iron pilings screwed into the ground. He received a patent for his invention
in 1833. Trinity House decided to use this unique design for the
Thames estuary light, and in 1838, Mitchell and his son directed the
construction of the screwpile foundation. The keepers' quarters were

Drawing of the original Minot Ledge lighthouse built off the coast of Cohasset, Massachusetts, in 1850. Although destroyed in a storm a year later, the screwpile construction influenced the architectural design for six iron pile lighthouses off the Florida Keys. (U.S. COAST GUARD PHOTO, NATIONAL ARCHIVES)

built over the iron pile base with the lantern placed on top of the structure. Completed in 1841, the Maplin Sand Lighthouse was the first of its kind.[9]

This innovative design had important implications for the expansion of navigational aids in Europe and the United States. In 1845 the United States government sent two naval officers abroad to study lighthouses in Europe. They were able to examine Mitchell's screwpile structure as well as study lamps and lenses. The officers' report on the advanced European designs for lighthouses and lighting gave new impulse to the Lighthouse Service in the United States.[10]

In 1847 Congress made an appropriation for the construction of the first iron pile lighthouse in the United States. A dangerous ledge off the coast of Cohasset, Massachusetts, seventeen miles southeast of Boston Harbor, needed a navigational marker. The ledge, known as Minot's Ledge, was visible only at low tide. Vessels often ran aground there, especially during a strong northwest blow, as they attempted to sail into Boston Harbor. The difficulties of constructing a masonry tower on the ledge seemed insurmountable. Captain William H. Swift of the U.S. Corps of Topographical Engineers suggested an iron pile lighthouse for the ocean site.

Workmen could work at the submarine site only in calm weather and at low tide. They drilled five-foot holes to accommodate the nine iron legs—one hole in the center, the others on the periphery. The workmen cemented the piles in place. The pilings formed an octagon twenty-five feet in diameter at the bottom and fourteen feet at the top. The men built the keepers' dwelling within this iron frame thirty-eight feet above the sea. The lantern at the top of the structure was seventy-eight feet above the base. Diagonal crossbracing connected and strengthened the pilings, but the engineer felt the lower bracing was unnecessary.[11]

Shortly after the light went into service in 1850, the principal keeper questioned the stability of the tower. When the engineer took no action to add the omitted bracing, the keeper resigned. Soon afterward, a violent storm raged along the northeast coast and swept the Minot's Ledge Lighthouse out to sea. All that was left of the structure were stubs of iron piles. The piles had broken at the juncture where the lower bracing should have been. Both keepers drowned.[12]

Commodore David Porter arrived on the island of Key West in 1823 to take command of the naval station and the West Indies Squadron. It was his responsibility to bring an end to piracy off the Florida Keys and in the Caribbean. (MONROE COUNTY PUBLIC LIBRARY)

This tragedy did not change the plans for constructing future iron pile lights. Two years later, Major Hartmann Bache, U.S. Army Corps of Topographical Engineers, initiated and directed the erection of a similar screwpile lighthouse at Brandywine Shoal in Delaware Bay, eight miles from the ocean. Major Bache originally surveyed the area for a lighthouse in 1834. Alexander Mitchell, the designer of the iron pile design, came from England to act as consultant during the construction of the forty-six-foot structure. It took two years to build the Brandywine Shoal Light, and it cost $53,317. Equipping the light with a third-order Fresnel lens, a type of lens designed by Augustine Jean Fresnel (pronounced fruh-NELLE) in 1823, required a special act of Congress. The keeper lit the light for the first time on the night of October 28, 1850.[13]

As early as 1848 Congress approved funding for an iron screwpile lighthouse on Carysfort Reef off Key Largo in the Florida Keys. Lieutenant David D. Porter, U.S. Navy, commanding the U.S. mail steamer *Georgia*, recognized the merits of these types of lighthouses and recommended them to mark the entire dangerous commercial shipping route off the Florida Keys:

> A large portion of our commerce passes daily along [this] coast, with scarcely anything to guide it; and now that our steam navigation is so rapidly increasing, and steamers have to run close [to the reef], and in all weathers, I would recommend lights to be placed on the following points: On Carysfort reef . . . New Matecumbe and Sombrero Keys. . . . Lighthouses could light the entire Florida reef nearly as well as Long Island Sound is now lighted, and the lights would be so distinctly marked that no one could possible [sic] mistake them . . . the object being to enable a vessel to get sight of a light a short time after leaving a known one, and before the current can have full effect upon her. No man can know the currents of the Gulf Stream, no matter how often he may have sailed there; consequently the necessity of having in sight some constant object. . . . The expenditure for these lights would be small in comparison with the amount of property wrecked every year. . . . No part of the coast of the United States is so badly lighted as the Florida reef.[14]

The Florida Keys had long been a menace to shipping. Early sixteenth-century charts often indicated the islands in the wrong places—sometimes closer to Cuba than to Florida, and the number of islands varied. They were called Islas de los Martires, or the Martyr Islands, a name suggesting tragedy and suffering. Perhaps the twisted appearance of the taller trees, as they appeared on the horizon, reminded Spanish sailors of the suffering bodies of martyrs; or perhaps mariners, as they sailed past the islands, recalled the many ships destroyed on the reefs and the crews lost.[15]

Ponce de León discovered the dangerous but advantageous sea route between the Keys and the Bahamas. After Spain established colonies in Central and South America, the riches of the New World began to pour back to Spain and into the rest of Europe by way of the Bahama Channel and the Gulf Stream. For centuries, the Spanish shipped the treasures of the Indies first to Havana and then past the Islas de los Martires. Vessels laden with copper, silver, gold, tobacco, and indigo used the swift current of the Gulf Stream passage to speed them on their homeward voyage. There were no lights to guide ships past the coral reefs. The captains and navigators knew the position of the reefs and tried to give them plenty of sea room, but they were helpless during violent storms and hurricanes. Through the years, countless Spanish ships were damaged or destroyed on the reefs—their cargoes of treasures and lives lost at sea.

Storms and reefs were not the only dangers along the Florida coast. As commerce increased, pirates established themselves throughout the Keys, the Bahamas, and the West Indies. The pirates showed no discrimination; they plundered Spanish, French, English, and American vessels. In the Bahamas, New Providence became an ideal base from which the pirates operated. On July 24, 1718, Woodes Rodgers arrived on the island with a group of colonists sent by England. These were brave settlers, for there were over a thousand pirates in port at the time and probably two thousand operating out of Nassau. As governor, Rodgers tried to encourage the pirates to become settlers and offered pardons as well as a free plot of land to all who would give up piracy. Six hundred men accepted his offer. Yet there remained many thousand pirates operating from Cuba to Florida in the early 1800s.[16]

When the United States acquired the Louisiana Territory in 1803, new ports developed along the Gulf Coast, and the Florida Straits became one of the busiest shipping routes in the world. Flatboats carried lumber, livestock, and farm produce from inland states down the Mississippi River. From New Orleans, sailing vessels transported the bounties of the new territory to Eastern seacoast ports and to Europe. All the ships sailed along the dangerous coast of the Florida Keys, vulnerable to piracy and to the navigational hazards of the reefs. Wrecks abounded. Salvaging, referred to as "wrecking," became almost as lucrative as piracy.[17]

In 1819, when Spain ceded all of Spanish Florida to the United States, families from some New England and Southern states arrived on the island of Cayo Hueso (Key West). The men came to fish; the fishing was excellent—and so were the salvaging opportunities. John Watson Simonton, a businessman who made frequent voyages between Havana, New Orleans, and New York, was quick to recognize the need for an American base for the wreckers (the word referred to both the vessels employed in salvaging and to the men who worked on such vessels). After the United States ratified the treaty for Florida with Spain in 1821, Simonton realized that the small island would be ideal as a wrecking center. He believed it was "the only eligible situation for a depot of wrecked property on the whole coast of Florida."[18]

Key West, located strategically near the Gulf of Mexico, the Florida Straits, and the Gulf Stream, had a natural harbor. It was the only deep, protected harbor south of Charleston, South Carolina. In 1821 Simonton purchased the island of Key West. Construction of houses, stores, wharves, and warehouses quickly began in preparation for receiving salvaged goods and repairing and refitting salvaged vessels.[19]

On May 7, 1822, Congress appropriated $6,000 for making a survey of the coast of Florida, including the Florida Keys and Key West. As a result of the survey, Secretary of the Navy Smith Thompson reported to President James Monroe:

> There can be no doubt of the importance of this island [Key West]. . . . From the peculiar dangers of navigation along the coast and among the Florida Keys, our merchant vessels are frequently driven by distress, to seek a harbor, and, for want of one in our own waters, are under the necessity of making a port in the Island of Cuba, which subjects them to considerable additional expense. This island also, affords a very eligible depot for wrecked property, which is highly necessary and advantageous, where the navigation is attended with so many dangers and difficulties. We are, at this time . . . dependent on the wreckers of New Providence, for the protection of our property in case of shipwreck. . . . This island [Key West] is considered so convenient a place of rendezvous for our public vessels on the West Indies Station, that it is intended to make it a depot for provisions and supplies, for the expedition against the pirates, lately authorized by Congress.[20]

Nine days before Thompson's report, Congress had appropriated funds for an additional naval force for the suppression of piracy. The stated purpose of this act was to afford "effectual protection to the citizens and commerce of the United States in the Gulf of Mexico and the seas and territories adjacent." The government designated Key

West (also called at this time Thompson's Island, for the secretary of the Navy) a naval base and depot. In 1822 the government placed Commodore David Porter in command of the station and the West Indies Squadron. It was up to him to expurgate piracy from the Keys and the Caribbean.[21]

Congress supported plans for establishing Key West as a wrecking center, but did nothing to mark the important harbor or the reefs, which were a major hazard to navigation. Companies, merchants, and foreign governments, as well as the owners and operators of ships, began to demand navigational aids and more accurate charts for the entire southeastern coast, particularly for the waters off the Florida Keys. The government felt the pressure, and on May 7, 1822, Congress authorized the first money for building lighthouses in the Keys.

The lighthouses were to be erected as soon as the Territory of Florida ceded the needed land to the United States. The government had chosen sites on Cape Florida and on the Dry Tortugas. Congress made appropriations for the construction of each of these lights, but made no provisions at that time for building a harbor light at Key West. However, the government did designate Key West as a port of entry and defined the Key West Collection District boundaries as extending from Cape Sable to Charlotte Bay.[22]

The emergence of Key West as a wrecking center and the development of navigational aids in the Keys were a direct result of the island's geographical location. Mariners knew that the shoal water and coral reefs, the strong currents, and the violent storms in the area created a need for both salvagers and lighthouses. When a ship ran aground or wrecked, the main hope of those aboard for personal rescue and for the salvaging of their ship and its cargo lay with the wreckers. Before Americans arrived in Key West, Bahamians, as they fished and caught turtles off the Florida coast, looked for vessels in distress. These fishermen/wreckers brought the salvaged ships and property to New Providence, where all claims were settled according to British salvage law.

As investments in salvaging businesses in Key West increased, the Americans wanted to eliminate Bahamian competition. The 1823 Florida Legislative Council called upon Congress to provide a law that would close the Florida coast to all but American wreckers. The council itself enacted a law regulating the process of awarding salvage through arbitration. Between December 1824 and December 1825, $293,333 worth of salvaged property was sold at auction at Key West. Salvage and all its related enterprises formed the basis for Key West's economy.[23]

The number of wrecks along the Keys and the loss of revenue from the transport of salvaged goods to the Bahamas began to concern Congress. In 1824 Congress made an appropriation for "a lighthouse on one of the Sambo Keys . . . a light vessel on Carysfort Reef . . . and a beacon and buoys between the Dry Tortugas and the coast of Florida." A year later Congress passed the law requested by the Florida Legislative Council, which stated that any vessel would "be forfeited if engaged in carrying any property, whatever, taken from a wreck on the coast of Florida to any foreign port." The law further specified that such property "be brought to some port of entry under the jurisdiction of the United States."[24]

Between 1825 and 1827, the government built lighthouses at Cape Florida, Key West Harbor, Sand Key, and Garden Key in the Dry Tortugas, and stationed a lightship at Carysfort Reef.[25]

As the navigational aids began lighting the coastal waters of the Keys, the *Pensacola Gazette* reported on July 29, 1826: "Employment for the wreckers diminishes daily and some of them have left the wrecking ground." This optimistic statement was without basis, for there was no noticeable decrease in the number of salvaged vessels brought to Key West or in the amount of salvage allowed by arbitration.

Salvage awarded by means of arbitration was questionable. Legal battles between salvagers and insurance companies were not infrequent. For example, in 1826, the *East Florida Herald* reported the arrest of Captain Charles Johnson, known for his extensive engagement in the wrecking business in the Keys. The arrest was made in connection with the "great number of suits brought by the insurance companies in that city, on the grounds of the illegality of the proceedings at Key West." Bringing suit in admiralty court was the underwriters' only recourse to rectify what they believed to be unfair salvage awards made through arbitration.[26]

Congress, aware of the situation and wanting to bring order and le-

Judge William Marvin served on the admiralty court in Key West from 1839 to 1863. His book, A Treatise on the Law of Wreck and Salvage, *published in 1858, had a profound influence on the development of American salvage laws.* (Monroe County Public Library)

gality to the wrecking business, passed a bill in 1826 establishing an admiralty court at Key West. Congress also empowered the judge of the court to license wrecking vessels. Florida was the only place in the United States where the federal government required salvagers to have such a license and where there were rules for wrecking. At last the salvage business was regulated by law.[27]

The first "Rule of Wrecking" required any vessel or "Master thereof, regularly employed in the business of wrecking on the coast of Florida" to be licensed. Before licensing a vessel, the judge had to be satisfied that the vessel was "seaworthy, and properly and sufficiently fitted and equipped for the business of saving property shipwrecked and in distress." To be licensed, the captain had to prove trustworthy and "innocent of any fraud or misconduct in relation to any property shipwrecked or saved on said coast." The rules and licensing, along with the salvage cases heard in admiralty court, resulted in encouraging honesty and professionalism in the salvors. Wreckers forfeited their salvage award and could lose their licenses for misconduct, em-

A wrecking license issued by the U.S. District Court, Southern District of Florida in Key West. Licenses continued to be required until the wrecking register of the court was closed in 1921. (MONROE COUNTY PUBLIC LIBRARY)

From 1848 through 1858, wreckers salvaged 618 ships along the Florida Keys. The cargoes carried by the vessels were valued at approximately $22 million. (S. G. W. BENJAMIN, *HARPER'S WEEKLY*, OCTOBER 19, 1878)

bezzlement, injury to property, fraud, negligence, or corrupting the master of the disabled vessel or its crew.[28]

The salvage award granted by the court varied from case to case, because it was not based solely on the value of the salvaged vessel and its cargo. Judge William Marvin served on the admiralty court in Key West from 1839 to 1863. Marvin said he used the award "not only as a reward to a particular salvor, but also as an inducement to others to render like services." In his book, *A Treatise on the Law of Wreck and Salvage*, Judge Marvin demonstrated that the court took into consideration the danger to the vessel in distress, and to its passengers, crew, and cargo; the value of the property involved; the skill and labor required on the part of the wreckers; and the duration of the salvage operations. Although the salvage cases involved local wreckers, the court's decisions had a broad impact and influence because the salvaged vessels and cargoes involved were from a wide variety of locations in the United States and Europe. Judge Marvin's book and his court decisions profoundly affected the development of American salvage laws.[29]

In 1848 Stephen Mallory, the collector of customs at Key West, emphasized in his report to Congress that three-fifths of the cargoes lost on the Florida reef came down the Mississippi River, and three-fourths of the vessels salvaged were owned in the Northern and Eastern states. He urged Congress to appropriate funds for a survey of the Florida reef for the purpose of compiling up-to-date hydrographic charts of the area. Mallory called the passage along the Florida Keys a "... great highway of commerce," and pointed out that along this sea route "... property of every section of our Union is afloat." He urged Congress to make every effort to ensure the route's safety and to "... remove every excuse for shipwrecks."[30]

Congress ordered another survey and new charts. In addition, in 1847 it approved appropriations for rebuilding the lighthouses destroyed in the 1846 hurricane at Key West and Sand Key. Congress also included funds for erecting a lighthouse at Carysfort Reef. During the next four decades, it made further appropriations for lighthouses. Commenting on that period, Theodore Leba Jr., chief structural engineer for the U.S. Coast Guard, wrote, "To give some idea of the treachery of this water, from 1831 to 1844 there was always work in the channel to keep fifty wrecker vessels busy. To alleviate this deplorable condition, a series of six lighthouses were constructed between 1852 and 1880 marking the Florida Reefs from Fowey Rocks to Sand Key. . . . [they] are all similar in construction, being of the wrought iron skeleton type. These sentinels of the sea are generally referred to as the Reef Lights."[31]

The establishment of the Reef Lights and the lights at Cape Florida, Rebecca Shoals, and in the Dry Tortugas was part of the Light House Board's ambitious plan for lighting the coasts of the United States. Ideally, the board wanted each coast to be "... so set with towers that the rays from their light shall meet and pass each other," and vessels sailing along the coast "... shall never be out of sight of a light, and that there shall be no dark spaces between the lights . . . From year to year the length of the dark spaces on [our] coast is lessened or expunged entirely, and the day will come when all coasts will be defined from end to end with a band of light by night and by well marked beacons by day."[32]

This was a lofty goal, for at the end of the American Revolution only two lighthouses marked the Southeastern coast: the Charleston Lighthouse, established in 1767 on Morris Island, South Carolina, and the 1773 Tybee Lighthouse near Savannah, Georgia. The entire coastline south of the Tybee Lighthouse remained unmarked for the next fifty years.[33]

The United States, in addition to establishing lights in South Florida, also erected a lighthouse at Saint Augustine in 1824 to mark the harbor entrance. The Saint Augustine light was not adequate for coastal navigation, nor was the lighthouse built in 1830 on a site east of Jacksonville. Called the Saint Johns River Lighthouse, the aid was originally built to guide vessels to the entrance of the river.

The government took no action to achieve a band of light along the Southeastern mainland coast of the United States until the construction of the lighthouse at Mosquito Inlet (Ponce de León Inlet) in 1835—and this light never functioned. Oil for the lamps had not been delivered when the light was completed, and before the oil arrived, a storm undermined the tower's foundation and it collapsed. Because of the Seminole War, the board did not attempt to rebuild the tower. It was not until 1887 that a new lighthouse was established at that site.

The sixty-five-foot navigational aid erected at Cape Canaveral was only slightly more successful. A powerful seacoast light for this prominent point had been recommended, but the one first displayed in 1848 was so ineffectual that many vessels ran up on the surrounding shoals as they searched for the light.[34]

The Jupiter Inlet Lighthouse, completed in 1860, was the most effective seacoast light in Florida outside of the Keys, but it took four years to build. Hundreds of tons of building materials needed to be off-loaded from oceangoing vessels and placed on shallow-draft boats to cross the Indian River bar and negotiate the shallow water surrounding the building site. In 1856 the Light House Board suspended work for two years because of Indian hostilities. In 1859 workmen refused to resume work on the lighthouse because of the extreme heat and the swarms of stinging insects. Two years later, after workmen completed the light, Confederate soldiers (or sympathizers) removed the illuminating apparatus. The following year Rebel forces destroyed the tower and lantern. The board could not have the light repaired until 1866.[35]

Difficult as it was to build lighthouses on land, the task was even more demanding in the Florida Keys, where engineers selected eight submarine sites for light towers. Nevertheless, the Light House Board finally realized its goal of establishing a band of light along the coast of southern Florida. The navigational aids did not, and still do not, prevent shipwrecks, although in 1921 the federal court in Key West finally closed the wrecking register.[36]

Of the twelve original lighthouses built from Cape Florida to the Dry Tortugas, seven still stand and are functioning today: Fowey Rocks, Carysfort Reef, Alligator Reef, Sombrero Key, American Shoal, Sand Key, and Dry Tortugas (on Loggerhead Key). The light-houses built at Cape Florida and at Key West replaced ones that were destroyed. The Coast Guard has discontinued the Key West Light, but the Cape Florida Light was restored and once again helps mark the sea route between Cape Florida and the Dry Tortugas. Nighttime sailing southwest and westward along the Atlantic side of the Keys remains a challenge, but the lights provide reassuring guidance. Each, with its special history, conjures in the mariner's mind the richness of the maritime heritage of the Florida Keys.

The notes for the Introduction begin on page 269.

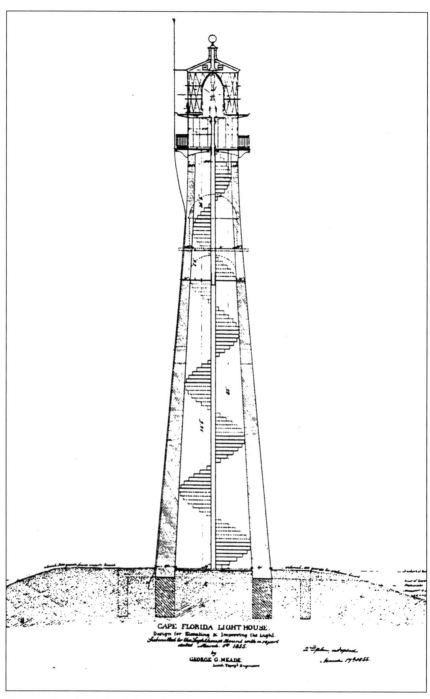

George Gordon Meade's design for elevating and improving the light tower built on Cape Florida in 1846. (NATIONAL ARCHIVES)

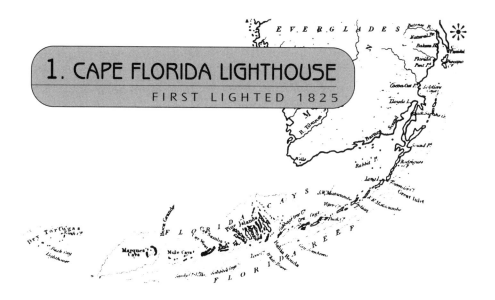

1. CAPE FLORIDA LIGHTHOUSE

FIRST LIGHTED 1825

One of the most tragic days in Florida's lighthouse history was July 23, 1836. The day started out routinely. The summer morning was hot and clear. The seas off the Cape Florida Light Station were calm. Brown pelicans soared over clear subtropical waters looking for fish. Laughing gulls screeched. The keeper, John Dubose, had gone to Key West, and John W. Thompson acted as temporary assistant keeper during Dubose's absence. Aaron Carter helped Thompson care for the station. Lighthouse reports refer to Carter, an elderly man, as temporary assistant, but he may have been Thompson's slave.[1]

Though things seemed routine, a sense of uneasiness, even fearfulness, had plagued everyone at the station since the outbreak of the Second Seminole War in 1835. The Indians had not threatened any lighthouses or lightships, but they had attacked settlements all along the Florida coast and massacred William Cooley's family on the New River. Even before the massacre, settlers on the New River, north of Miami and the lighthouse, felt unprotected and vulnerable. Many left their homes and sought refuge in the Keys. On their way, many stayed briefly at the Cape Florida Light Station before traveling farther southwest to Indian Key or Key West. The Cooley family had not made the journey to safety, but remained at their home on the river. The Indians called the area Coontihatchee because the coontie plant grew abundantly in the region. William Cooley, who arrived on the New River from Maryland in 1824, built a mill powered by the river and processed arrowroot starch from the coontie plant. Cooley shipped the starch by schooner to Key West, and from there it was transported to other American and European ports.

Cooley was a popular man in the small community. The settlers made him justice of the peace. Besides processing coontie, he was also a licensed master pilot and an appraiser of wrecked vessels and their cargoes. When the hurricane of September 1835 destroyed many of the ships along the Florida coast, Cooley was hired to salvage the *Gil Blas*, a two-hundred-ton Spanish brigantine blown ashore near Hillsboro Inlet. While he was at work on the brigantine, a group of white men killed Alibama, the Indians' old chief. As justice of the peace, Cooley took the accused men into custody. They were tried in Key West but, because of lack of evidence, the case was dismissed. The trial's outcome outraged the Indians, and they accused Cooley of withholding vital evidence.[2]

On January 6, 1836, the Indians attacked the Cooley house. Cooley was away salvaging the *Gil Blas*. The Indians killed the children's tutor, then shot Mrs. Cooley as she fled from the house carrying her baby in her arms. The bullet passed through her body, killing her and the infant. The Indians clubbed Cooley's nine-year-old son to death and shot his eleven-year-old daughter. Word of the attack reached Cooley at the wreck, and he returned home to find his family dead, his home burned to the ground, and his property plundered. Cooley buried the victims and left the New River. He joined about sixty other settlers who had fled to Cape Florida. Without provisions or arms, the settlers realized they had little chance of surviving at the light station if the Indians attacked. They sailed south to Indian Key.

The *Key West Inquirer* reported on January 11, 1836, that a boat, dispatched from Indian Key, arrived ". . . within sight of the [Cape Florida] Light House shortly after the inhabitants left there, and found on approaching the shores that the premises were already in possession of the Indians." The loss of the light at Cape Florida created a dangerous situation for mariners who did not know of its abandonment and might run aground while looking for the light at night. Cooley volunteered to return to Cape Florida and take charge of the

An artist's interpretation of the July 23, 1836, Indian attack on Cape Florida Light Station. (HISTORICAL ASSOCIATION OF SOUTHERN FLORIDA)

lighthouse. On January 23, Cooley obtained the position of temporary keeper. Five men, acting as guards, accompanied him to Cape Florida. After several weeks, the Indians moved inland and the light station no longer seemed to be in danger. Dubose returned from Key West, where he had left his family, to resume his duties as keeper, and Cooley sailed back to Indian Key.[3]

During the time Cooley served at the station, and in the five months afterwards, there was no further indication that the Indians planned to attack the lighthouse, which they called "the white man's moon." Yet as each day passed, the danger seemed more imminent. When Dubose left once again for Key West, Thompson and Carter remained at the station. They went about their duties with a feeling of foreboding. Suddenly, on the afternoon of that seemingly calm and peaceful July day, their worst nightmares took on the reality of flesh and blood. The Indians attacked. Thompson vividly recalled his agonizing experience:

About 4:00 P.M. as I was going from the kitchen to the dwelling house, I discovered a large body of Indians within twenty yards of

me, back of the kitchen. I ran for the Lighthouse, and called out to
the old Negro man that was with me to run, for the Indians were
near. At that moment, they discharged a volley of rifle balls, which
cut my clothes and hat and perforated the door in many places. We
got in, and as I was turning the key the savages had hold of the door.
I stationed the Negro at the door, with orders to let me know if they
attempted to break in. I then took my three muskets, which were
loaded with ball and buckshots, and went to the second window.
Seeing a large body of them opposite the dwelling-house, I discharged my muskets in succession among them, which put them in
some confusion; they then, for the second time began their horrid
yells.

Thompson, firing at the Indians whenever he saw one approach,
managed to keep them away from the lighthouse until dark. At night-
fall, the Indians discharged a heavy barrage of bullets. They set fire to
the door of the light tower, and the flames quickly spread, igniting a
225-gallon tank of oil. Thompson and Carter retreated to the top of
the light tower. Thompson managed to take a keg of gunpowder and
his musket to the top of the tower and then began to cut away the
stairs. The flames forced the keepers to further retreat to the two-foot-
wide outside gallery surrounding the lantern.

"The lantern was now full of flame," wrote Thompson, "the lamps
and glasses bursting and flying in all directions . . . my flesh roasting, and
to put an end to my horrible suffering I . . . threw the keg of gunpowder
down the scuttle. Instantly it exploded and shook the tower from top to
bottom. It had not the desired effect of blowing me into eternity."

The Indians had fatally wounded Carter. Thompson was about to
throw himself off the top of the lighthouse when the winds shifted and
he noticed the fire was abating. "I had to lie where I was, for I could
not walk, having received six rifle balls, three in each foot. The Indians, thinking me dead, left the lighthouse."

After loading as much plunder as they could into their canoes and
the light station's sloop, the Indians set fire to all the buildings and left.
Though the Indians were gone, Thompson expected to die, for he had
little hope of being saved. "I was almost as bad off as before; a burning
fever on me, my feet shot to pieces, no clothes to cover me, nothing to

eat or drink, a hot sun overhead, a dead man by my side, no friend near or any to expect, and placed between seventy and eighty feet from the earth with no chance of getting down. My situation was truly horrible."[4]

Thompson thought rescue was beyond hope, but at nine o'clock on the night of July 23 the U.S. Transport Schooner *Motto* was about seven miles offshore when those aboard sighted the fire at the lighthouse. The wind was light, with a strong current setting to the northward. It was not until daylight that the captain of the *Motto*, Lieutenant Thomas J. Leib, endeavored to reach the still-smoldering lighthouse. At 11:00 A.M. the *Motto* anchored in Bears Cut. In his report to Alexander J. Dallas, Esq., Commanding U.S. Naval Forces in the West Indies, Leib wrote:

> . . . hoisted out the boats, manned and armed them and steered thro [sic] the cut for the Light House. About an hour after leaving the Vessel came upon a Canoe evidently just abandoned by the Indians. . . . Took her in tow and steered for the Light House. About a mile further on took possession of a Sloop loaded with the plunder from the dwelling of the Light House. Oil Jugs &c, there was also a few bunches of fresh grapes and a hog's liver apparently not more than three hours killed . . . towed the Sloop off the Light House and anchored her to cover our landing which we effected about 5 P.M. and proceeded to the Light House where we found the Keeper still surviving on the top of the house very much burnt and his ankles and feet very much shattered with rifle balls.[5]

The men from the *Motto* were incredulous when they discovered the keeper alive and able to talk. Thompson told Lieutenant Leib that fifty or sixty Indians attacked the lighthouse about 4:00 P.M. the previous day. Leib reported that Carter was dead and had "five rifle balls in him and was so much burnt that in lifting him into his grave the skin wherever it was touched would slip from the flesh."

"We used all possible means in our power to extricate Thompson from his perilous situation, but in vain," wrote Leib. "We then went on board our boats . . . and made every preparation we could devise . . . such as making Kites &c."[6]

It was not until the next day that the men improvised a way to bring Thompson down from the top of the tower. They fired twine from their muskets, made fast to a ramrod, and Thompson was able to secure the twine and haul up a two-inch rope. Thompson recalled that two men were hoisted to the platform and "soon landed me on terra firma." Thompson, placed aboard the *Motto*, sailed to Key West where he was admitted to the hospital. The people of Key West, according to a grateful Thompson, "gave their sympathy and kind offers of anything I would wish that was in their power to bestow."

Thompson later transferred to a military hospital and reported, "I am still in the land of the living, and am now in Charleston, S.C., where every attention is paid me. Although a cripple, I can eat my allowance and walk without the use of a cane." Thompson's recovery was little short of miraculous.[7]

After the disastrous fire, Stephen Pleasonton, the government official in charge of navigational aids, sent a lighthouse inspector from Key West to examine the remains of the Cape Florida Lighthouse. The inspector discovered more than the damage caused by warring Indians—he found evidence of fraud perpetrated by the builder of the light tower. The plans for the sixty-five-foot lighthouse stipulated that the tower should have solid brick walls, five feet thick at the bottom and two feet thick at the top. The inspector, examining the crumbling walls after the Indian attack, discovered that rather than being built solidly of brick they were "hollow from the base upwards . . . one-half of the bricks and materials required to erect a solid wall were saved, to the benefit of the contractor."[8]

When Pleasonton received the inspector's findings of fraud on the contractor's part, he reported to Congress: "Every precaution was taken by this office to insure the erection of a substantial building of the first class." The contract for the lighthouses for Cape Florida, Key West, and Garden Key on the Dry Tortugas had been "entered into by Collector Dearborn of Boston, with Samuel B. Lincoln." The first shipment of materials and workmen was lost at sea. Mr. Dearborn was then "directed to appoint a respectable and suitable mechanic to proceed to Cape Florida to oversee the materials and work; and he appointed Noah Humphries, of Hingham [Massachusetts]."

Humphries verified that the builders completed the Cape Florida

Lighthouse Station and fulfilled their contract to his satisfaction: "Cape Florida, December 17, 1825. This is to certify that the lighthouse and dwelling-house on Cape Florida are finished in a workmanlike manner, agreeably to the within-written contract. Signed Noah Humphries."[9]

The bricks used in the Cape Florida light tower originally came from demolished buildings in Europe and America. Brick, because of its durability, was the favored construction material for lighthouses, which encountered harsh environmental conditions. Since there were no facilities in Florida for manufacturing bricks, sailing ships brought used bricks as ballast.[10]

The Cape Florida Lighthouse, shoddily built or not, was the first seacoast light established in Florida. A harbor light was erected in 1824 for St. Augustine, 355 miles to the north-northwest, and another harbor light at Key West was being built approximately 120 miles to the southwest. The Cape Florida Light, located on the east point of Key Biscayne, did not mark a harbor but the shallow reefs offshore. The light was built to aid coastal shipping.

By 1822 the government recognized the need for a lighthouse at Cape Florida to mark the northern extreme of the Florida reefs. Congress had endorsed the original appropriation for $16,000 on May 26, 1824. In 1837 Congress approved $10,000 for rebuilding the tower, but because of the continual Indian threat, construction could not begin for almost nine years. Cape Florida's second light tower began service on October 24, 1846. Reason Duke, who had moved to the area from Tampa, became keeper at a salary of $600 a year. Duke remained at the light until 1853.[11]

Engineers designed the new tower with a height of seventy feet, but the additional five feet seemed to do little to aid navigation. The light remained fixed, with a range of thirteen miles. However, many who used the light for navigation reported that the tower did not project the light beyond the reefs.

The problem was not only with the height of the tower but also with the power of the light. During Pleasonton's tenure as general superintendent of lights, he considered it too expensive to equip lighthouses with Fresnel lenses. After the Light House Board assumed responsibility for navigational aids in 1852, it reported, "The Cape

Florida light, marking as it does a prominent point on a most dangerous coast, should necessarily be of the most powerful illuminating apparatus. The present apparatus is composed of seventeen lamps and 21-inch reflectors . . . giving it a range of not more than thirteen nautical miles. The currents and dangerous reefs along the Florida coast, render it of absolute importance that it should be increased to the rank of a first-class sea coast light."[12]

Captain Thomas J. Heler of the ship *Shirley* out of Boston wrote Congress in 1851, "I have been many years in the coasting trade, and I have passed the Gulf of Florida more than one hundred times, and in all the time I have seen the Cape Florida light only twice." Commanders of U.S. mail steamers whose routes took them past Cape Florida had their own critical comments to make. Lieutenant H. J. Hartsterne, commanding the *Illinois*, suggested that if the light on Cape Florida were not improved, it "had better be dispensed with as the navigator is apt to run ashore looking for it." Lieutenant David Dixon Porter, commanding the *Georgia*, declared, "The Cape Florida light is a beacon for all persons to avoid . . . badly lighted and badly kept. . . . I saw a vessel ashore six miles to the southwest of it, no doubt having been deceived by the light, which I do not think can be seen six miles." Porter felt that engineers should raise the tower and extend the light's range to twenty miles.[13]

In 1853 Lieutenant George Meade, who was building the Sand Key Lighthouse at the time, also suggested that the Cape Florida tower "be raised as far as the present structure will permit. . . . I think a light iron structure could be placed on top of it, that would add twenty or thirty feet elevation to the focal plane." He suggested that a second-order Fresnel lens replace the reflectors then in use with the lamps. The next year Congress appropriated $15,000 "for elevating and fitting with the most approved illuminating apparatus for the light tower at Cape Florida." Engineers submitted the plans and estimates for the tower, and the board approved adding twenty feet to its height. In 1856 workmen completed the brickwork and surmounted the tower with an iron watch room and lantern. The board also purchased a second-order Fresnel lens for the light.[14]

The focal point of the improved light was 100 feet above sea level. In spite of these improvements, several months later the *Ellen Hood*, carrying 3,039 bales of cotton, ran up on the surrounding reefs fifteen miles north of the light. Ten wreckers with eighty men aboard removed 961 bales before they could pull the vessel off the reefs. The next year the British ship *Crown*, transporting cotton and grain, grounded on Ajax Reef near the lighthouse. Judge Marvin, who heard the salvage case in Admiralty Court in Key West, wrote, "Fifteen wrecking vessels . . . carrying 152 men, saved the ship's materials and 2,916 bales of cotton. They were employed in this service thirteen days, though they were unable to work at the wreck every day on account of the tempestuous weather. Before they could get the cotton all out, the ship broke up and went all to pieces, with 300 bales of cotton in her, which were totally lost. One of the wrecking schooners . . . while loading alongside the ship, took fire from the accidental upsetting of a lamp among the cotton and was totally consumed with 250 bales of cotton in her."[15]

Judge Marvin heard four other major salvage cases during 1859 and 1860. Each case involved ships wrecked off the Cape Florida Light. The *Ocean Star* went aground on the outer side of a reef. Marvin wrote, "The ship was in a very dangerous situation, demanding the utmost skill and care to extricate her . . . she leaked badly, requiring constant pumping on her way to this port." The *Eliza Mallory* wrecked north of the light. The ship carried 4,923 bales of cotton, each weighing 180 pounds. The water in the ship came up about two feet over the lower deck. The men salvaging the cargo dove repeatedly into the lower hold in order to save the cotton stowed there. Not long afterward, nine wrecking vessels salvaged the cargo of the *Yucatan* when the British ship sank off Cape Florida. When the *Brewster*, laden with cotton, struck the reef, it immediately began taking on water. Twelve wrecking vessels carrying 133 men were able to save the cargo, but the ship broke up on the reef. Soon after the *Brewster* sank off Cape Florida, the Light House Board received reports that "a band of lawless persons visited" the lighthouse and destroyed the lens.

The Confederate sympathizers who attacked the Cape Florida Light in 1861 wrote to the governor of Florida, Madison Starke Perry, giving an account of what had occurred: "At Cape Florida the Light being within the immediate protection of Key West and most indispensable at this time to the enemy's fleet, as well as knowing it to be useless for us to try and hold it, we determined to damage it so that it will be of no possible use to our enemies. The Keepers at Cape Florida were armed, and instructed not to surrender the Light with their lives. . . . The seizure and surrender was made at midnight of the 21st of August, while the two Keepers were in the tower, and the Iron door below bolted and locked on the inside."

The attackers lured the keepers down from the watch room by pretending to have news about supplies they were expecting from Key West. "As soon as the door opened," they reported, "we secured them as prisoners. The party being small, and having only a small Boat to return in, we concluded not to take them prisoners, they professing to be strongly in favor of the South, although they had repeatedly boasted that they would defend the Light to the last. . . . We brought away from the Cape . . . two Muskets . . . two Colt Revolvers, and three lamps and burners belonging to the Light." They also smashed the center prism of the lens.[16]

During the Civil War, the Light House Board found it impossible to have the light repaired or to obtain exact information concerning the extent of damage inflicted. The board knew from ships' reports that the light no longer functioned, but that was all. Florida had seceded from the Union and the U.S. Government no longer retained control over the Cape Florida Lighthouse. In 1863 the board sent ". . . the necessary materials for repair and a suitable illuminating apparatus to replace the one destroyed by the enemy to Key West for storage until it was . . . safe and prudent . . . to work on the light." Three years later workmen made the needed repairs and the keeper, Simeon Frow, relit the light April 15, 1866.[17]

Throughout the war, Frow had retained his designation as the keeper of the Cape Florida Light. When the Light House Board reactivated the light, Charles Howe, Collector of Customs in Key West and superintendent of lights, assigned Charles Russell and Charles F. Salas as Frow's assistants. In 1867 Frow's son John became keeper and moved with his wife, Adelaida, to the station. Two years later, another son, Joseph, became assistant keeper.[18]

In 1875 the board decided that an iron pile tower could more effectively mark the dangerous reef area off Cape Florida. The board selected a submarine site directly on a reef known as Fowey Rocks.

Cape Florida Lighthouse and keepers' house in 1901. After the light was discontinued in 1878, the area on the cape was planted with coconuts. At one time the lighthouse property was leased to the Biscayne Yacht Club, and afterwards the land was bought and sold several times. In the late 1960s plans were made for the development of the area, but Miami newspaperman Bill Baggs, along with many others, worked for the establishment of a state park that included the light station. (HISTORICAL ASSOCIATION OF SOUTHERN FLORIDA)

Although plans were under way to discontinue the Cape Florida Light, the board decided to maintain the light and the station until the completion of the Fowey Rocks Lighthouse. Workmen repaired the keeper's house; rebuilt an open square between the keeper's house and the tower, referred to as "the old piazza"; and installed new wooden gutters on the keeper's dwelling that supplied rainwater to the cistern.

The Fowey Rocks Light was first exhibited on June 15, 1878. The board discontinued the Cape Florida Light and had the lens and illuminating apparatus removed, packed, and shipped to the lighthouse depot at Staten Island, New York. Keepers Simeon and John Frow transferred to the new Fowey Rocks Lighthouse. Though the Cape Florida tower no longer displayed a light, it remained an important day mark along the South Florida coast.[19]

After 1910 the Bureau of Lighthouses did little to maintain the tower or the buildings on the property. Over the years, storms destroyed the keeper's house and the cookhouse. In 1946, Cuban José Alemán purchased Cape Florida. The location, with its natural beach and water on three sides, seemed ideal for development. In the late 1950s, real estate entrepreneurs platted the property for housing and began advertising for buyers. Bill Baggs, news editor of the *Miami News*, and many other private citizens considered the light station a historic landmark. They spearheaded a campaign to save Cape Florida and to protect the light tower, recognized as South Florida's oldest standing structure.

As a result of the outcry, Governor Haydon Burns announced in 1965 that the state would buy the Alemán property. This 510-acre parcel, together with later additions of land, became the 900-acre Bill Baggs State Park. To protect the surrounding waters, in 1968 Congress designated the area extending almost twenty miles south of Cape Florida as Biscayne National Park. The park comprises Biscayne Bay and the offshore reefs northeast and east of Elliot Key.

In the light station within Bill Baggs State Park, masons built a duplicate of the 1846 keeper's house. The two-story, Cape Cod–style house served as a museum. Workmen also reconstructed the kitchen building, the outhouse, and the cistern, helping to preserve both the natural and the historic values of the cape. In 1971 the lighthouse was listed on the National Register of Historic Places.[20] One hundred

Living room of Cape Florida Lightkeepers Cottage. (PHOTO BY MERYL NOLAN, VILLAGER)

years after the Lighthouse Board discontinued the Cape Florida Light, the Seventh Coast Guard District, Aids to Navigation (ATON) decided to activate the light once again. At night, from 1978 until 1991, near the busy port of Miami where millions of lights are shining, the Cape Florida Light could be seen from sea almost exactly as it had appeared a century before. Then in 1992 the light was once more extinguished when Hurricane Andrew severely damaged the tower and inspectors declared it unsafe for Coast Guard servicing personnel.[21]

The future of the lighthouse was in jeopardy. However, the people of Miami, the Dade Heritage Trust, and the Florida State Parks Department believed that the light tower and the station deserved preservation. The undertaking included replacing approximately 23,000 damaged bricks on both the inside and outside walls of the tower, installing a new steel interior stairway, and replacing the deteriorating cupola and lantern room. As a day mark, the color of the tower was originally white. This identifying color was restored by applying a

The Cape Florida Lighthouse and keepers' house in 1998. The light is now a privately maintained navigational aid. The station and the park are open for the benefit and enjoyment of the public. The Florida Department of Environmental Protection, Division of Recreation and Parks manages the 415-acre Bill Baggs Cape Florida State Recreation Area where the light station is located. It took contractors and volunteers eight years to restore the light station. (PHOTOGRAPH BY NORA DENSLOW)

coat of lime plaster whitewash over the bricks. On July 27, 1996, workers completed the restoration of the tower, and the Cape Florida Light functioned once again as a navigational light. The Dade Heritage Trust, in helping to finance the $1.5 million project, raised $900,000 in private contributions. Maggi Cook, executive director of the trust at the time, said, "What the Statue of Liberty is to New York, the Cape Florida Lighthouse will be to Miami."[22]

At the light station, workers refurbished the keeper's house and the small outside kitchen. The keeper's cottage now contains cultural displays depicting early island life. The re-created cookhouse serves as a theater for a video showing what life was like at the lighthouse in the 1820s.

Preservationists consider all the structures on the property, as well as the landscaping, an integral part of the overall character of a light station. Hurricane Andrew severely damaged the non-native Australian pine trees on Key Biscayne, and park officials took the opportunity to remove these exotics from the station. A 350-foot walkway, lined with coconut palms, leads to the front door of the lighthouse. Visitors may now climb the 109 cast-iron stairs and step out onto the circular gallery that offers a breathtaking 360-degree view of the ocean, southern Biscayne Bay, Key Biscayne, and the mainland. From the top of the tower, there is also a bird's-eye view of the station similar to the view keepers enjoyed in the 1850s.

The Florida Department of Environmental Protection, Division of Recreation and Parks, manages the 415-acre Bill Baggs Cape Florida State Recreation Area where the light station is located. They have restored wetlands and freshwater ponds and have planted thousands of native trees and plants on this southern tip of the cape. They have also built a walkway with interpretive signs that winds through subtropical gardens of native fruit and hardwood trees, such as Jamaica dogwood, key lime, cashew, star apple, and sour sop.[23]

The Florida State Parks Department maintains the light. ATON has assigned the light the same characteristic as it had in 1979 when it was reactivated—an isophase six-second signal. The light is on for three seconds, then off for three seconds. It has a range of seven nautical miles.[24]

The restoration of the light station took eight years. "Hundreds of volunteers poured their heart and soul—and money—into the massive effort to 'Save Our Lighthouse'," wrote Becky Roper Matkov, current executive director of Dade Heritage Trust. "Today the Cape Florida Lighthouse stands as a gleaming white beacon . . . uniting our community with its fascinating past."[25]

Not only will the Cape Florida Light Station be a symbol for Miami and Dade County, but by preserving this station and others in the country, the maritime heritage of the nation can be enjoyed and appreciated by all.

The notes for this chapter begin on page 271.

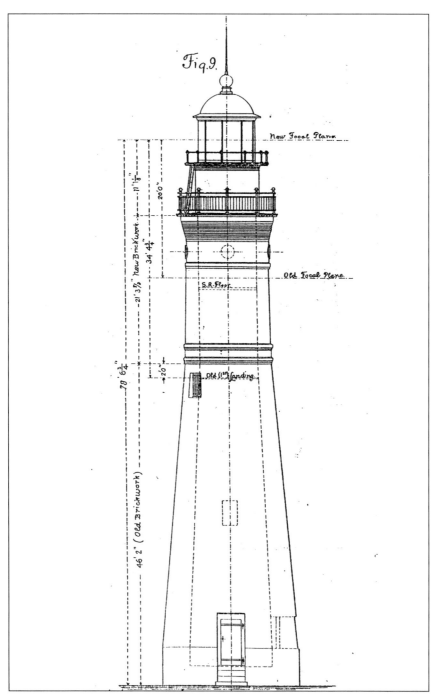

Architectural drawing of the Key West Lighthouse in 1894 after the height was increased. (NATIONAL ARCHIVES)

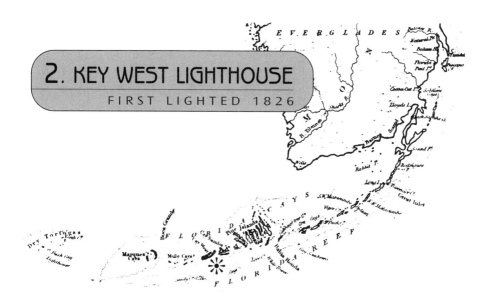

2. KEY WEST LIGHTHOUSE
FIRST LIGHTED 1826

The tiny island of Key West lies more than one hundred miles southwest of Cape Florida and only ninety miles north of Cuba. The island, about one and a half miles wide and four and a half miles long, is surrounded by the waters of the Gulf of Mexico and the Atlantic Ocean. On December 20, 1821, John W. Simonton, a wealthy New Jersey merchant, purchased Juan P. Salas's claim to the island for $2,000. Simonton was familiar with the Florida Keys and Key West (Cayo Hueso), having sailed past them many times en route to Cuba, where he had commercial interests. A shrewd businessman, Simonton quickly recognized the economic potential for the island as a wrecking center.

Fifty to sixty Bahamian vessels, and more than five hundred seamen, regularly engaged in wrecking on the Florida reefs. The salvage trade was one of the chief economic supports of the town of Nassau on the island of New Providence in the Bahamas. However, fishermen from New England ports began making wrecking voyages to the Florida Straits in 1820, and perhaps earlier. Simonton could clearly visualize the wealth gained from the business of wrecking shifting to Key West and the Americans.[1]

Two weeks before Simonton completed his purchase of the island, he wrote to Secretary of the Navy Smith Thompson suggesting that

Key West be made a port of entry. He emphasized that the island's location and harbor made it ideal for both a Naval base and a salvage depot. Five months later President James Monroe signed an executive order declaring Key West a port of entry. Establishing a Naval station and a depot for wrecked property took a bit longer.

On February 1, 1823, Thompson ordered Commodore David Porter, commanding the West Indies Squadron, to set up a base at Key West for the suppression of piracy. Porter set up the base; however, the government took no action to establish a wrecking depot. After petitioning Congress without results, the territorial Legislative Council passed a wrecking act of its own on July 4, 1823, but the act lacked authority. The *Pensacola Gazette* on February 19, 1825, reported, "Legislative Council . . . was clamoring for Federal Regulation of wrecking, spurred on, perhaps, by the fact that some of its members were shipwrecked during their passage from St. Augustine to Pensacola to attend its first session." Congress responded on March 3, 1825, by passing legislation making it illegal to transfer wrecked property salvaged on the Florida coast to any foreign port and declaring that such property would have to be landed at a designated United States port of entry. This meant that wreckers would have to bring property salvaged off the Florida Keys either to Key West or to St. Augustine, 475 nautical miles to the north of the Keys.[2]

Congress was well aware of the need for salvaging because of the hazards to navigation in the Florida Straits. After taking formal possession of Key West for the United States in 1822, Lieutenant Commander Matthew C. Perry, aboard the USS *Shark*, made a careful examination of the area. In his report to Thompson, he noted the high number of wrecks off the Keys and recommended the construction of four lighthouses. He suggested building one lighthouse at each of the extremes of the reef and two lighthouses at intermediate points. In 1824 Congress provided funds for a lightship and for constructing lighthouses at Cape Florida, in the Dry Tortugas, and "on one of the Sambo Keys." The Sambos are three islets approximately seven nautical miles from Key West harbor, on the Atlantic side of the island.[3]

Building lighthouses in such remote areas was a difficult and complicated feat. Construction materials, tools, and all the specialized parts for the lighthouses, as well as workmen, had to be shipped in from the more industrialized areas of the north. After lighthouse engineers drew up plans and specifications for the brick light tower and keeper's house, Congress designated $16,000 for a lighthouse station on the Sambos. Stephen Pleasonton, the fifth auditor of the Treasury Department, acted as the general superintendent of lighthouses. He advertised for contractors to submit bids on the construction. A Boston firm, with the lowest bid, received the contract.[4]

On August 29, 1824, a vessel carrying Samuel B. Lincoln, one of the contractors, along with workmen and a portion of the needed building materials embarked from Boston to St. Augustine. Lincoln was to meet a collector of customs there and proceed with him to determine the site for the lighthouse on the Sambo Keys.

The collectors of customs also acted as the field representatives of Pleasonton, and he designated them "superintendent of lights." Their duties included the selection of sites for lighthouses, supervision of construction contractors, and authorization of repairs. These officials, however, had little or no construction experience. The contractors were solely responsible for the design and the supervision of construction.

The collector of customs at St. Augustine awaited the arrival of the contractor's vessel, but it did not arrive on schedule. Months passed, and there was still no sign of the ship. In December, Pleasonton reported to the secretary of the Treasury. "His [Lincoln's] sureties . . . concluded that he had been lost at sea, and applied for permission to go on themselves with the work, and for an extension of time for finishing one of the Light Houses, that at Sambo Keys."[5]

On January 29, 1825, the *Pensacola Gazette* reported that the vessel was presumed lost with all persons on board. The firm obtained from the government an extension of time for completing the lighthouse. The newspaper believed that in spite of the disastrous setback the contractors would be able to meet the deadline, which Pleasonton extended to June 1825.

The contractor again assembled workmen and supplies, and the schooner *George Stodder* sailed from Boston with all aboard. The contractors planned to have the schooner remain as tender to the workmen until they completed the work. The *George Stodder* arrived in Key West on December 12, but work could not begin. The collector of customs, William Pinkney, was in St. Augustine and could not leave until a revenue cutter, sailing from Georgia, could bring him to Key West. The contractor in the meantime was paying for the schooner and the workmen while he waited for Pinkney to arrive. Impatient at the delay, he applied to Commodore Porter, who was in Key West, to designate a site on the Sambo Keys, so he could land the materials and start building the light station.[6]

Porter knew that high tides completely inundated the Sambos, and he considered them an unfit site for a permanent lighthouse. He recommended Whitehead's Point on the southern point of the island for the lighthouse station. Pinkney, finally arriving on February 8, 1825, approved the site selection. Soon after building began, the ill health of the workmen caused the contractor to postpone further construction.

When work resumed, the construction proved more difficult than anticipated. After several delays, the masons eventually completed the keeper's house and the brickwork on the tower. The structure was readied for the lantern, which was built in the north and shipped to the site. Section by section, workmen raised the lantern's parts, joined the sections, and secured the assembled lantern in place at the top of the tower. The tower, sixty-five feet tall from base to lantern, rose eighty-three feet above sea level.

Keeper Michael Mabrity first lit the lamps on January 13, 1826. At night, its fixed white light guided mariners to Key West harbor. Whale oil was the illuminant used for the fifteen lamps required for the light. During the day, the lighthouse, the tallest structure on the island, proved a readily identifiable navigational aid.

Pinkney officially appointed Barbara, Mabrity's wife, assistant keeper. Mabrity and his family originally came from St. Augustine and were among the first permanent settlers of Key West. A seafaring man, Mabrity was familiar with coastal and offshore waters and occasionally served as part-time harbor pilot. Unlike many light stations located in isolated areas, the Key West Light was situated within a growing community, and Mabrity took an active interest in local affairs. In 1828 he served on the town council.[7]

When Mabrity died in 1832, Barbara became keeper. She did not have an assistant keeper and maintained the light by herself. Three years after Mrs. Mabrity assumed her post, the first hurricane of great intensity officially recorded in the Keys occurred September 15, 16, and 17, 1835. The hurricane's unrelenting wind and the huge waves generated by the wind drove vessels up on the reefs off Key West and sank them in the harbor. Amazingly, the lighthouses at Sand Key (lit in 1827) and Key West both withstood the buffeting of the gale. Mrs. Mabrity maintained her lighthouse throughout the three days of turbulent weather. When hurricanes again swept the island in 1841 and 1842, Mrs. Mabrity again stood her post.[8]

In 1843 a group of concerned Key West citizens wrote to Stephen Pleasanton, who was in charge of lighthouse administration:

> The undersigned inhabitants of Key West respectfully call attention . . . to the circumstance that Mrs. Mabrity, the keeper of the light upon this island, has for a number of years performed the duties of her office with fidelity, and to the satisfaction . . . of the Collector and of Navigators; that she has practiced and still practices rigid economy in her mode of living and yet she has not been able to accumulate any property to support her in her old age; that she is now becoming considerably advanced in her age; that she is less able to perform the labor and endure the fatigue of her office than she has been, and that in our opinion a just appreciation of her past services, and her present situation give her an equitable claim upon the government for assistance.[9]

What Pleasonton's response was to this appeal, or if he offered Mrs. Mabrity financial help, does not appear in extant records.

On October 10, 1846, a hurricane again slashed Key West. Stephen Mallory, collector of customs, described the storm as the most destructive "of any that has ever visited these latitudes." U.S. Navy Lieutenant William C. Pease, aboard a small vessel in the harbor when the hurricane struck, reported, "The air was full of water, and no man could look windward for a second." Around his ship, the *Morris*, were ". . . wrecks of all descriptions: one ship on her beam end, three brigs dismasted, also three schooners; three vessels sunk . . . four vessels bottom up. How many persons attached to these vessels I am unable to say. We have picked up only two. The lighthouse at Key West and Sand Key washed away, and Key West is in ruins. A white sand beach

By 1838 Key West was a thriving port town. Salvaged goods were stored in large warehouses built near the harbor. More than twenty vessels were regularly engaged in the wrecking business. (MONROE COUNTY PUBLIC LIBRARY)

covers the spot where Key West lighthouse stood, and waves roll over the spot where Sand Key was."[10]

There were six people at the Sand Key Light when it collapsed, and everyone was killed. No one knows how many people took refuge at the Key West Light, but fourteen died. Miraculously, Barbara Mabrity survived.

With the Key West Lighthouse destroyed, Mallory suggested that "a temporary light be placed on Whitehead's Point. A tripod with a large signal lantern elevated thirty feet would answer the purpose until a tower can be erected." This temporary light remained in operation until another tower was built.[11]

On March 3, 1847, Congress appropriated $12,000 for the second lighthouse. Mallory selected a site on higher ground for the tower, east of the original lighthouse location. (Evidence of the foundation for the 1825 tower is still visible.) The House of Representatives Executive Documents notes: "A new site has been purchased and jurisdiction obtained; a contract been entered into with the lowest bidder and work to be completed by 1st January 1848. Price $6,975 with $2,050 for fitting up."

The government purchased almost one acre of land for the tower and keepers' dwelling from John Simonton for $200. Pleasonton awarded the firm of Smith, Keeney, and Hallowday the building contract. On November 21, 1847, construction began on the new tower and keeper's quarters. Lighthouse architects again chose brick as the building material for the tower. Brick and stone masonry were the most commonly used construction materials for light towers. The work progressed rapidly, and by January 15, 1848, the masons completed the tower. The total cost of the lighthouse construction was $7,247.77.[12]

The new tower was only fifty feet high but built substantially. Plans called for the walls at the base to be four and a half feet thick and gradually diminish to two and a half feet at the top. The diameter of the tower tapered from ten feet at the foundation to nine feet at the top where the lantern was secured. Surprisingly, the designers made no provisions for a watch room, and the iron staircase led directly to the lantern. The lantern was seven feet high. To facilitate cleaning the panes of glass in the lantern, Stephen Pleasonton stipulated that the keeper be supplied with a "stool and railing inside and out." The keeper, Mrs. Mabrity, continued to use fifteen lamps with reflectors to produce the light that retained its original fixed white characteristic showing 360 degrees.[13]

In 1849, after the carpenters completed the wooden keepers' house, Pleasonton officially announced the operation of the light station. Mrs. Mabrity, with a salary of $500 a year, moved in as soon as the house was habitable. It was a comfortable one-story building with an attic, two bedrooms, a parlor, and a dining room. Workmen built the kitchen as a separate building, following the custom of the times. This arrangement kept the living quarters cooler during the hot tropical summer months. There was also an outdoor privy. The only source of water was rain, which was collected in a 4,000-gallon brick cistern. All the buildings were painted a lead color. The lighthouse service wanted each station to have an identifiable and uniform look that would define the overall character of the station.

The service expected keepers to maintain light stations properly at all times. The keepers' jobs included keeping the light burning, trimming wicks, washing the glass panes in the lantern, polishing brass, and all the duties related to the maintenance of the lighthouse and the light. The keepers' responsibilities also included the upkeep of the grounds and the inside and the outside of all buildings on the station. Inspectors periodically inspected the stations and made thorough reports on every detail of the property's condition. The two most repeated summary comments by inspectors of the Key West Light seem to be either "Hurricane caused considerable damage to tower. Repairs made," or "The light is well kept, and the station is in good order and condition."[14]

When William Richardson became assistant keeper, lightkeeping duties became a bit easier for Mrs. Mabrity. Richardson served from 1854 to 1860, then Edwin Halseman took his place. In 1858 the Light House Board made a great improvement in the Key West Light. The board purchased a third-order Fresnel lens, had it shipped from Paris and installed within the lantern.[15]

These were politically explosive times in Key West. Historian Jefferson B. Browne wrote, "The cultivated and wealthy citizens were nearly all strongly pro Southern." On December 12, 1860, the citizens held a meeting to nominate delegates to the Florida State convention. The convention, about to assemble in Tallahassee, would convene for the purpose of voting on secession. The candidates chosen from Key West were avowed secessionists. It seemed assured that Florida would withdraw from the Union and Key West would most certainly be a part of any future confederacy along with the rest of Florida.

However, one man's action changed the role Key West was to play in the Civil War. His decision assured that the navigational lights of the Florida Keys would remain under federal control. Captain James M. Brannan of the First Artillery was stationed at the army barracks at Key West. He had written to Washington for instructions on whether he should "prevent Fort Taylor from being taken or allow the State authorities to have possession." Builders had not yet completed Fort Zachary Taylor. When Florida seceded, Brannan still had not received any orders. He decided to act on his own. Brannan proceeded to move his men through the sleeping town of Key West and occupy the fort. This act, in effect, retained Key West for the federal government. According to Browne, Key West was "the most strategic point within the Southern Confederacy. . . . [Its] being in the hands of the Federal Government during the entire war and used as a naval base, was one of the determining factors in the result of the war between the States."[16]

When hostilities began, the Light House Board reported that "a band of lawless persons" attacked the Cape Florida Light and destroyed the lens; but the lighthouses established at Carysfort Reef, Sombrero Key, Sand Key, Key West, and the Dry Tortugas remained undamaged. Some of the keepers of these lights found themselves in a political quandary, for though their sympathies lay with the South, they felt duty-bound to maintain the lights. At one time, certain citizens of Key West accused Barbara Mabrity of being loyal to the Southern cause and therefore unfit to continue as lightkeeper. She cleared herself of this charge and retained her position until 1864, when Frederick Anderson took her place.

Mrs. Mabrity died in 1867, at the age of eighty-five. She served thirty-two years on the Key West Light, and she and her husband, Michael, had spawned a dynasty of lighthouse keepers. Their granddaughter, Mary Armanda Fletcher, married John J. Carroll from New York, who became assistant keeper and then keeper of the Key West Light in 1866. Mary served as assistant keeper from 1876 until her husband's death in 1889, when the board appointed her keeper of the light. The Mabritys' daughter, Nicolosa, married Captain Joseph Bethel in 1831. Captain Bethel served first at the Dry Tortugas Station at Garden Key and then as keeper of Sombrero Key Light from 1858 to 1879. Their son, William A. Bethel, became the Key West keeper in 1889. He remained in that post until his death in 1910, when his wife, Mary Elizabeth, took over the position. The Mabrity family and their descendants were associated with lighthouses, and in particular the Key West Light, for over seventy years.[17]

There were many deaths, diseases, and dangers through the years for the keepers of the Key West Light. Records include reports on sporadic outbreaks of yellow fever, the devastating Key West fire in 1886, and the almost yearly damage to the lighthouse by severe storms and hurricanes. Although the Key West Light did not have to contend with fog obscuring the light, keepers often reported insects swarming

The Key West Lighthouse in the 1880s. In 1886 a new picket fence was put up around the station, and in 1887 a new keepers' house was built. The station was in excellent condition, but mariners believed the sixty-foot tower was not high enough to make the light as visible as it should be. (KEY WEST LIGHT- HOUSE MUSEUM)

around the lantern so thickly that mariners could barely observe the light! By 1868 the lantern was old and defective. The door to the lantern room would not shut properly and ajar it allowed the insects to invade the lantern and even the lamps.

In 1873 workmen installed a third-order lantern and raised the focal plane of the light five feet. This made a great improvement in the light's visibility. The keeper observed that "the wide sash bars of the old lantern caused a marked diminution of the brilliancy of the light in certain directions."

The Light House Board also specified improvements throughout the station. The board ordered the construction of a new cistern by "cutting out the coral rock and building inside." In the 1880s keepers whitewashed the buildings instead of painting them a lead color and put new shingles on the roof of the keepers' house. The house needed constant repairs and an inspector recommended tearing it down and building a new one "on the site of the old." Lighthouse Engineer W. H. Meuer suggested that "the Amelia Island design of Keeper's quarters with modifications be used at Key West."[18]

In 1886 J. H. Gardner signed a contract to build a new keepers' quarters for $4,975. One year later he completed the dwelling and erected a new picket fence around the reservation. The station, with its variety of structures and well-kept grounds, made a picturesque addition to the town of Key West. The townspeople enjoyed strolling by to look at the attractive keepers' quarters, the graceful light tower, the ample cistern, and the tidy wash and chicken houses. The spacious keepers' house was painted white with green shutters and had a shingle roof. It was designed to provide privacy for one keeper and two assistants and their families. Each family had a private room with a separate exit door. They shared the parlor, the dining room, and the kitchen. Lighthouse architects used this design for many keepers' houses in Florida.[19]

The first keepers to live in the new house were John Carroll and his wife Mary (the Mabritys' granddaughter). When John died of typhoid fever on March 19, 1889, Mary became keeper of the light. Three months later, she, too, died of typhoid. The next keeper, William Bethel, was another Mabrity descendant. He had served on the Alligator Reef, Dry Tortugas, Pensacola, and Northwest Passage lights

William Bethel and his family in front of the Key West Lighthouse, where he served as keeper from 1889 until his death in 1908. Bethel previously served on the lighthouses at Northwest Passage, Alligator Reef, Pensacola, and Logger-head Key in the Dry Tortugas. Born in Florida in 1839, his father Joseph Bethel was the first keeper of the Sombrero Key Lighthouse. (KEY WEST LIGHTHOUSE MUSEUM)

before his assignment to the Key West Light. As keeper the board paid him $720 a year and paid his wife Mary Elizabeth, the assistant keeper, $420. The other assistant keeper at Key West in 1889 was Henry Shanahan.[20]

In 1891 workmen completed building a storeroom and kitchen with a hip roof adjoining the main house. They also constructed a new brick oil house for storing kerosene. The superintendent of lights, John F. Horr, pronounced the station in good condition except for certain reservations he had about the height of the tower. He also observed that the area the keeper used as a watch room was so low that the keeper could not stand upright and the balcony too narrow for practical purposes. The tower, Horr said, "was not high enough to make it as conspicuous as it should be. Tall trees obstruct the view of the light from the northwest. It is an important light of the third order, and is a leading light for not less than seven different channels in the vicinity. The tower is but sixty feet high. It would be an immense improvement . . . to build up the tower about twenty feet to increase the height of the watch room section about three feet, and to provide a suitable balcony."[21]

The Light House Board estimated that it would take about a month to complete the construction (a temporary light could be set up during that time) and would cost about $4,500. Congress approved appropriations in 1893. Construction began sometime in December 1894, and masons completed the work on February 5, 1895.

In 1900 the Bethels' grandson, Stephen F. Whalton, was born in the front room of the keepers' quarters. As an adult, Whalton remembered the lighthouse as a fascinating place to grow up. "The keepers were constantly engaged in a variety of activities . . . and there was a horse and a mule at the station. The horse could wiggle an outside water pump enough to make a puddle of water from which it could drink." The mule pulled Whalton around the lighthouse station in a buggy.[22]

One of Whalton's favorite things to do as a young boy was to sleep at the top of the tall tower under the light. "The lightkeeper had to stay there to make sure nothing went wrong with the light," he explained. "I used to love to sleep there; it was so cool." Whenever there were tourists, Whalton's parents allowed him to be the official guide. The keepers kept the buildings and equipment spotless, since unannounced inspections were not unusual. "As a kid, I had the run of the place, but I knew better than to make a mess."

One of Whalton's tasks was hanging the curtains in the lantern room after the keepers extinguished the light for the day. "The curtains were hung by hand onto rings all around the lantern." The curtains protected the lens from the sun and the keeper removed them each evening before he lit the light. Besides the duties at the station, the keepers were also responsible for two range beacons, one at Fort Zachary Taylor and one at the wharf warehouse near Greene Street.

By 1908 the Light House Board had introduced incandescent oil vapor (i.o.v.) as the illuminant for the Key West Light. The board considered the i.o.v. system a strong rival of electricity and acetylene gas and selected Key West as one of the first lighthouses to have the system installed. By 1910 about forty-four stations were using i.o.v. lamps. The lamps used kerosene that was forced, under pressure, into a vaporizing chamber. The vapor then passed through a series of small holes where it was ignited by a Bunsen burner. The mantle, when placed over the flame, became white-hot and produced a light that was eight to ten times brighter than that achieved with an ordinary kerosene-wick lamp.

Whalton recalled that the i.o.v. system at Key West was initially difficult to use. There were two tanks, one with kerosene and one with compressed air, which were mixed in the line leading to the lamp. Evidently, there were several leaks in the line that were difficult for the keepers to locate. After the keepers solved the problems, Whalton agreed that the new illuminant burned much brighter than the kerosene.[23]

In 1909 a hurricane lashed Key West. Whalton, with his father, grandfather, and uncle, stood in the back of the lighthouse, in the lee, and watched what was happening around them. The light tower swayed. "It was no illusion," Whalton declared.

The October 2, 1952, edition of *The Key West Citizen* reported how the Bethels' lives changed because of the storm, based on their daughter's recollections. During the hurricane of 1909, William Bethel climbed on the roof of his house to clear the gutters so that the water running into the cistern would be clean. He fell and injured his back and was still confined to bed when the big blow of 1910 came. Though his wife and children assured him that the light was burning in the tower, he continued worrying. Finally, he got up and went to take care of the light himself. Someone later found him outside in the storm and brought him home. Six months later he died and Mary Elizabeth became keeper.

Her devotion to duty was no less than her husband's. Jennie De Boer, the Bethels' daughter, recalled that "the following year when a hurricane whirled in over Key West . . . the wind rose and it was so strong that it threatened the light. . . . My mother headed for those steep winding stairs. She thought she could save the light. I pleaded with her not to go, and finally had to drag her back with force when she started up the steps. Just then, up above us, we heard the glass break and the pieces came crashing down inside the tower. That was the first time the light ever failed."[24]

The hurricane also damaged the wharf at the Key West Lighthouse Depot, which was the principal depot of the district.

The Bureau of Lighthouses shipped supplies for the entire area to the depot. From the depot, the lighthouse tender took supplies wherever they were needed. The buoys were also stored there. The facilities did not impress the lighthouse inspector. He reported, "The blacksmith's shop is a cheap wooden structure. The store house is part of the buoy shed. . . . There is no railway for moving buoys to and from the shed, and they have to be rolled along the wharf, to the damage of the decking."[25]

The bureau ordered the necessary repairs for both the depot and the light station. Mary Elizabeth, with her son, Merril A. Bethel, as assistant, remained keeper of the light until 1914. Years later, she married Henry Shanahan, who had once served with her on the Key West Light.

In 1915 when the Light House Board converted the light to acetylene, it also changed the characteristic from fixed white to six seconds white flashing (six seconds of light alternating with six seconds of eclipse). With the acetylene system installed, the services of a keeper were no longer necessary and the Key West Light became automated.[26]

The keepers' quarters did not remain unoccupied for long. In 1917, William Demeritt, the lighthouse superintendent, recommended "that the lighthouse property be under observation at all times during the war due to storage of kerosene in the oil house," and that he and his family "be allowed to live in the keeper's quarters." The board granted permission and had the first sanitary plumbing system installed, rendering the privy an obsolete structure. The Demeritt family lived in the keeper's house for the next thirteen years.

Demeritt, who was born in Key West, came from a family involved with the sea and lighthouses for generations. His father, also born in Key West, held the post of chief engineer in the lighthouse service, and Demeritt worked under him as a coal passer on lighthouse tenders. He enrolled with the International Correspondence School of Scranton, Pennsylvania, and became a marine engineer. Four years later Demeritt succeeded his father as chief engineer. In 1911, at thirty-one years of age, he became superintendent of the Seventh Lighthouse District. This district included the Florida coast from Hillsboro Inlet on the Atlantic side to the Cedar Keys on the Gulf side. Demeritt was responsible for property valued at $15 million, and he had eight hundred people and ten vessels under his direction. On July 1, 1939, Franklin D. Roosevelt's Presidential Reorganization Order No. 11 provided for the consolidation of the United States Lighthouse Service with the United States Coast Guard. Demeritt was out of a job and a house.[27]

The keepers' house, located on the northwest corner of Whitehead Street and Division Street (now Truman Avenue), underwent many changes by Demeritt, by the Coast Guard, and by private tenants, all leaving their individual marks. In 1966, the Key West Art and Historical Society took over the dwelling and made it into a military museum. Three years later, the Coast Guard decommissioned the lighthouse as an aid to navigation, and the society opened the tower to the public.

The light tower has always been a popular attraction for tourists (Thomas Edison was once a visitor), but by the 1980s cracks and water damage were apparent. In 1987 a restoration project got under way. Preservationists painstakingly and authentically restored the 1895 light tower. The work included repairing structural problems that had developed over the years. The brick addition to the tower made in 1894 may not have been erected properly, and through the decades moisture eroded bricks and mortar. Bricks of the same type and age were needed to replace the damaged ones. Such bricks are not easy to

Mary Elizabeth Bethel, wife of William Bethel, was born in the Bahamas in 1854. She served as assistant keeper of the Key West Lighthouse from 1891 to 1908 and as keeper from 1908 to 1913. After retiring she continued to live in Key West. She died in 1941 and is buried in the city cemetery. (KEY WEST LIGHTHOUSE MUSEUM)

come by, but a cistern at Fort Zachary Taylor was built with a similar type, and permission was given to salvage what was needed for the restoration work.

Workers, many of them volunteers, refurbished the lighthouse equipment and fittings; they even polished the brass acetylene gas tubing that once supplied the illuminant for the automated light. (Electricity was not used for the light until 1927.) When they completed the restoration of the tower, Susan Olsen, executive director of the Key West Art and Historical Society, announced that a restoration of the 1887 keepers' quarters and the rest of the station would begin. Money for the projects came from private and corporate donations, and local, county, state, and federal funds, including the 1989 Bicentennial Lighthouse Fund. The latter was the federal government's way of helping to celebrate two hundred years of American lighthouses. In 1990 the light station was at its turn-of-the-century prime.[28]

The saving and restoration of the Key West Light Station are part

William Wellesley Demeritt and his family in front of the keepers' house on the northwest corner of Whitehead Street and Truman Avenue in Key West. Demeritt was the last superintendent of the Seventh Lighthouse District. The restored house is part of the Key West Lighthouse Museum. (MONROE COUNTY PUBLIC LIBRARY)

of a nationwide struggle to preserve this part of the maritime heritage of the United States. The keepers' house is now a lighthouse museum. Here people have an opportunity to explore a way of life that is forever gone. Visitors can again climb the eighty-eight spiral stairs to the watch room and outside gallery of the light tower. It is there, at the top, looking at the city, harbor, and ocean beyond from the keeper's vantage point, that one can visually appreciate the unique role the lighthouse has played in Key West's history.

The job of lightkeeper became defunct in the United States in 1990, when the Coast Guard automated the last of America's lighthouses— but America's lighthouses will survive. Though many of our most picturesque and historically important lighted navigational aids have

Department of Commerce Lighthouse Service building on the northwest corner of Front and Whitehead Streets. Built circa 1856, it was the first permanent naval building and the second oldest brick building in Key West. It is on the National Register of Historic Places. (MONROE COUNTY PUBLIC LIBRARY)

become obsolete, individuals and communities have rallied to save these romantic and symbolic structures on our shores. Key West is one of the maritime communities that have restored their historic light stations.

The notes for this chapter begin on page 273.

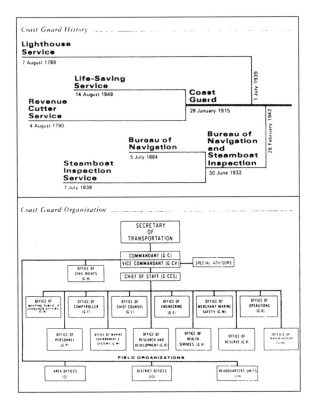

Illustration of Coast Guard history compiled by Robert L. Sheina, U.S. Coast Guard historian. From 1789 to 1939 the Lighthouse Service was reorganized a number of times. Secretary of the Treasury Alexander Hamilton adminis-tered lighthouses from 1789 to 1792, when the responsibility was transferred to the Commissioner of Revenue. In 1802 Albert Gallatin, secretary of the Trea-sury, resumed the job. In 1813 aids to navigation were once again administered by the Commissioner of Revenue. In 1820 the fifth auditor of the Treasury, Stephen Pleasonton, became the general superintendent of lighthouses and re-tained the office until the formation of the Light House Board in 1852. The board was composed primarily of officers from the Army and the Navy. The country was divided into twelve new lighthouse districts. In 1910 the nine-member board was replaced by the Bureau of Lighthouses headed by George R. Putnam, Commissioner of Lighthouses. The Bureau of Lighthouses was as-signed to the Department of Commerce when it was separated from the De-partment of Labor in 1913. Four years after Putnam's retirement, the Presidential Reorganizational Act of 1939 incorporated the aids to navigation into the Coast Guard, part of the Department of the Treasury. On April 1, 1967, the Coast Guard was transferred to the Department of Transportation.

In 1966 the Key West Art and Historical Society took over the keepers' house and made it into a military museum. In 1969 the Coast Guard decommissioned the light as a navigational aid, and the society opened the tower and the station to the public. (FLORIDA DIVISION OF TOURISM)

The Key West Light Station's restoration project was undertaken by the Key West Art and Historical Society in 1987 and completed two years later. The keepers' house, now the Key West Lighthouse Museum, has been restored to its turn-of-the-century prime, just as it was when the Bethel family lived there. (HISTORIC FLORIDA KEYS PRESERVATION BOARD)

3. DRY TORTUGAS

LIGHTHOUSE AT GARDEN KEY
FIRST LIGHTED 1826

LIGHTHOUSE ON LOGGERHEAD KEY
FIRST LIGHTED 1858

It was early in the morning on July 24, 1857, when Silas Denison, master of the wrecking sloop *Plume*, sighted the bark *Pacific* aground on East Key Reef in the Dry Tortugas, approximately sixty-three miles west of Key West in the Gulf of Mexico. Though the morning sky seemed to portend a storm, visibility was still good, and Denison could clearly see the light tower on Garden Key, four and a half miles west by south. During the previous night the light from the tower, which warned vessels of the surrounding shoals and reefs, should have been readily identifiable to the captain and crew of the *Pacific*. The wind was fresh and there was a heavy sea from the east as the *Plume* approached the disabled vessel. Every wave caused the bark to lift and then smash down on the rocky, irregular coral reef. As the *Plume* drew near, the men on the wrecker could see the *Pacific*'s crew heaving cargo overboard in an attempt to lighten the bark and float her off the reef.

What happened next could only have occurred off the coast of Florida—Captain Denison boarded the *Pacific*, and as he offered assistance, presented his wrecking license to Charles F. Gardner, master of the bark. The United States District Court, Southern District of Florida, had granted the license. Florida was the only state in the

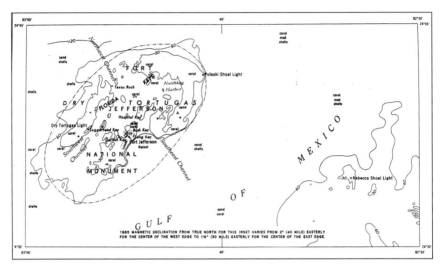

United States Geological Survey Map of the Dry Tortugas, 1965. The map shows the extent of Fort Jefferson National Monument; also note the location of Dry Tortugas Light on Loggerhead Key in the west and the Rebecca Shoal Light to the east. (U.S. DEPARTMENT OF THE INTERIOR, NATIONAL PARK SERVICE)

Union where the federal government required salvagers, known as wreckers, to have such a license. The law required Denison, as a wrecker, to go to the aid of the *Pacific*, but the law did not require Gardner to accept his offer of assistance.

The salvage cases heard in the admiralty court in Key West reveal the pattern of wrecking operations. If the captain of a grounded vessel gave the wrecker permission to help save the ship and its cargo, the salvager then became the "wreck master" and directed the salvage operations. When other wrecking vessels arrived on the scene, the wreck master could include them in the operation at his discretion. However, the timing was imperative—it was important to free the vessel, if possible, during the first high tide of salvage operations (if the wreckers accomplished this the salvage award was frequently higher). Therefore, the wreck master usually needed all the help he could get. The owners or masters of two or more wrecking vessels often made an agreement, called *consortship*, for the particular salvage job at hand, or sometimes for a longer period of time.[1]

The case of Silas Denison versus the bark *Pacific*, New York to Mobile, illustrates consortship well, and how imperative it was to have the help of other salvagers. It also demonstrates that the establishment of lighted navigational aids could not prevent wrecks if captains or navigators were incompetent, or unaware of the dangerous and sometimes unpredictable effects of the current on their vessel as they sailed through the Florida Straits.

Testimony revealed that soon after Captain Gardner accepted Denison's offer of assistance, three more wrecking vessels arrived on the scene: the sloops *Elisha Beckworth* and *Shepard*, and the schooner *Champion*. The *Pacific* continued to pound with great violence against the rocks. Pieces of her keel broke off and tossed alongside the vessel in the waves. The *Shepard* took the anchor and chain from the bark's bow, carried it out, and set it in five fathoms.

One after another salvage vessel came alongside the disabled ship to receive cargo. The *Champion* suddenly struck bottom and had to withdraw. The *Plume*, which drew less water, took her place. Then it too struck the reef heavily. The wind and sea increased in violence as the day advanced, and the *Plume* was in a position of great danger. "It was difficult to keep her alongside or from breaking adrift." Denison testified. "The sea boarded the bark and wet every part of her decks. She leaked beyond the power of the pumps to keep the water out."

The wreckers kept pumping and removing cargo from the holds as quickly as possible throughout the night. Denison continued: "At 2:00 A.M. on July 25th the water inside the bark was on a level with that outside her and the pumps were abandoned. The wind and sea were very heavy." The *Plume*, loaded, struck the reefs again, unshipped her rudder, lost her anchor, "and was compelled to haul away." Denison declared, "No vessel could lie alongside the bark." The sea swept over the *Pacific* fore and aft. Denison and other wreckers remained on board the stricken vessel to aid and encourage the crew and be ready to assist in their escape should the bark go to pieces.

After Judge William Marvin heard the testimony of the salvagers he called on Captain Gardner to testify. Gardner stated that he had seen the light from the Tortugas lighthouse bearing west-southwest, but that the distance from the lighthouse to the bark seemed to him to increase, and he therefore thought the light was a vessel. Captain

Gardner did not change course, and the *Pacific* grounded on East Key Reef. After hearing the case, Judge Marvin stated that although the *Pacific* had been lost, the wreckers salvaged most of the cargo at a risk of losing their own vessels. On August 24, 1857, Judge Marvin awarded the wreckers $10,129.57, approximately eight percent of the value of the salvaged goods. Judge Marvin made no mention of Gardner mistaking the lighthouse on Garden Key for a ship at sea.[2]

The currents, which deceived Captain Gardner into believing that the light he saw was moving (when indeed his own vessel was being carried sideways), were particularly strong and tricky around the Dry Tortugas. The Tortugas, comprising islands, islets, reefs, and shoals, stretch about eleven miles in a northeast, southwest direction in the Gulf of Mexico. They lie approximately ninety miles north of Cuba and 120 miles west-southwest of the southern extremity of the mainland of Florida. The Tortugas are the last in the 150-mile string of coral reefs and islands, now known as the Florida Keys. It is here, where the waters of the Gulf of Mexico mix with the Atlantic Ocean, that the skill of even the most experienced navigator is tested.[3]

Ponce de León was the first European explorer to sight these islands. On June 13, 1513, he successfully navigated the reefs and shoals and anchored offshore of one of the islands. Turtles were everywhere, and because of this Ponce de León named the isolated group of islets "Las Tortugas." ("Dry" was added later because of the absence of fresh water.) During the night the crew captured 160 sea turtles and might have taken many more if they had wished. The log reveals that the men also killed "fourteen seals . . . many pelicans and other birds that amounted to five thousand." (The Caribbean Monk seal, *Monachus Tropicalis*, was abundant at that time.)[4]

The Spanish soon began to use the knowledge gained by navigators sailing off the Florida Keys and in the Gulf Stream. By the mid-sixteenth century, Spanish ships, homeward bound and loaded with treasures from South America and Mexico, plotted their course across the Gulf of Mexico and through the Florida Straits and the Bahama Channel to take advantage of the Gulf Stream current, which flowed north at about three knots. The number of vessels taking advantage of the Gulf Stream route continued to increase as ships sailed from colonial ports established on the Gulf coast.[5]

In the 1770s, during the time the British controlled Florida, George Gauld surveyed and mapped the Tortugas and named the islands. East Key, near the reefs where the *Pacific* wrecked, has retained the same name throughout its history. Once there were large breeding colonies of terns on the island, but continual egg collecting by humans may have driven them away. Today, no birds nest on East Key; however, it is a primary nesting site for green and loggerhead turtles.

The eleven rocky islets seen by Ponce de León, where a "great amount of turtles there do breed," have not only changed shape—five of the islands have slowly eroded away or been destroyed by hurricanes. The action of the sea caused some islands to disappear and then reappear, and the seas created one new island. Bird Key is one of the islands that vanished. The new one, Bush Key, appeared in the 1830s, but forty years later a hurricane destroyed it. Since the 1870s, Bush Key has steadily built back up again, and now it is the second largest island in the group.

Adjacent to Bush Key is Long Key. Mariners and mapmakers have often interchanged the names of the two islands, making early descriptions of the islands unreliable. The 1922 chart of the Dry Tortugas established the current use of the names.

Middle Key is another island that was more substantial before the twentieth century. Gauld called the island Bird Key on his 1773 chart, and it was probably an important nesting site. In recent years Middle Key has appeared only intermittently as a low strip of bare sand where few plants can survive and few birds nest. North, Northeast, and Southwest Keys were all barren sand islands when Gauld surveyed them. In the hurricane of 1875 they all washed away, but sometime in the future Southwest Key may again develop into an islet. Recent charts indicate that the sandy bar is bare when the water is low.

Garden Key remains much the same as when Gauld charted it and is one of the more stable islands. To the northeast of Garden Key lies the tiny islet of Sand Key (later known as Hospital Key). Gauld's chart identifies Loggerhead Key as "Loggerhead Turtle" Key. It was and still is the largest island in the Tortugas.[6]

After the United States acquired the Louisiana Territory and shipping increased in the Dry Tortugas area, navigators continued to use Gauld's chart. The newly established settlers along the Ohio, Missouri, and Tennessee Rivers transported their produce down the Mississippi, and from there shipped it to ports in Europe and on the Atlantic seaboard of the United States. All vessels sailed by way of the treacherous Florida Straits route, considered after 1821 to be territorial waters of the United States.

After Florida became a territory, the government sent Lieutenant Commander Matthew C. Perry to Key West. While cruising the Keys and Dry Tortugas aboard the U.S. schooner *Shark*, Perry observed that ships were exposed to imminent danger. He reported that many vessels bound for the Gulf of Mexico sailed to Cuba and set a course from the Morro lighthouse to help avoid the dangerous reefs and islands in the Dry Tortugas. This course often left the ships vulnerable to attacks by pirates, who infested the area. To reduce the navigational hazards of sailing the Florida Key coast, Perry suggested locations for four lighthouses: Cape Florida, Key Largo, Sand Key, and Southwest Key in the Dry Tortugas.[7]

Congress responded to Perry's report by recommending appropriations for lighthouses at Cape Florida, Key West, and the Dry Tortugas. The amount requested for the Dry Tortugas Light was $8,000. The act, passed on May 7, 1822, illustrates the procedure for establishing lighthouses during that era:

> As soon as the jurisdiction of such portions of land on the Dry Tortugas, or in some place in the vicinity, as the President of the United States shall select . . . shall be ceded to, and the property there of vested in, the United States, it shall be the duty of the Secretary of the Treasury to provide, by contracts, which shall be approved of by the President, for building a lighthouse on such site, to be so lighted as to be distinguishable from other lighthouses near the same; and also to agree for the salaries, wages, or hire of the persons to be appointed by the President for the superintendence of the same.[8]

The site selected was Garden Key, not Southwest Key. Lighthouse engineers drew up plans for the tower. Congress appropriated funds two years later, but engineers deemed the original estimate for the Dry Tortugas Light too low, and Congress added an additional $2,790.85. A Boston firm received the contract to build the lighthouses at Cape

Florida, Key West, and the Dry Tortugas. Stephen Pleasonton, fifth auditor of the Treasury and the man responsible for navigational aids, decided to place a lightship off Key Largo as an additional aid to navigation in the Keys. In August 1824 the vessel carrying the workmen and materials needed to construct the lighthouses was lost at sea. Because of this tragedy, Pleasonton extended the contractor's deadline for completion of the lighthouse on Garden Key to June 1825.[9]

Other setbacks plagued the construction of the seventy-foot conical brick tower, and workers did not complete it until late March 1826. The delayed arrival of the keeper, John R. Flaherty, further postponed the lighting. The lighthouse superintendent at Key West, William Pinkney, reported in April that "it would be of immense advantage to have the light in operation speedily, but it would be improper to entrust it to anyone except its keeper." Three months later, Flaherty and his wife, Rebecca, arrived on Garden Key. The lighthouse was equipped with twenty-three lamps set in fourteen-inch reflectors. Flaherty prepared the lamps and lit them—displaying the first navigational light in the Tortugas on July 4, 1826.[10]

In 1829 the United States government considered the Dry Tortugas as a possible site for a naval station. Commodore John Rodgers, one of the officers sent to examine the islands, enthusiastically reported the potential of the Tortugas. The islands, he said, were "encircled by an immense reef or bank formed of coral, which breaks off the sea in every direction, and contains within its embrace an outer and inner harbor." The harbors, he believed, would provide a safe anchorage during all seasons. The geographical position of the Tortugas offered many advantages for the defense of the southern coast, "lying as it does, directly in the track of all vessels passing to and fro, not only between the Mississippi, but every part of West Florida having intercourse by sea with our eastern states." At the same time, observed Rodgers, "the commerce of Cuba, and even the homeward bound trade of Jamaica, would be subjected to the grasp of a naval force located in the Tortugas." He recommended erecting suitable works for the protection and convenience of a competent naval force. The government kept Commodore Rodger's report on file, but took no action.[11]

The wreckers from Key West used the harbors described by

Rodgers. Anchored off Garden Key they could observe almost any vessel that ran aground or needed assistance. Unfortunately, they were not anchored in the Tortugas harbor on the night of October 2, 1831, when the brig *Concord* stranded. Strong gales along the Atlantic coast shredded the vessel's rigging, and when the *Concord* met with turbulent winds in the Tortugas it was driven ashore. Edward Glover, the lightkeeper, saw that the ship was in danger of breaking up. He sailed out to the *Concord* and offered to assist the captain. The court libeled the goods saved from the *Concord* for $15,000. Judge James Webb, who heard the salvage case, decreed Glover only $750 and expenses— he did not want to encourage lighthouse keepers to engage in the wrecking business.

The month after the *Concord* wreck, Glover was returning from Key West aboard a wrecker when the crew sighted the *Florence*, aground on a shoal off the lighthouse. Rather than participate in the salvage, Glover talked with the captain of the *Florence* while the wreckers lightened the ship. The captain told him that he had been unable to see the Garden Key Light from the deck and had sent a man aloft, who reported that the light was so dim he could barely see it from the top of the mast. Glover explained that he had been absent from his post for a week, leaving his invalid wife and a black woman to care for the light. He assured the captain that he would soon improve it.[12]

The light appeared to be in good condition when the well-known painter and ornithologist John James Audubon visited the Dry Tortugas in 1832. Audubon, aboard the U.S. revenue cutter *Marion*, observed not only the birds, but the geography and marine life of the Tortugas as well. Audubon, who had heard gruesome stories about the wreckers, was invited aboard one of the salvaging vessels and was astonished by what he discovered. "We were welcomed aboard with all the frankness of our native tars. Silence and order prevailed upon her decks." The crew was from "down east . . . stout, active men, clean and smart in their attire. In a short time, we were all extremely social and merry." Even with the establishment of the lighthouse, Audubon could see the need for the services of the wreckers in the Tortugas. The captain of the *Marion* told him that a "great coral reef, or wall, lies about eight miles from these inhospitable isles, in the direction of the

Gulf, and on it many an ignorant or careless navigator has suffered shipwreck."[13]

One of these navigators was Lemuel S. Akin, captain of the packet ship *America* en route from New York to Mobile in 1836. After sighting the Tortugas Light to the west, Akin set his ship on a northwest course. The thirty passengers aboard retired, not expecting to see land again until they reached Mobile. Several hours later the *America* stranded on a shoal. Akin believed that the lightkeeper had purposely dimmed the light to lure his ship to destruction and exclaimed, "We are victims of the piratical wreckers!"[14]

During that time, John Thompson served on the Garden Key Light as an assistant keeper. As a result of his experience in the Tortugas, Thompson made certain suggestions he thought would aid navigation in the area.

Thompson described the shoals as extending eight miles northeast and six miles southwest of Garden Key. The reefs and shoals on the southwest side were the most hazardous to ships. He reported numerous complaints from captains who could not accurately judge their distance from the light in a thick squall or even in bright moonlight. Thompson suggested that the government build additional lighthouses—one on the westermost key (Loggerhead), and another on one of the easternmost keys. This would give navigators three navigational aids to accurately determine their positions.[15]

The additional lights would have solved the navigational problems in the Tortugas. A June 18, 1836, editorial in *The Key West Inquirer* backed Thompson's idea. However, it was unlikely that Stephen Pleasonton would agree to the expense of two additional lighthouses when he had not requested funds for a first-order Fresnel lens to improve the light on Garden Key.

Pleasonton refused to equip U.S. lighthouses with Fresnel lenses even though they were proven to be far superior to the reflector system. The reason he gave was that Fresnel lenses were too expensive, but Pleasonton was also a close associate of Winslow Lewis, who originally equipped all U.S. lighthouses with his Argand lamp and parabolic reflector system. Pleasonton continued to have this system installed on new lights despite the development of the Fresnel lens.[16]

Edmund M. Blunt and G. W. Blunt, publishers of *American Coast*

Pilot, an essential guide for navigation, severely criticized Pleasonton. The Blunts firmly believed that British and French lighthouses were superior in management and equipment to those in the United States. They specifically stated that the navigational light on Garden Key was inadequate. In their letter of November 30, 1837, to Secretary of the Treasury Levi Woodbury, they wrote, "The light at the Tortugas should, from its position, be a light of the first class; it has long been noticed by mariners as a very bad one, and we felt justified in our last edition of the *American Coast Pilot* in remarking on the very bad manner in which this light is kept. Lieutenant Gedney, of the U.S. Navy, who has been much employed by the government about the Florida reef, gave notice to Mr. Pleasonton that the management of this light needed reforming; it still remains a very bad light."[17]

This letter must have had some effect, for on October 9, 1838, Adam Gordon, the superintendent of lights at Key West, reported that the Tortugas light was "refitted with English plate-glass in the lantern, new reflectors, and twenty-three new lamps instead of the fifteen old ones . . . an excellent light."[18]

Pleasonton could not hold out forever, and in 1840 he finally purchased two Fresnel lenses: a fixed first-order and a revolving second-order. However, the lenses did not help the situation in the Tortugas—Pleasonton had them installed in the Twin Lights at Navesink, New Jersey.[19]

On September 4, 1842, a hurricane swept through the Dry Tortugas. The high surf washed away Long Key and took out a section of Garden Key. The water came within twenty feet of the tower, but the light remained undamaged. The storm broke only the vane on top of the lighthouse and the frame for turning the smoke pipe. Two small lighthouse boats, which the keepers moored in the harbor, tore loose from their anchors and washed up on Garden Key. The keepers made the needed repairs, and when the inspector arrived for the semiannual inspection he found the station in good condition.

No matter how well the keepers tended the light there continued to be complaints about its short range. The government sent captains William H. Chase and George Dutton, U.S. Army Corps of Engineers, to investigate. The officers found the light station "well and neatly kept." They reported that, on clear nights, they could see the light for twenty miles, and that, when the distance diminished, it was due to the hazy atmosphere. The officers believed engineers could remedy this situation by raising the seventy-foot tower to 120 feet. They also recommended building a lighthouse on Loggerhead Key.[20]

Another severe hurricane struck the Dry Tortugas in 1846, cutting a deadly and destructive path through Key West and the lower Keys. On November 6, 1846, the *New York Herald* ran an article entitled "Authentic Particulars of the Terrific Gale of the 11th of October." It stated, "The Light at the Tortugas was uninjured.... The new lantern for the Tortugas Light was lost in schooner *William* on the 10th on its way to Tortugas. The contractor and crew all saved."

Pleasonton did not have the lost equipment replaced, and he did not order any improvements to the light. Records indicate that within a ten-year period there were thirty shipwrecks in the Dry Tortugas area. Several captains reported that they had thought they were at least ten miles from the lighthouse when their vessels ran aground on the reefs. Others said that when the light bore northeast-by-east the iron door leading to the lantern partially blocked the light. The captains often requested more lamps and reflectors, or a Fresnel lens to be installed on the light. Finally, Pleasonton sent Winslow Lewis, the designer of the reflector lighting system, to Garden Key. Lewis adjusted the seventeen lamps and the twenty-one one-inch reflectors, improving the light somewhat, but dissatisfaction still remained.[21]

A full-blown investigation of the entire U.S. lighthouse system took place in 1851–52. Congress directed the Secretary of the Treasury to establish a board to investigate the Lighthouse Service, and they began by circulating a letter to all "commanders of mail steamers, packet-ships, &c," requesting their firsthand knowledge of U.S. lighthouses. Information about the navigational aids had to be collected in order for Congress to enact legislation to "extend and improve the system of constructing, illuminating, inspecting, and administrating" the lighthouses in the United States.

John Young, captain of the *Venice*, out of Philadelphia responded, "The Tortugas light, though much improved, is very far from being perfect. In fact, two lights are required at this place, one lower than the one now in use; for owing to some local cause, the light is frequently invisible, even with the lighthouse in sight. On one occasion this writer was becalmed off the Tortugas all one night close enough to see . . . the lower part of the lighthouse, but could not see the light. As much fault was laid to the keeper's charge for neglect; I feel sure that instead of any censure being due him, it is owing to the peculiar state of the atmosphere."[22]

While engaged in the freighting business between the Gulf of Mexico and Europe, Captain George Baker made two or three yearly voyages through the intricate and dangerous Florida Straits. Coming from New Orleans, the first navigational light he saw was the one at Garden Key. He did not think the light had "sufficient brilliancy and power to be seen over ten miles in very clear weather." He wanted a light of the first magnitude placed at the extreme point of the Florida reef (Loggerhead Key). Captain Thomas S. Budd of the U.S. mail steamship *Union* considered the Garden Key light to be poor and "unsafe to run for unless the weather is very clear."[23]

The captains' letters and documented comparisons between the navigational aids in the United States and Europe resulted in a total reorganization of the lighthouse administration. On October 9, 1852, Congress created a nine-member Light House Board under the auspices of the U.S. Department of Commerce and Labor. Congress charged the board with all administrative duties related to the Lighthouse Service.[24]

The board intended to equip all existing and future lighthouses with Fresnel lenses and to establish new aids where needed. In 1855 and 1856 the board's attention focused on the Dry Tortugas. Ten years earlier, the government had selected Garden Key as the site for Fort Jefferson and had placed Captain Horatio Governeur Wright, U.S. Army Corps of Engineers, in charge of building the six-sided casemented work. This would become the largest nineteenth-century brick fortification in the United States, and it enclosed most of the sixteen-acre island.

The lighthouse continued to function as the engineers built the fort around it. One engineer working on the fort project wrote, "About midway the length of the island, in the angle of Bastion C, towers the slender lighthouse, and fenced off at its foot are the light keeper's quarters." Construction on the fort was still under way when the

Light House Board decided to build a new seacoast lighthouse and reduce the Garden Key Light to a fourth-order harbor light.[25]

On August 15, 1855, Lieutenant T. A. Jenkins, U.S. Navy, and secretary of the Light House Board, wrote Captain Wright at Fort Jefferson requesting an estimate for a lighthouse and keepers' quarters. The board may not have determined the location for the new lighthouse at that time, but Wright assumed he would build on Garden Key. He wrote, "There is now a wooden house, built for the keeper in 1847, which contains two lower rooms, with hall, two half attic rooms, and a detached kitchen, which if sufficiently capacious, will answer the purpose for some years to come. An addition may be made to it at a small expense."[26]

Jenkins also was not specific about the dimensions for the light tower, only suggesting that the focal plane for the light be about 150 feet above sea level. Wright drew up sketches for the tower and made detailed estimates, but reminded Jenkins that he did not have any means of "ascertaining what experience has shown to be suitable in regard to convenience and stability for the upper and lower diameters, and the thickness of the walls of the tower so much higher than our ordinary structures."

Wright felt that the most important factor in the stability of the tower was a "sufficient foundation." Still assuming the tower would be built on Garden Key, Wright proposed "to first lay a grillage . . . the top of which shall be on a level of those in the bastions of the fort, and being always underwater is secured from decay." Unbeknownst to Wright, the engineers had not built Fort Jefferson on solid coral as supposed, but on coral rubble that had washed up, accumulated in the shallows, and been covered with sand. Over the years the fort kept sinking, and the Army abandoned plans for a third tier.[27]

In Wright's final plan for the tower, he called for brick-faced concrete walls, six feet thick at the bottom and gradually decreasing to two feet at the top. He wanted the tower to be 146 feet above the foundation, making the deck 150 feet above low water. In his design the structure tapered in circumference from thirty feet (above the foundation) to fifteen feet (at the top, where the lantern would be placed). Wright estimated it would cost $14,968 for a concrete tower faced with brick, and $16,187.50 for an all-brick tower. Additional costs were $3,000 for the 146-foot cast-iron stairway, $5,000 for the lantern, and $10,000 for the first-order Fresnel lens.

When making the estimates, Wright implied that the price of materials included labor. In his analysis of the masonry costs he itemized the cost of masons and tenders to masons. He wrote, "No allowance is made for expense . . . for shelter of workmen or transporting workmen to this place; as most, if not all of these may be avoided by putting the work under the control of the officer in charge of the fort." The Lighthouse Service used part of Fort Jefferson's labor force to work on the light tower, and a large number of the workers were slaves. The artisans employed at the fort mostly came from the north, but the government used predominately slave labor to build and maintain the fort from 1846 until the Emancipation Proclamation was signed on January 1, 1862. Many families in Key West bought slaves in order to hire them out to the government during the construction of Fort Jefferson and the lighthouse in the Dry Tortugas.[28]

On August 18, 1856, Congress appropriated $35,000 for building a lighthouse—on a proper site—in the Dry Tortugas, and to fit it with a first-order lens. The Light House Board chose a site on Loggerhead Key. Before construction began, the U.S. Army Corps of Engineers reassigned Wright to another duty station and placed Captain Daniel P. Woodbury in charge of construction for both the fort and the lighthouse.

Woodbury changed and refined Wright's plans for the tower. He reduced the size of the base to twenty-eight feet in circumference, and specified eight-foot, nine-inch walls. Woodbury also designed a winding staircase of cut granite blocks that would lead from the base of the tower to the watch room. The lantern room was above the watch room. The point at which the lantern joined the brick tower was to be thirteen and a half feet in diameter and 150 feet above sea level. Woodbury designed the brickwork to corbel out from the tower twelve feet below the watch room. The intricately worked courses of masonry, like steps in reverse, would form the floor of an exterior galley around the watch room.[29]

Construction began in 1857. Wright had anticipated one of the problems encountered in "raising the material for so high a tower." The usual way of carrying brick was with a hod—a wooden trough with a wooden handle—carried on the shoulder. After workers reached a certain elevation on the tower, this method became impractical. As Wright had suggested, Woodbury used a steam engine to hoist the brick.

After completing the tower, workmen secured the lantern to the top. A narrow gallery encircled the lantern room's polygonal arrangement of windows. With delicate care, the men raised and installed the sections of the jewel-like Fresnel lens, supplied by L. Sautter & Company of Paris, France. Atop the copper roof with its decorative spire, workmen added the last detail—a tall lightning conductor. The Light House Board considered the most important lighthouse structures under way at that time to be the Sombrero Lighthouse and the first-class masonry tower at Dry Tortugas. Workmen completed both structures in 1858.

Although *Hunt's Merchant Magazine* published the March 29, 1858, "Notice to Mariners" notifying all those involved with shipping and commercial interests that there was a new lighthouse on Loggerhead Key, Dry Tortugas Group, the lighthouse was not officially put into operation until July 1. The Light House Board assigned the light a fixed characteristic with a range of twenty miles.[30]

Lighthouse architects used brick throughout the light station. The station contained the light tower, two-story keepers' house, separate cookhouse, two cisterns, and an oil storage building. The 1857 construction drawings show the oil house connected to the light tower, but it was built as a freestanding two-story structure, measuring sixteen feet by fourteen feet, with a gabled roof. The keepers' quarters housed the principal keeper, one of his assistants, and their families. Each floor had two rooms off a central staircase hall with two interior chimneys, one for each side of the house. Porches extended across the front and back, with the rear porch partially enclosed.

A smaller, two-story kitchen building with a gabled roof was built next to the main house. The building, with an interior staircase, was approximately twenty by seventeen feet. The downstairs served as a communal kitchen, where masons built a large bake oven into the base of the chimney. The upstairs was designated as living quarters for one of the assistant keepers. The two cisterns, each fourteen feet in diameter, extended four feet above the ground. Gutters ran from the roof

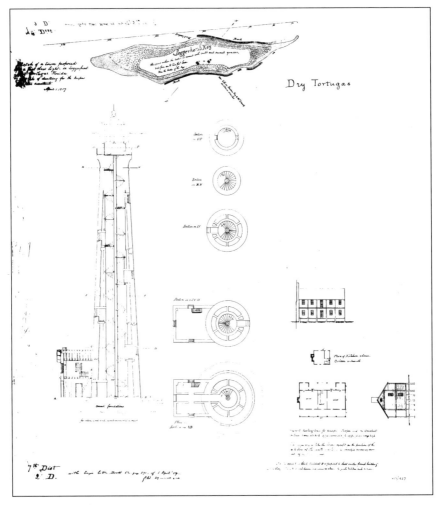

Sketch of proposed lighthouse and keepers' quarters on Loggerhead Key, dated April 1, 1857. (NATIONAL ARCHIVES)

of the keepers' house into one and from the cookhouse roof to the other. This method of collecting and storing rainwater was used throughout the Keys.[31]

The lighthouse station occupied the center of Loggerhead Key, the entire island being about 4,200 feet long and 700 feet at its widest point. In 1858, the sparse vegetation consisted of scrub brush, cacti, and grasses. The keepers were soon busy planting vegetable gardens and coconut trees, and the light tender *Activa* brought most of the other food and provisions, as well as lighthouse supplies, for the keepers and their families. The *Activa* left the Staten Island Lighthouse Service Depot in New York Harbor on December 1, 1846, and arrived at the islands fifteen days later. She transported materials, supplies, and personnel for the fort as well as the Loggerhead Light Station.[32]

When the lamps were ready to be lit at the Loggerhead Light, the Light House Board transferred Benjamin H. Kerr, the keeper of the lighthouse on Garden Key, to the new station. The board assigned William Solomon keeper of the Garden Key Lighthouse, still designated as a fourth-order harbor light. Kerr and his wife, Henriette, both forty-one years old at the time, had seven children. Kerr had served at the Garden Key Light for nine years, and his salary as principal keeper was $600 a year.

Kerr had a series of assistants from 1859 through 1860, and it is difficult to document who was on duty at the Loggerhead Light Station during what G. Phillips, stationed at Fort Jefferson, referred to as the "incident." Phillips, in his written report to Captain Woodbury, related that the keeper had been having trouble with his assistants. Phillips explained that one day in June 1860, Kerr and his nearly-naked daughter, "who had been bathing in the ocean when the incident occurred," arrived at Garden Key in a small boat. They told the officer in charge that both assistant keepers, Kerr's wife, and their oldest daughter had banded together to make an attempt on Kerr's life. The keeper managed to defend himself "with a carving knife and fled with his sympathetic daughter" to Fort Jefferson. Several of the officers from the fort tried to help the family reconcile but failed. "Kerr and his younger daughter were forced to leave for Key West," wrote Phillips, ending his report. The family must have eventually resolved their problems, since according to lighthouse records, Kerr remained the head keeper at the Loggerhead Key Light until 1861, when James P. Lightbourn took his place.[33]

Lightbourn was on duty when the Civil War broke out, and the Dry Tortugas remained under Union control during the entire war. Though Fort Jefferson was still not completed (nor ever would be), the first troops were garrisoned there on January 18, 1861. The Light House Board reported to Congress that the "lights at Tortugas, Key

West, Sand Key, Dry Bank, and Carysfort Reef, on the Florida Reefs, have thus far been protected."[34]

Members of the 47th Regiment of Pennsylvania Veteran Volunteers recorded many of the most detailed descriptions of life at Fort Jefferson and Loggerhead Light Station. The Army stationed this regiment at the fort from December 15, 1862, through March 2, 1864. During that time there were approximately two thousand people at the fort, including officers and their families, soldiers, former slaves, and prisoners. There were also dogs, horses, cats, chickens, and turkeys. The regiment kept hogs and cattle on Bush Key, and the latter, "with a hawser fastened to their horns . . . were compelled to swim across the channel to the fort to be butchered."

Local fishermen sold their catches to people at the fort and the light stations, and, when possible, the keepers and the soldiers at the fort went fishing themselves. It was their favorite pastime, as well as a necessity. The men collected turtle and bird eggs by the barrel from adjacent keys during the nesting seasons, and the soldiers went regularly to Loggerhead Key to "turn turtle." (Captured turtles, when turned on their backs, are unable to right themselves and escape). The turtles, each weighing two hundred to five hundred pounds, provided much of the meat for the keepers, their families, and for the inhabitants of the fort. Fruits and vegetables were seldom eaten, although one report noted, "Sgt. Hutcheson left for Loggerhead Key again with four men to bring back vegetables for the command."

Six families lived at the fort, "with twelve or fifteen respectable ladies." These families socialized with the lightkeeping families at the fort and at Loggerhead Key, three nautical miles away. Balls and parties were held regularly at the officers' quarters at the fort, and afternoon teas also were fashionable. An army band played for public and private functions.

Occasionally parties were held in conjunction with turtle hunts on Loggerhead Key. One officer's wife wrote, "We took three boats, with music for dancing and supper, making a grand frolic of the occasion. After supper, which everyone enjoyed in the lighthouse living room, the ample kitchen was converted into a ballroom, and dancing indulged in until it was time for the turtles to come up." (Female turtles would come ashore to lay their eggs.)[35]

The one common complaint of everyone in the Tortugas was the mosquitoes that plagued the islands from time to time. Private journals, letters, and official reports describe the discomfort endured when the mosquitoes were exceptionally bad. On some occasions the insects infested the buildings, and everyone that could slept under netting at night, daubing liquid ammonia on their bites during the day. No one knew at the time that a particular species of mosquito was a carrier of yellow fever, and there was an outbreak at the fort in 1867. The army set up a quarantine station for military personnel on Loggerhead Key.[36]

The yellow fever outbreak affected the maintenance of the lighthouse as well. An inspector of the light tower on Loggerhead Key in 1868 reported that heavy rains washed out "much of the mortar on the south and southwest sides." He noted that some parts of the plastered walls and ceilings in the oil storage house and the cookhouse had fallen down. Workmen could not make repairs because the yellow fever quarantine prevented them from landing on the island.

In 1871, after the quarantine was lifted, the Light House Board acted on the inspector's rain damage report. The board also approved a variety of other projects, including repainting the tower. Although the board considered the recommendation that the tower be "painted with alternate white and black bands from the base to the lantern to render it a better day mark," the board decided to keep the tower's original markings. The bottom half of the tower was painted white and the top half, including the lantern, black. A new boat house was also built. On Garden Key, repairs were made to the lantern room, keepers' dwelling, and outbuildings.[37]

Now that everything was in good repair at both lighthouses, nature delivered a devastating blow with the hurricane of October 1873. The pounding storm seriously damaged the tower on Loggerhead Key, and the inspector determined that the tower was "in dangerous condition and should be rebuilt or replaced." He believed that the upper portion was unsafe during high winds. Once more, the islands were under a yellow fever quarantine, and the keepers could make only temporary repairs. The Light House Board estimated that a new tower would cost $150,000 and requested an appropriation of $100,000 to begin the work; Congress granted $75,000.[38]

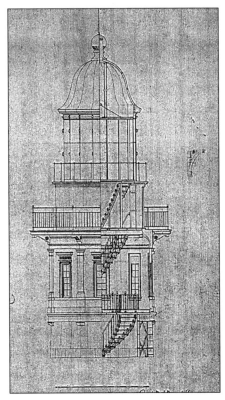

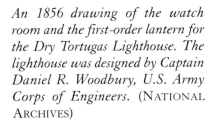

An 1856 drawing of the watch room and the first-order lantern for the Dry Tortugas Lighthouse. The lighthouse was designed by Captain Daniel R. Woodbury, U.S. Army Corps of Engineers. (NATIONAL ARCHIVES)

The violent hurricane also badly damaged the light tower on Garden Key. The keepers made extensive temporary repairs, but lighthouse inspectors suggested that the old tower be torn down and an iron tower erected on one of the bastions of Fort Jefferson. Although the Army abandoned Fort Jefferson in 1874, the War Department remained responsible for the fort. The department approved the plan, and in March 1875 Congress appropriated $5,000 for erecting the proposed tower.

In order to keep the Loggerhead Key light functioning until a new tower could be built, the Light House Board ordered substantial repairs to be made as soon as the yellow fever quarantine was lifted. In 1875 the board reported:

The old part [of the tower], for a distance of eight or nine feet below the lantern, including watch-room walls, was entirely rebuilt, and the anchors of the lantern extended downward through the entire distance without in any way interfering with the regular exhibition of the light. When it is remembered that the tower is about 150 feet high, the difficulty in making these repairs will be better appreciated. They were accomplished by cutting out the old masonry in narrow vertical sections, replacing each section entire before removing the next. The black portion of the tower has been painted, and the remainder whitewashed. The lens has been readjusted and secured in position. The walk in front of the keeper's dwelling has been cemented and the water-conductors to the cisterns repaired. The cisterns have been cleaned and repaired, and wooden shutters for the tower-windows have been made, painted, and hung. It is proposed, during the coming season, to make a careful examination with a view to determining on plans for the foundation of a new tower.[39]

No sooner had the masons made these meticulous repairs than the hurricane of September 1875 severely tested the work. Despite the battering of the storm, the top of the tower remained secure. However, reports from the keepers stated that in high winds "the vibrations are very great and injure the masonry." In 1876 the board reported it would postpone work on a new Loggerhead lighthouse in the hope that it may not be necessary. Inspectors reported that the new brickwork on the old tower seemed to be holding up amazingly well.

Work for the new light tower on Garden Key began in February 1876. Engineers selected a site on Bastion C overlooking the harbor. Their plans called for a tower, hexagonal in shape, to be constructed of boilerplate iron. After the harbor light was completed on April 5, the old light tower was demolished.[40]

For the next three years, inspectors on Loggerhead Key thoroughly inspected the repaired tower to determine whether it needed replacing. Each year they pronounced it in good condition, so the Light House Board abandoned the plan to replace the tower. For the next nineteen years the light station received only routine maintenance. Then in 1899 the board decided it was time to make extensive repairs and renovations and ordered the metal work on the lantern scaled and painted, new storm doors and windows installed, a new ceiling built

The Dry Tortugas Light Station on Loggerhead Key was completed in 1858. Brick was used to build the 150-foot-high conical light tower, the original two-story keepers' house, and the smaller separate cook house with keepers' quarters on the second floor. (Monroe County Public Library)

in the watch room, new floors laid throughout the keepers' house, and the roof replaced. The boathouse was enlarged by ten feet, and walkways were constructed between the buildings.[41]

George R. Billberry (or Billborg, in some records) was the keeper of the Loggerhead Light from 1888 to 1910. He was born in Prussia in 1845; his wife, Sarrah, was a native Floridian. The Billberrys were living at the Sand Key lighthouse where George was keeper when their two children were born in 1867 and 1868. Before being stationed on Loggerhead, Billberry also served at the Northwest Passage, Alligator Reef, and Sombrero Key lights.

The Light House Board made several improvements to the light while Billberry was keeper. On April 30, 1893, the keepers added a red sector to warn mariners of the reef just offshore. (Red sectors were created by installing a panel of red glass in a specific area of the lantern, which would enable the light to illuminate dangerous areas in red.) The board bought a new first-order bivalve lens from Henry Lepaute of Paris, France, in 1909 and shipped the lighthouse the lens with an

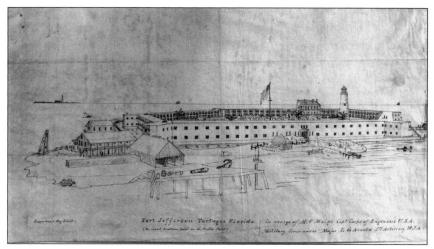

A pen-on-cloth drawing of Fort Jefferson showing the lighthouse on the parade grounds of the fort on Garden Key, and in the background the Dry Tortugas Lighthouse on Loggerhead Key. (M. AND M. KAROLIK COLLECTION, COURTESY OF THE MUSEUM OF FINE ARTS, BOSTON)

incandescent oil vapor (i.o.v.) system. The i.o.v. system replaced the kerosene oil wick lamps, and the lens changed the characteristic of the light from fixed to flashing.[42]

Billberry was also at Loggerhead Key when the Light House Board granted the Carnegie Institute a site for laboratory buildings on the lighthouse reservation. In 1905 surveyors marked the limits of this site as specified in the grant, and the buildings and concrete specimen tanks were built on the northern tip of the island. Scientists studying marine biology used the laboratories during the summer, and during their stays they planted more coconut palms and introduced a variety of non-indigenous plants to the island, including date palms, rubber trees, bananas, azaleas, and ornamental cacti.

In 1908 the government declared the Dry Tortugas a wildlife refuge for the protection of the endangered Sooty Tern. Decades of egg collecting had taken their toll.

In 1912 a fire on Garden Key burned many of the fort's buildings, destroying the keepers' dwelling as well as the soldier's barracks. The loss of the keepers' house may have motivated the installation of an automated acetylene light for the Dry Tortugas Harbor Light. At that time the other lights in the Keys were manned and used the new i.o.v. illumination system.[43]

After the Light House Board discontinued the harbor light on Garden Key in 1921, it took the first steps to modernize the Dry Tortugas Light Station on Loggerhead Key. A new house was built for the principal keeper and his family in 1922, and architects designed it in the typical bungalow style common in suburban housing communities of the period. It was a one-story, yellow-brick bungalow with an asphalt shingle–covered hip roof. The front porch wrapped around the northeast side of the house, and tapered wooden columns supported the roof. The columns rested on brick piers trimmed with coral that had washed up on the island. The piers, porch foundation, and brick balustrade for the porch steps were built of yellow and red brick set in a diamond pattern. The small rear porch off the kitchen had the same decorative brick design.

Concrete cisterns replaced the brick ones built in 1858. The water from the new cisterns now went directly into the new plumbing systems installed in the light station buildings, rather than being collected and manually pumped from the cisterns.[44]

One of the most important improvements to navigational aids in the 1920s was the development of the radio beacon. The Lighthouse Service began experimenting with the use of radio in navigational direction finding in 1917, and by 1921 the first radio beacon was established at the Sea Girt Light Station on the New Jersey shore. In 1926, the Light House Board ordered a radio beacon station for Loggerhead Key. A structural steel tower was erected, and the oil house was converted to accommodate the electronic equipment to operate the radio signal. A twelve by six and a half foot concrete passageway connected the converted building to the tower. Engineers took care to design a new oil house that was in keeping architecturally with the original buildings of the station. Though it was a one-story concrete structure, sixteen by fourteen feet, it appeared similar to the two-story 1858 oil house and kitchen. The lintels over the door and windows, as well as the sills and frames, were crafted to duplicate the originals.[45]

With generators installed, electricity became available for the station and for the light. The i.o.v. system was retained only as a backup in case the electricity should fail. The civilian keepers and later the

The Dry Tortugas Lighthouse on Loggerhead Key in 1998. Completed in 1858, the top of the tower was so badly damaged in the 1873 hurricane that the Light House Board planned to build a new lighthouse. Masons replaced the upper nine feet of brickwork with such expertise that the tower has re-mained in good condition ever since. The light station is now part of the Dry Tortugas National Park. (U.S. COAST GUARD OFFICIAL PHOTO)

A preliminary sketch for a cast-iron lighthouse proposed for Loggerhead Key, Dry Tortugas, after the hurricane of 1873 severely damaged the 1858 brick light tower. The brick tower, however, was repaired so successfully that it withstood subsequent hurricanes and was never replaced. (NATIONAL ARCHIVES)

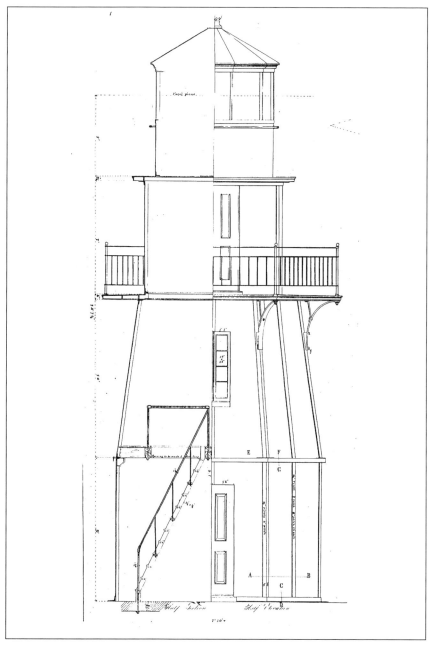

An 1876 drawing for the hexagonal light tower to be constructed of boiler-plate iron and erected on bastion C at Fort Jefferson, Garden Key. (NATIONAL ARCHIVES)

The Dry Tortugas Harbor Light in 1897. Note a small section of the keeper's house showing on the left. In 1912, a fire destroyed the dwelling. Soon after the loss of the house, the light was automated. (LANGLEY COLLECTION)

Coast Guardsmen spent most of their time, not in the watch room, but in the radio room monitoring both the radio signal and the light.

In 1986 an accident with the mercury float disabled the Fresnel lens. Technically, the revolving lens was referred to as a "bivalve" or a "clam shell," but this describes its shape rather than its beauty and intricate design. As the lens revolved, the arrangement and angles of panels produced the light's flashing characteristic. After the Coast Guard Aid to Navigation Team (ANT) disposed of the mercury, the lens no longer revolved and was removed. The classical lens is now on display at the National Aids to Navigation School in Yorktown, Virginia.

In place of the lens, ANT personnel installed a modern optic known as a DCB-24. The DCB (Directional Code Beacon) was a standard optic used by the Coast Guard for landfall lights that must have a minimal range greater than eighteen nautical miles. The DCB-24 (twenty-four inches in diameter) emitted a beam of light that swept

The Coast Guard removed the second-order, bi-valve lens from the Dry Tortugas Lighthouse on Loggerhead Key circa 1986. It is now on display at the U.S. Coast Guard National Aids to Navigation School, Yorktown, VA. (PHOTOGRAPHY BY GAIL FULLER, CURATOR, U.S. COAST GUARD)

the horizon at a predetermined number of revolutions per minute, creating the flashing white, twenty-second characteristic. Mariners could see the Dry Tortugas Light twenty-four miles at sea.[46]

The Coast Guard Aids to Navigation (ATON) officially automated the light in June 1987, after which members of the Coast Guard Auxiliary volunteered to run the station along with the Coast Guard. Generators used to produce the electricity for the light and the radio beacon needed monitoring and maintenance at all times. The radio beacon, a whip antenna on a platform located about 269 yards from the light tower, emitted a "dash, dash, dash" Morse code signal. The beacon, often non-operational from 1993 to 1994, was decommissioned in January 1995.[47]

In 1992 Loggerhead Key, Garden Key, and all the islands and surrounding waters became part of the Dry Tortugas National Park. The National Park Service owns and manages Loggerhead Key and the light station. Volunteers, who stay at the station from two to four weeks, have replaced the Coast Guard Auxiliary personnel. ANT still

Loggerhead Light Station in the 1980s. The brick bungalow surrounded by coconut trees (lower left) was built for the keeper and his family in 1922 and later housed U.S. Coast Guard personnel. The radio beacon (lower right) was erected in 1926. (U.S. COAST GUARD OFFICIAL PHOTO)

maintains the light, which was replaced in July 1995. A Coast Guard helicopter delivered the new Vega VRB-25 and took away the previous optic, the DCB-24. The VRB-25 is currently ATON's standard twelve-volt rotating beacon with solar powered batteries. The characteristic of the light changed from flashing white twenty-seconds to flashing white six-seconds; the range of the light decreased from twenty-four to nineteen nautical miles.[48]

When working on the island, ANT crews stay in the 1922 two-bedroom keepers' bungalow. The old keepers' house burned down in 1945, and the site was razed, leaving only the outline of the foundation. Volunteers stay in the original kitchen building, which workmen updated with modern kitchen appliances, a bathroom, air conditioning, a sofabed, and a second story with bunks and lockers. Although only the stairs leading to the second floor remain the same, the building retains a historic flavor.[49]

*The Dry Tortugas Harbor Light at Fort Jefferson in 1998. In 1935 the gov-
ernment proclaimed Fort Jefferson a National Monument. In 1992 the fort
and the light tower became part of the Dry Tortugas National Park.* (PHOTO-
GRAPH BY BM2 RAY POTTER, AIDS TO NAVIGATION TEAM, KEY WEST)

Rainwater, still collected from the roofs of the buildings, is now stored in fiberglass tanks. Concrete additions were built on the south and west walls of the original oil storage building, and Coast Guardsmen also built a new generator building and a hurricane shelter, both maintained by the National Park Service. Only the light tower seems unchanged. The 203 pie-slice stairs lead upward and dovetail into the ever-decreasing concentric circles of white-washed brickwork.

Reefs are distinctly visible from the top of the tower. On calm days, spotted eagle rays can be seen swimming across the shallows. Offshore on the lee side of the island, large and small dark blue-brown pools dot the aquamarine water. It is here that strawberry groupers, yellowtail, and mangrove snappers hide in deep holes near the reefs. To the north, there remains a plaque honoring Alfred Mayer, the first director of the Carnegie biological laboratories. A few foundation stones are all that remain from the institute's scientific compound.

Vegetation on the island today looks different than it did in 1858. The light keepers, the Carnegie scientists, and the Coast Guard have all contributed plantings. Many native species also flourish on Loggerhead; in spring, clusters of orange-red blossoms cover the Geiger trees, and the delicate white flowers of the spider lilies are in bloom. Agaves, which have tall flowering stalks that look like giant asparagus, can be seen here. Growing nearby are prickly-pear cactus and sharp-pointed yuccas. Along the sandy shoreline trail grow long vines of goat-foot morning glory. The rare sea lavender seems to thrive on the island, as does the bay cedar, sometimes growing ten feet tall. Just above the reach of the storm tide, sea oats bow their heads in the wind.

Despite all the changes over the years, the island retains its feeling of isolation. Nature is still in command, and the surrounding sea offers the same beauty and dangers to mariners that it always has.

The notes for this chapter begin on page 275.

4. SAND KEY LIGHTHOUSE

FIRST LIGHTED 1827

Nine miles south-southwest of Key West's harbor there is sometimes a small, white-sand islet. When it's there it is an enticing spot surrounded by warm, clean, multi-hued blue and green waters and coral reefs that team with life. A few miles to both the west and east are reefs that are visible at low tide. Toward the north-northwest the sea grows deeper, and the coral is covered in some places by twelve feet of water, and in others by twice that depth, forming a natural channel.

The islet, known as Sand Key, was once called Porpoise Island, named perhaps for the many porpoises (dolphins) in these waters, or maybe because the key looks like a porpoise as its arching back breaks the surface of the water. When George Gauld surveyed the area in the 1770s, he supposedly erected a large flagpole-like structure on the island to make it more conspicuous to mariners. In the early 1820s a wooden daybeacon marked Sand Key. The island, barely above sea level, is unstable; storms change its shape and sand builds up on one side and recedes on another. Sometimes it disappears altogether. Nevertheless, because of Sand Key's location, just offshore and near a channel leading into Key West's harbor, the government chose it as the site for a coastal lighthouse.

On May 18, 1826, Congress appropriated $16,000 for the construction of the light station. Lighthouse engineers chose brick building

The Sand Key Lighthouse, designed by I. W. P. Lewis. The skeleton frame-work of iron pile lighthouses had less wind and water resistance against gales and hurricanes, which was imperative in their exposed locations. (NATIONAL ARCHIVES)

material for the light tower and the keepers' house. Their architectural plans were similar in design to the lighthouse stations built at Cape Florida, Key West, and on Garden Key in the Dry Tortugas. They designed a sixty-three-foot light tower. The lantern atop the brickwork raised the height of the structure to seventy feet above sea level. The narrow central part of the 350-foot-long island would be the site for the tower, placing the keeper's house, cookhouse, and privy just to the south. Rainwater, collected in a cistern built next to the house, provided the keepers with fresh water.[1]

Since the characteristic of the Key West Light was fixed, a revolving light was chosen for Sand Key. The light required fourteen lamps with twenty-one-inch reflectors, and on a clear night it supposedly could be seen twenty miles at sea. The first keeper selected for the lighthouse was Joseph Himmenez, but he exchanged posts with John Flaherty and his wife, Rebecca, who kept the Dry Tortugas Light seventy miles west of Key West.[2]

The Flahertys found life less isolated on Sand Key. Shipping activity in the vicinity increased as Key West developed, and turtlers, fishermen, and wreckers often stopped on the island to collect birds' eggs and socialize. The island also became a favorite picnic spot for Key Westers. Unfortunately the Flahertys' enjoyable new social life ended in May 1828, when health problems forced John to take sick leave. Rebecca remained on Sand Key to keep the light while he was away. Records do not indicate whether John returned to Sand Key, but he died in 1830, and Rebecca received the keeper's appointment.

William Randolph Hackley, an attorney in Key West, described a trip he made to the island on June 5, 1831, in his diary. He wrote, "The wind was so light that we did not get to the key until 12 . . . I went up to the lighthouse. The light is revolving and is one of the best in the United States. It is kept by Mrs. Flaherty. . . . She, with her sister and a hired man, are the only inhabitants of the key and sometimes there are none but the two females. . . . The length of the key is from 150 to 200 yards and the average breadth 50. . . . [We] remained till evening and, having spent a pleasant day, returned to town at 8:00 P.M."[3]

On November 22, 1834, *The Florida Herald*, a St. Augustine newspaper, reported a special celebration on Sand Key, "Mrs. R. F. Flaherty, formerly of Fredrick City, Maryland . . . was married to Captain

Engraving titled "Supply Boat To Sand Key Light House" by F. Townsend Morgan, a W. P. A. artist-in-residence, 1935. (MONROE COUNTY PUBLIC LIBRARY)

Fredrick Neill. . . . The ceremony was performed by Richard Fitzpatrick at the Sand Key Lighthouse." Rebecca Flaherty Neill remained keeper of the Sand Key light until 1837, when Captain Joshua Appleby took her place.

Appleby experienced many adventures before settling down, at the age of sixty-seven, as keeper of the Sand Key Light. Born in Rhode Island on December 5, 1773, Appleby went to sea as a young man. His first wife, Sara Viall, died when she was twenty-three, leaving Appleby with the care of their one-year-old daughter, Eliza. Records show that Appleby owned property on Elm Street in Newport, Rhode Island in 1806, and had married Mary Forrester by 1820.[4]

Appleby sailed from Rhode Island to the Florida Keys sometime in 1820. He became one of the earliest settlers on Key Vaca, an island approximately thirty-seven nautical miles east-northeast of Key West. A "Notice to Mariners" that appeared in the March 8, 1823, edition of *The Floridian Pensacola* reads, "The public are informed that this settlement commenced November 19, 1822, by Joshua Appleby of Newport, Rhode Island, and John W. Fiveash of Norfolk, Virginia. Immediately at the west end of the Key is the settlement, where there is a flag staff erected. This port has . . . boats and provisions of all kinds to relieve those who may be so unfortunate as to get on the Florida Reef. . . . At present there are four families residing at this place; corn, potatoes, beans, onions, cotton and all West India fruit thrive rapidly."

As Appleby fished and turtled along the keys he also looked for shipwrecks to salvage. In 1823 he was accused of conspiring with Charles Hopner, who commanded the Colombian privateer *La Centella*, to "run ashore gently" the vessels Hopner captured. The vessels, after grounding on the coral off Key Vaca, could be salvaged and sold as wreck property. Whether the accusations against Appleby were true or not, Commander David Porter, whose charge it was to eradicate piracy in the Keys and the West Indies, acted quickly. He sent a squad of marines to arrest Appleby, place him in irons, and ship him to Charleston, South Carolina, for trial.[5]

The case against Appleby drew the attention of two top men in government, Secretary of the Navy Smith Thompson, and President James Monroe. Thompson wrote to Porter on July 24, 1823: "As regards the conduct of Joshua Appleby, detained under arrest, it is not expedient to institute against him any further proceedings; his offense does not amount to a positive violation of any law of the United States; you will, therefore, direct him to be forthwith liberated."[6]

Porter had Appleby released, and in 1825 Appleby returned to Newport. Five years later the 1830 census lists him living with his wife in Key West. When Appleby returned to the Keys, he once again engaged in wrecking—admiralty court records list him as one of the salvagers in a case heard April 6, 1830, and in another January 7, 1831. Court records show that he owned the wrecking schooner *Mary Ann*, but to become a licensed wrecker at that time the Key West court would have had to clear Appleby of any charges of wrongdoing.[7]

On May 23, 1828, Congress established the district court at Key West in order to license wreckers and hear salvage cases. Congress gave the judge the means to control the wrecking industry by decreeing that only vessels under his authority could be employed as a wrecker and no person could be employed who had made a collusive agreement with the master of a wrecked vessel. The court apparently exonerated Appleby once he was granted a license.[8]

Appleby continued his career as a wrecker for several years. Then on July 27, 1837, he received an appointment as head keeper of the Sand Key Light. Appleby kept the light burning through the hurricanes of 1841 and 1842. The 1842 storm wrecked the keepers' house and seriously damaged the lantern, which required all new plate glass panes and lamp reflectors. In his September 26, 1843, report, Adam Gordon, superintendent of lights for the district, observed, "with these improvements the light is exceedingly brilliant and powerful." Gordon also oversaw the construction of a sea wall, which he hoped would protect the island from the effects of storm surge. When the wall was completed, Gordon called it ". . . a fine piece of masonry. At the earnest solicitation of the keeper and with the advice of others who are good judges, I have employed the contractors to extend the wall about thirty feet longer . . . to give protection to the kitchen and . . . the whole south side. I am of the belief that you may now safely construct a keeper's house. . . . A keeper's house should be prepared at the earliest convenience of the Government; for both the keeper and his assistant have lacked ordinary comfort for the year past."[9]

Almost as soon as the contractors completed the improvements, the hurricane of 1844 blew half of Sand Key away and demolished the keepers' new home. The steep, cresting waves severely damaged the seawall, erected to protect the shifting sands. It took a year to repair the wall and build another house.[10]

In October 1846, Appleby's daughter, Eliza, visited him. Appleby's second wife died in 1833, and he felt especially close to his daughter and grandsons. On this particular visit to the lighthouse, Eliza brought her three-year-old son, Thomas. There were also two other guests at the light station, Mrs. Mary Ann Perry Harris and her adopted daughter, who were visiting from Newport, Rhode Island. No one at Sand Key knew that a hurricane had just devastated Havana and that it was moving rapidly toward Key West.[11]

The day of October 10 had been unusually stifling at Sand Key, with only an occasional breeze—yet the waves were building. Their rhythmic pattern around the island was erratic. During the night storm clouds scudded across the sky, and the barometer began to drop rapidly. Part of Appleby's job as keeper was to read the barometer and make notations on the weather in his log. When Appleby read the barometer, he had to have known that a storm of unusual severity headed his way. As hurricane-force winds approached, Appleby probably brought everyone to the light tower, remembering that during the 1842 and 1844 hurricanes the tower survived while the keeper's house washed away.

The high winds produced surf all around the key, and waves broke violently against the seawall. As the tide rose, water rushed over the wall and flooded the island. The sand gradually washed away, undermining the stability of the house and the tower, and both structures collapsed. The helpless victims were either buried or washed away.[12]

In a letter dated October 19, 1846, Stephen Pleasonton, the official in charge of lighthouses, wrote to Stephen R. Mallory, the district lighthouse superintendent, saying, "I am very happy to learn that you have repaired the sea wall at Sand Key." As he wrote these words he had no way of knowing that six feet of water covered the island.

When Pleasonton received the report that the hurricane had destroyed both the Key West and the Sand Key lighthouses and that only the Dry Tortugas Light remained, he proposed a temporary light for Key West and a lightship for Sand Key. The *Honey*, a 140-ton vessel, was purchased in New York and recommissioned as a lightship to mark the Sand Key reef. Pleasonton appointed a captain, along with a cook, for the vessel, and what he described as "five sober seamen." As the *Honey* set sail for the Florida Keys, part of the cargo included a small frame house for the future keeper of the Key West Light.

The captain moored the lightship close to where Sand Key had been, about seven miles southwest from Key West and about five miles west from the main entrance to Key West harbor. Mariners used the ship's navigational light not only as a seacoast light, but as a reference for Rock Key Channel, Southwest Channel, and the main ship channel; all of the channels provided access to Key West from the Florida Straits. The *Honey* remained on station for seven years.[13]

Almost immediately, plans were under way for another lighthouse on the island—but there wasn't an island. On March 3, 1847, Congress appropriated $20,000 for a lighthouse on or near Sand Key. To compensate for the site's instability, lighthouse engineers decided to use a wrought iron screwpile design to secure the foundation piles to underwater coral reefs. In 1848 Congress granted an additional $39,970.74 for the erection of a "durable structure adapted to the locality."[14]

Before work could begin on the new Sand Key Light, the Lighthouse Service underwent significant administrative changes. The upheaval and reorganization stymied lighthouse building; however, this delay proved to be fortuitous. While construction was delayed the islet slowly reappeared. Sand again built up behind the outcropping reefs, and an island of a somewhat different shape than what existed in 1846 formed over the large masses of coral just below the surface of the water.

J. V. Merrick and Son had already been awarded the contract for the construction of the lantern and watch room and John F. Riley Iron Works in Charleston, South Carolina, would manufacture the wrought iron structure. The Light House Board sent I. W. P. Lewis, the lighthouse engineer, to South Carolina to supervise the construction of the iron work. When the tower was completed, it was then assembled to make sure all parts fit perfectly, then it was dismantled for shipping. Lewis sailed to the Keys with the disassembled lighthouse, the needed building supplies and tools, and the trained workmen.

Lewis directed the installation of the foundation piles. The iron piles were eight inches in diameter and thirteen feet long. All seventeen piles had a cast-iron screw with a flange two feet in diameter at the lower end. Each piling was bored through the sand and into the coral to a depth of ten feet under water. In addition, the twelve exterior piles were passed through heavy cast-iron disks, four feet in diameter, that rested on bases of concrete. At this point in construction, Lewis suspended operations for lack of funds.[15]

The *Honey* continued on station, but there were numerous complaints about the vessel. John C. Hoyt, an insurance underwriter in Key West, reported in 1850, "The light-ship stationed near Sand Key is old, and the light is miserable. Several vessels and much valuable cargo have been lost by the neglect of the government to build a lighthouse on Sand Key." Eight vessels ran aground from May 1850 to August 1851 with a total loss of $425,000, and Hoyt once again complained, "The three light-ships on this coast are faithfully kept, but the power of their lights is by no means what it ought to be."[16]

One of the lightships Hoyt referred to was stationed off Carysfort Reef to the east-northeast of Sand Key, where an iron screwpile light-house was being built. The light was completed in March 1852, and in May the Light House Board transferred the engineer in charge, Lieu-tenant George Gordon Meade, to the Sand Key project. Meade re-ported, "After I was placed in charge, funds were not appropriated until September and did not actually become available 'til December."

As soon as Meade received the needed funds, he assembled me-chanics and laborers, and appointed civil engineers William C. Den-nison of Boston, and James W. James of Philadelphia, to direct the construction. The group landed at Sand Key on January 22, 1853, to begin work. Reporting on the details of construction, Meade said, "This pyramidal framework is divided into six sections, the piles at both ends fitting into cast-iron sockets at the juncture of each section, and being united together by a uniform system of horizontal tension and diagonal braces. The dimensions of the piles, sockets, and braces of each section diminish proportionately to its elevation."[17]

Over 450 tons of iron went into the construction of the light. On top of the first series of piles, above the reach of the waves, workers built a keepers' dwelling within the skeletal structure. The house had wooden floors and ceilings, and a roof of corrugated iron. There were nine rooms, each twelve feet square. One room contained tanks used for storing water and oil. One tank held five thousand gallons of fresh water and the other one thousand gallons of oil. Rainwater, collected from the roof, fed into the water tank. "There is no doubt," wrote Meade, "the house will be constantly supplied with good water." The Light House Board supplied all of the furniture, as well as the neces-sary items for daily living and maintenance of the light. Two work-boats were also provided; one was a whaleboat with four oars, and the other a centerboard sailboat.

An open stairway, attached outside to the piles and braces of the first tier, led to the keepers' house and its surrounding gallery. In the house's center room an enclosed stairway with 112 steps led from the keepers' quarters to the watch room and lantern. The watch room, containing the revolving machinery for the light, was about twelve feet in diameter and eight feet high. Outside and inside galleries, encircling the lens and lantern, facilitated cleaning and maintenance.[18]

One of the most important decisions of the newly organized Light House Board was to use the Fresnel lens on all new lights. The board members agreed that the Fresnel lens system of lighthouse illumination was four times more effective than the best reflector system, yet used one-fourth as much oil.

After the first-order lens and revolving machinery were installed, Meade instructed the keepers how to use a new type of hydraulic lamp he invented. "It is, in fact, a carcel lamp, except that instead of pumping up the oil by clockwork, it is raised to the level of the burner by being discharged from a reservoir in the dome of the lantern."[19]

The first keepers assigned to the lighthouse were Latham Brightman, head keeper, and Charles Bowman and Charles B. Berry, assistant keepers. Meade was clever when he introduced his new lamp design to the men. The first five nights they attended the light Meade had them use the standard French lamp. "The lamp had to be constantly watched and something done to it," Meade reported. He then set up the hydraulic lamp. "Its simplicity and uniform working afforded great relief to the keepers, who ascertained it required but one adjustment of the wicks during the night."[20]

Meade's hydraulic lamp, as well as the French lamps, used sperm oil. The lamps required approximately 240 gallons for a four-month period, at a cost of $1.47 per gallon. The Light House Board spent almost as much money for the oil as it did for three keepers' salaries. Brightman received $550 a year and his assistants received $300 each. Salaries increased over the next ten years, and in 1864 the head keeper at Sand Key, Edward Hudson, received $820; the first assistant keeper $465 and the second assistant $460.[21]

On July 20, 1853, the keepers officially put the lighthouse into operation. The characteristic for the Sand Key Lighthouse was a series of signals: a fixed white light for one minute, a partial eclipse of twenty-five seconds, a white flash of ten seconds, and finally another partial eclipse of twenty-five seconds.

The durability and strength of this second iron pile lighthouse built off the Keys thoroughly satisfied Meade. He knew the foundation would not settle because of the screwpile construction, and even if the

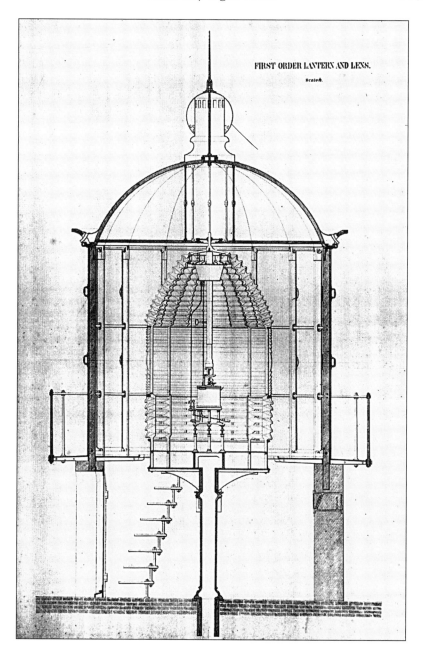

FIRST ORDER LANTERN AND LENS.

Scale.

The Light House Board adapted and used George Gordon Meade's hydraulic lamp in 1853. This vertical section of the first-order Fresnel lens and lantern shows the hydraulic lamp in the lens. (NATIONAL ARCHIVES)

sand island washed away and the island vanished, the structure could not be undermined. He believed that the braced open-ironwork design of the superstructure would withstand high winds and the force of the sea. Meade insisted that no platform or structure be built below the keepers' dwelling that would impede wave action during a storm. He advised frequent examination of the braces, which the keepers could tighten if necessary, and ordered the keepers to periodically scrape and paint the ironwork to prevent rust. Meade ended his final report to the board by saying, "It was a source of satisfaction that the work was closed with all parties returned to their homes without the slightest accident, or without a serious case of illness."[22]

Meade wrote detailed and articulate reports, and his encyclopedic description of the Fresnel lens impressed the Light House Board. The board invited him to New York to help exhibit the lens at the Crystal Palace Exposition in 1853. Meade's interesting response was, "Many thanks for your complimentary notice of me. . . . I will cheerfully attend . . . with two provisions—1st, that it is made a matter of duty—2nd, that it is not to cost me anything. This latter is an imperative condition with me. I don't ever ask to make money. I only compromise that I shall not sink any." It is not known if the Light House Board responded to Meade's unique acceptance; however, Meade did attend.[23]

These were challenging years for the keepers. The history of Sand Key is entwined with the history of the hurricanes that swept across the Keys. On August 29, 1856, the Light House Board reported that, "many lives were lost and much property was destroyed and damaged . . . the sand island, upon which the Sand Key light-house was, with the wooden buildings, wharf, and boats, was destroyed, leaving, however, the light-house tower uninjured. The water, during the gale, rose to six feet around the tower, and at the last dates from Key West, it remained at a depth of two feet. The gradual reformation of this little sand island gives strong hopes that there will be no permanent injury to the site and foundation."[24]

Sand Key disappeared again in the October 1865 hurricane, which carried away everything on the island except the lighthouse. The Light House Board ordered extensive repairs and renovations. For the fifth time since 1842 the light station was rebuilt, including a boathouse, privy, storehouse, and wharf on the newly formed island. Five

Sand Key Light Station in 1903, shortly after the boathouse was completed and the entire wrought iron lighthouse from the lantern to the waterline had been scaled, scraped, and painted. The house on the right is the weather station, which had been recently completed. Six years later, Sand Key and everything on it except for the lighthouse was destroyed by a hurricane. (LANGLEY COLLECTION)

years later the infamous 1870 "Twin Hurricanes" arrived with full force.

On October 8, the first storm struck Sand Key, and the wind and sea did not subside until October 11. The keepers no sooner repaired the damage and cleaned up debris when the second hurricane, lasting two days, washed the island away. The inspector scrupulously examined the iron pile light tower and recommended such extensive repairs that the Light House Board asked Congress for a special appropriation of $20,000. Congress granted the funds in 1874, but according to the board, work was unavoidably delayed. The delay turned out to be fortunate, for once more Sand Key took the brunt of another powerful storm. The tower withstood the action of the avalanching waves, but the tempestuous winds ripped through the keepers' quarters. When the inspector examined the house he reported that it was scarcely inhabitable.[25]

In 1781 Ami Argand invented a lamp for lighthouses with a hollow, circular wick that enabled oxygen to pass inside and outside of the wick, causing the flame to burn without smoking and to emit an intense and bright light. Before the development of the Fresnel lens, as many as thirty lamps were required to produce the required illumination. The lamps pictured were an improvement on the Argand lamps and used concentric wicks. Only one of these lamps was needed with the Fresnel lens; the larger size lens required the lamp with the greatest number of wicks. Left to right, two-wick lamp, five-wick lamp, and three-wick lamp. (NATIONAL ARCHIVES)

The board made plans to replace the quarters rather than try to repair them, and it turned out to be a complicated project. Workmen first constructed temporary buildings on the island for themselves and the keepers, and workshops were built to accommodate the equipment and shelter the workers as the project was completed. Contractors planned the repair work on the tower so that it would not interfere with the regular exhibition of the light. The damaged keepers' house was removed, and the construction report noted that this was a time-consuming job, "as parts were so thoroughly rusted as to

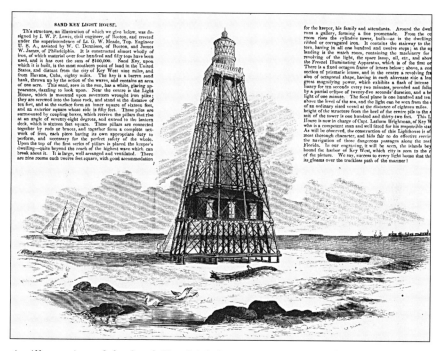

An illustration of the Sand Key Lighthouse appearing in Gleason's Pictorial Magazine *on September 9, 1854, and again on December 10, 1859. In describing the island, the author of the caption writes, "The sand seen in the sun, has a white, glaring appearance, dazzling to look upon." Key West is shown in the distance on the right of the drawing.* (Monroe County Public Library)

require much cutting of the iron, as well as all the bolts and rivets." The report continues:

> All the girders, plates &c. were so rusted as to greatly impair their strength, and as the weight of the new work greatly exceeded the old . . . a system of iron beams supported by brackets was fitted to the columns beneath the floor of the dwelling. . . . The new dwelling has the same dimensions as the old one . . . 38 feet square, but is better arranged for the convenience of the keepers. . . . The outer walls and roof of the dwelling are cast-iron plates bolted together. . . . No iron doors, windows, or shutters have been used, as previous experience in this climate shows that they rust so that they

are not easily moved. . . . Excepting the lantern, the structure is now one of the best arranged in the district.[26]

The Sand Key Lighthouse required little attention after these repairs, but the Light House Board ordered improvements to the light itself. In 1889 a lampost brought new mineral oil lamps from the Lighthouse Service Depot, Staten Island, New York, on the supply steamer *Fern*. In 1891 the superintendent oversaw the installation of red glass panels in the lantern, making light appear red over the reefs. The flashing characteristic of the light remained the same.[27]

In the early 1900s, one building was constructed on Sand Key that had nothing to do directly with the light station—a weather station. Fortunately, the man in charge, C. J. Doharty, was not at the station during the hurricane of 1909, when the wind gusted up to one hundred miles per hour. During a storm of this intensity along the coast, the sea, acted on by the high winds, is probably the most destructive force. A great mound of water, topped by steep raging waves, rushes toward the shore. The storm surge raises the water level many feet above normal and carries with it almost everything in its path.

On October 13, 1909, *The Key West Journal* reported:

Weather observer Doharty returned last night from Sand Key where he went to examine the damages sustained by the weather station there. He states everything on Sand Key was blown completely away except the lighthouse, and that was damaged to some extent. No lives were lost . . . as every person there repaired to the lighthouse during the first part of the storm. The barometer fell to 28.32 inches, 14 points lower than at Key West. The sea overran Sand Key twenty feet high, coming to the top flight of steps on the lighthouse. Several windows were blown out, and the draft was so strong that the combined strength of several men could not open the doors below.

When the island reformed, the weather station was rebuilt and Doharty resumed his duties. The weather station journals contain the only exact account of life on Sand Key, as the keepers' journals have been lost. On April 22, 1910, Doharty observed Halley's comet and noted, "It was at first faintly seen by the naked eye after which it was observed with the telescope . . . it appeared to be at a height of about 25 or 30 degrees above the horizon in an almost easterly direction. The tail extended upward at an angle of about 65 degrees, leaning towards the south."

In October 1910 Doharty reported:

> This station was visited by two severe hurricanes on October 13th, 14th, and 15th, and October 17th and 18th. The wind velocity steadily increased and much rain fell. . . . Waves began to wash over the island, and soon all the sand was carried from under the lighthouse, and the island shifted to a position further north . . . an outhouse was washed away . . . at noon on the 17th the wharf and wood pile were washed away, and the lighthouse began to sway in the gusts. Great trouble was experienced in keeping the doors closed on the windward side, the force of the wind pulling out nails repeatedly . . . rain fell in torrents, making it impossible to see farther than 100 feet. . . . The wind velocity increased and the swaying and the trembling of the lighthouse stopped the clock several times . . . the boathouse went to pieces and was washed to sea. At 1:30 P.M. the brick oilhouse broke up. At 1:50 P.M. the barometer reached its lowest point, 28.40 inches . . . braces at the bottom of the lighthouse began to break, and the force of the waves kept striking them against the other iron like sledgehammers.[28]

The wind blew 125 miles per hour during this hurricane, with winds above gale force for more than thirty hours.

While storms are an important part of the history of Sand Key Light Station, so is the wildlife—more specifically, birds. In the 1800s and early 1900s, thousands of roseate terns, least terns, and sooty terns came to nest on Sand Key in March. The locals considered their eggs to be quite a luxury. Charles G. Johnson, the lightkeeper on Sand Key, wrote to William Dutcher, chairman of the American Ornithological Union, in 1902. Johnson told Dutcher that the small eggs had a "rich flavor more so than larger eggs . . . and the keepers used to get them by the baskets for their friends in Key West." He reported that "nine to twelve thousand birds used to nest on Sand Key, but so many eggs were taken only two to three hundred young ones hatched."[29]

Plume hunters on other islands in the Florida Keys were killing egrets, herons, and roseate spoonbills for their plumes and feathers, which would often end up adorning fashionable ladies' hats of the day. The depletion of these birds and their eggs attracted nationwide attention, and Dutcher formed a Bird Protection Committee. In 1902 lightkeepers and others were hired as bird wardens to prevent the slaughter of the birds and to protect their eggs. Johnson was one of those Dutcher hired, and he became a conscientious warden. He sent Dutcher detailed reports on the types of species represented and the number of birds nesting on Sand Key and the surrounding islands. He posted notices warning people that the birds were protected, and he wrote Dutcher that "fishermen, pilots, and sportsmen used to take all the eggs, but I run them off the island, and I have not allowed one of the nests to be troubled at all . . . this season we have had no trouble as [people] are fully satisfied they will be punished for any offense . . . they are all law-abiding and stand greatly in fear of the law."[30]

Terns no longer nest on Sand Key, but laughing gulls often roost along the shore. When picnickers arrive by boat, the birds quickly take wing. Visitors have always been welcomed on Sand Key by the keepers. Keeper Thomas Kelly brought his bride, Kathleen, to live at the lighthouse in 1924. "There was hardly a day when we didn't have company," Kathleen told reporter Ann Smith of the *Miami Herald*. The people partying on the island always invited the Kellys to share in the meals and festivities. "It never got boring or lonely; I wouldn't have minded living there forever."

Neither the keepers nor the Coast Guardsmen stationed on the Sand Key Light ever experienced the isolation that Chief Boatswain Mate David L. Cipra recognized. "Few people even remotely realize what isolation means to the men living under restricted conditions, such as prevailed on these lighthouse stations. Unless adequate measures are taken to neutralize the ill effects it has on the men, rancor, hostility, and even enmity of the most serious nature may result. The record of the Lighthouse Service over a period of years reveals cases of friction, violence and insanity among keepers who have inadvertently been too long isolated."[31]

The Coast Guard automated the light in 1941, and the island was left to the birds, the locals, and the tourists. The Coast Guard Aid to Navigation Team (ANT) needed only to check and maintain the light every three to five months, and the Civil Engineering Branch inspected the structure every six years. On January 3, 1975, Sand Key became part of the Wilderness Preservation System under the administration of the U.S. Department of the Interior's Fish and Wildlife Service. The lighthouse is listed on the National Register of Historic Places.[32]

In 1982 ANT removed the Fresnel lens and replaced the incandescent light with a "flash tube array," powered by solar-charged batteries. Problems with the flash tubes forced the Coast Guard to replace them with a standard solar-powered three-hundred-millimeter lantern in 1983. Then in 1987 ANT installed a rotating 190-millimeter optic, providing a light range of sixteen miles—a range comparable to what was produced by the Fresnel lens. Solar panels and a bank of six 780-amp-hour rechargeable batteries powered the rotating optic.[33]

In 1989 major renovation work began on the Sand Key Lighthouse. The work included structural repairs, new handrails, a deck replacement, sandblasting, and painting. At 5:30 P.M. on Sunday, November 12, the Key West Coast Guard base received a report that there was a fire at the lighthouse. The historic lighthouse was ablaze!

The Coast Guard called in the Bureau of Alcohol, Tobacco, and Firearms to investigate the incident, but they were unable to determine the cause or origin of the destructive fire. The fuel that fed the intense blaze came from highly flammable paints and chemicals left by the contractors in the lower level of the keepers' house. A team of engineers went to Sand Key on July 3, 1990, to inspect the condition of the lighthouse, and they found that "much of the damage to the structural elements was superficial. Most of the damage . . . was concentrated in the central core . . . the stairwell to the watchtower, and the keepers' quarters. The walls of the stair tower and the majority of the braces stabilizing the stairwell were severely damaged. . . . The stairwell walls buckled at the base and collapsed . . . the staircase collapsed . . . the roof-framing fell to the floor below and all interior furnishings lost."[34]

The Sand Key Lighthouse before the 1989 fire. The platform for the keepers' house is supported by seventeen pilings, twelve exterior and five interior. The six sections of exterior pilings are joined at each juncture by cast-iron sockets. United by an iron webbing of horizontal and diagonal braces, the pilings rise at an angle of seventy-eight degrees from a fifty-foot square to the sixteen-foot square watch room gallery. In the center rises the cylindrical tower, containing 112 stairs. The stairwell and the keepers' house, both badly damaged in the fire, have been eliminated. (U.S. COAST GUARD OFFICIAL PHOTO)

*In 1989 after a disastrous fire roared through the 109-foot Sand Key Light-
house, a temporary beacon was built nearby. Note the missing section of Sand
Key Light's stairwell to the watch room.* (JENINE C. COUILLETTE, THE KEY
WEST CITIZEN)

To determine whether the lighthouse could be repaired and put
back into service, the Coast Guard developed a three-dimensional
computer model of the lighthouse structure. Engineers used the historic data and the original 1849 drawings by I. W. P. Lewis to develop
the model. From tests done on the computer model, they established
that the maximum loads, due to gravity, occurs on the four interior
columns of the lighthouse near the stairwell. Their report stated,
"These columns carry a load of about 49,000 pounds. The maximum
load to any of the columns occurs during hurricane-induced forces."
Based on field investigations, laboratory testing, and analysis, the
Coast Guard concluded that the structure was still serviceable and
should be salvaged. Aids to Navigation (ATON) made the decision to

renovate the Sand Key Lighthouse, and scheduled the project to begin in 1994 at a cost of approximately $500,000.[35]

With the Sand Key Light out, ATON needed to place a light nearby as quickly as possible. In the meantime, personnel from ANT installed the undamaged rotating 190-millimeter beacon on the lower level of the burned-out tower. The characteristic remained the same— a flashing white, fifteen-second light.

Establishing the new light took longer than expected. Site selection proved difficult, since ATON needed a location close to the light tower, but one that did not contain living coral. "NOAA (National Oceanographic and Atmospheric Agency) divers finally found a suitable site," according to Chief Charlie Pantelakos, ANT, Key West, "but afterwards, there were many delays due to rough weather." The construction tender *Hudson* had to be stable before building could begin. The tender used forty-five-foot steel legs, called "spuds," to secure its position. If the seas were over two feet, the spuds tended to sway with the wave action, causing the *Hudson* to spring back and forth.

After much delay, calm conditions prevailed and the workers were able to drive four sixty-five-foot-long H-beams vertically into the sea bottom. A square metal skeletal structure supported the beacon forty feet above the water. "Originally the Coast Guard installed a rotating optic with the same characteristics as the Sand Key Lighthouse," Chief Pantelakos said. However, the structure vibrated so intensely from the strong buffeting of the waves that the rotation of the light was affected. ANT replaced it with a three-hundred-millimeter optic with no moving parts, which has a quick flash characteristic visible for thirteen nautical miles. "The characteristic was changed," explained Chief Pantelakos, "to draw attention to the light; to let boaters know that something is different. The light flashes are produced at a rate of sixty flashes a minute."[36]

Solar-charged batteries power the temporary light, and the optic contains a six-lamp switcher that automatically changes lamps if one burns out. However, these lamps have a life of almost two thousand hours each. "The switcher only needs servicing about every two years." Chief Pantelakos says. That's good news for the men with

ANT, because the strong winds and high seas, especially in winter, make getting to the light difficult.

Every year winter storms cause major groundings on the reefs near the Sand Key Lighthouse. When the "storm of the century" in mid-March 1993 took a destructive path from the Yucatan Channel to Maine, the coastal freighter *Miss Beholden* was one of the maritime victims. En route from Miami to Mexico with a twenty-ton cargo of cigarettes and candy, the storm drove the 147-foot vessel aground on Western Sambo Reef. A barge removed all of the recoverable five-thousand gallons of fuel. Personnel for NOAA marked a safe path through the coral heads to deeper water, and seven days after the grounding the "Candy Boat" was refloated.[37]

Storms are not always the cause of groundings; human error is often to blame. On February 3, 1997, the 660-foot freighter *Contship Houston* ran aground on Maryland Shoal northeast of the Sand Key Lighthouse. The Coast Guard inspected the navigational aids in the area and found them to be operating properly. The grounding caused the usual environmental concerns: the possibility of a major oil spill, and the damage to the ancient coral reef. The owners guaranteed to pay up to six million dollars to satisfy any settlement or judgment for damage claims associated with the grounding.[38]

NOAA determines the amount of fines for coral damage in the National Marine Sanctuary, and the money is used in a variety of ways for the reconstruction of the reefs and prevention of future groundings. Some of the funds received by the Coast Guard will be used by ATON to purchase Radar Beacons (RACONS), which will be located on each of the Reef Lights. These radar responder devices, each costing about $40,000, will enable mariners to determine their positions with greater certainty. Once work on the light tower is completed, ATON will equip it with a radar beacon and restore its familiar white flashing light. The Sand Key Light remains a vital navigational aid, but hopes for a restored keepers' house have vanished.[39]

The notes for this chapter begin on page 278.

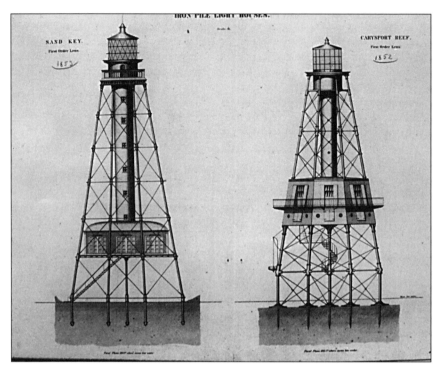

Proposed designs for the Sand Key and Carysfort Reef Lighthouses. The final plan for the 132-foot Sand Key Lighthouse differed considerably from the original design. The engineer, I. W. P. Lewis, used twelve exterior iron pilings for the tower, and designed a one-story square keepers' house. The drawing of the 112-foot Carysfort Lighthouse accurately depicts the completed tower with nine pilings and a two-story octagonal house. (NATIONAL ARCHIVES)

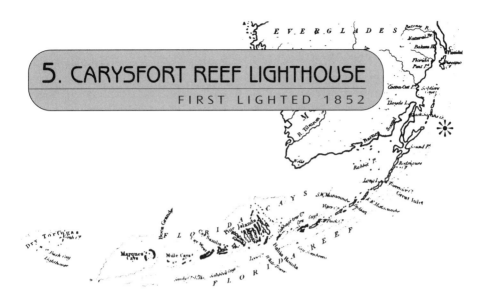

5. CARYSFORT REEF LIGHTHOUSE
FIRST LIGHTED 1852

Carysfort Reef Lighthouse is the oldest functioning lighthouse of its kind in the United States. It is an iron pile lighthouse, equipped with broad-bladed screws at the end of each foundation piling. This innovation not only makes it easier to secure the pilings into the coral bottom of the reef, but the large blades on the screws add additional bearing surface. Before the development of the iron screwpile design, offshore towers on submarine sites could not be erected.

The U.S. Corps of Topographical Engineers built the Carysfort Lighthouse off the island of Key Largo. The light, located at the easternmost point of the Florida Keys reefs, is as important to navigation today as it was in 1852. The reef on which this lighthouse stands takes its name from the HMS *Carysfort*, a twenty-eight-gun frigate that ran aground there on October 23, 1770. In 1775 Thomas Jefferys, a geographer, compiled a chart of Florida and the Bahamas for Robert Sayer of London, noting the soundings along the coast and locating the grounding of the frigate, misnaming it Carysford. In 1837 John Lee William's edition of *Territory of Florida* also refers to the reef as Carysford. Eleven years later, the 1846 chart of the area compiled by the U.S. Corps of Topographical Engineers has a notation: "A great extent of dangerous shoals and sunken rocks is commonly known among the wreckers as Carysfort Reef."[1]

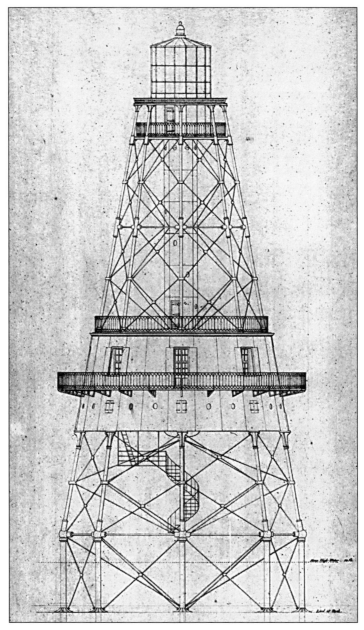

Original drawing for Carysfort Lighthouse. Open skeleton, wrought iron lighthouses were originally designed by Alexander Mitchell in 1836. His screwpile design made it possible to erect lighthouses on the reefs off the Florida Keys. (NATIONAL ARCHIVES)

Wreckers were familiar with Carysfort Reef. The first salvage case decided by the admiralty court in Key West concerned the bark *Nanna*, which ran aground the reef one night in 1828. Three wrecking vessels came to the bark's assistance, but before they could tow the *Nanna* off the reef, they had to remove 456 bales of cotton. Once this cargo was offloaded the *Nanna* floated higher in the water, and the wreckers were able to pull the vessel off the reef.[2]

Of the 324 known vessels that were lost on the Florida Reefs between January 1, 1833, and December 31, 1841, sixty-three were on Carysfort. From January 1844 to May 1847, there were 123 wrecks along the reefs with a total value of $3,266,000. The value of the wrecks on Carysfort alone amounted to $650,000. According to a report made in 1848 by Captain Howard Shansbury, U.S. Army Corps of Topographical Engineers, twenty percent of the wrecks between Cape Florida and the Dry Tortugas, a distance of two hundred miles, occurred on Carysfort Reef.[3]

The admiralty court, established in Key West in 1847, kept accurate records of the number of wrecks and the specific reefs on which the groundings occurred. It is difficult to determine how many vessels were in distress off Key Largo before that time, but it is safe to guess that long before the reef was charted or named it claimed many Spanish, French, and English ships.

One of the more famous wrecks still found on the reef today is the English sailing vessel TMS *Winchester*, which sank on September 14, 1695. (King William III and Queen Mary II reigned together; therefore, the *Winchester* was referred to as TMS, Their Majesties' Ship.) The 1939 discovery of the sunken wreck by Charles Brookfield generated great interest among both historians and divers. The 933-ton square-rigged *Winchester* was a fourth-rate ship-of-the-line. The ship, 146 feet long with a beam of thirty-eight feet, carried sixty guns. The square-rigger was only two years old when it struck the reef. A hurricane seemed to be the obvious cause of the wreck, but historians did not fully understand the sinking until 1960, when Brookfield obtained a copy of the *Winchester*'s log. From this record Brookfield learned that 160 of the men aboard died after the square-rigger departed from Port de Paix, Haiti. Brookfield theorized that scurvy plagued the *Winchester*'s officers and crew, but other historians suggest the crew con-

A diver retrieves coral chipped from one of the cannons from the wreck discovered on Carysfort Reef by Charles Brookfield in 1939. The coral contains signs of iron rust, indicating the cannon was made of iron and was therefore British; brass cannons were used on Spanish ships. The wreck was later identified as the TMS Winchester, *which sank September 14, 1695.* (HISTORICAL ASSOCIATION OF SOUTHERN FLORIDA)

tracted yellow fever when the *Winchester* engaged the Spanish in Haiti in June 1695. The *Winchester*'s log, beginning on August 1, 1695, reports deaths of one to three men almost every day until September 16 through 19, when forty-five men were buried at sea. When the hurricane struck, only seven men aboard were able to walk; all the others were either dead or too ill to help pump the bilge or handle the sails. Because of this, the ship's destruction was inevitable when the storm struck. A more fortunate ship accompanying the *Winchester* rescued eight men, the only survivors of *Winchester*'s 350-man crew.[4]

There would not have been any survivors of the *Winchester* disaster if there had not been another ship nearby. In the nineteenth century, when a ship went up on the reefs, the captain and crew were dependent on the help of the wreckers. The wreckers, who mostly lived in Key West, would fish and turtle as they sailed northeast along the reefs, keeping a sharp lookout for vessels in need of help.

Although charts noted the position of Carysfort reef when the United States acquired Spanish Florida, the Spanish had not established any navigational aids to mark the reef. It seemed impossible at the time to build a lighthouse on the reef itself. In 1824 Congress made an appropriation of $20,000 for a lightship to be stationed eight miles off Carysfort reef on the ocean side.[5]

The lightship, built under contract with Isaac Well & Company, took more than a year to construct. When completed in June 1825, the vessel *Caesar* sailed from New York for the Keys. John Whalton, one of the original settlers of Key West, applied to President John Monroe for the appointment as keeper of the lightship on July 24, 1824. His many letters of recommendation all attested to his nautical knowledge, seamanship and "habits of vigilance."[6]

Whalton secured the appointment and waited in Key West to take command of the *Caesar*. However, off the coast of Key Biscayne, Florida, a severe storm blew the *Caesar* up on the nearby reefs. The grounding did not damage the *Caesar*, but a greater part of the vessel's equipment was lost or destroyed. Isaac Well & Company informed Stephen Pleasonton, the Treasury Department official in charge of lighthouses, that the *Caesar* "had been gotten off [the reef] by wreckers" and towed to Key West, "where she will be dealt with according to wrecking laws." Pleasonton wrote the builder that "the floating light must be delivered in complete working order agreeably to the terms of their contract before payment can be made." The company paid a large salvage award before it regained possession of the lightship.[7]

Once on station, the lightship showed, according lightship records, "... two fixed lights at 50 and 60 feet above the sea, visible four leagues off [twelve nautical miles]." Although there were probably more than ten lightships in service in the late 1820s, most anchored "inside," in sounds and bays. The *Caesar*, moored off Carysfort Reef, was one of only three on "outside" stations, and problems due to its exposed position constantly plagued the lightship. Storms often blew the ship off station, and in 1827 it went aground on Carysfort Reef. The ship was both expensive and difficult to maintain.

The *Caesar* was also the shortest-lived lightship in the Lighthouse Service's history. The ship was only three years old when Whalton reported its deteriorating condition. He notified William Pinkney, the superintendent of lights in Key West, that the *Caesar*'s "plank sheer is entirely rotten, there are three planks on the starboard bow, two on the larboard, and seven bad places under each tuck, which cannot be caulked. The copper on both sides is much injured below the surface of the water, I fear, myself, that the worms will soon get hold of her if some measures are not taken for her preservation."[8]

Two years later Stephen Pleasonton wrote Congress:

> The decay of the first light vessel built for Carysfort Reef was extraordinary and unaccountable. She was built ... under the superintendence of an experienced shipbuilder, and examined by the collector. ... I saw the vessel myself after her timbers were up, but before she was planked; and every other person who saw her pronounced her a very superior vessel in every respect ... [yet] in five years she was examined, and found so entirely dry-rotten in every timber that a new vessel was found to be necessary to take her place.[9]

In 1830 Congress appropriated $20,000 for a new lightship. The second vessel, the *Florida*, experienced the same mooring difficulties as its predecessor. The hurricane of 1835 drove the lightship off station, demolished part of the decking, and smashed the lanterns. The crew expected hardships while attempting to keep their vessel on station during storms, but unexpected tragedies befell the men when the Second Seminole War began in 1835. Although the Indians had not threatened any lighthouses or lightships, they had attacked settlements along the Florida coast. The settlers on the New River and near Key Biscayne felt threatened, and many moved to Indian Key and Key West.[10]

Edmund Smith, a twelve-year-old boy traveling from Saint Augustine to Key West, described the tense situation in a letter to his mother. He told her that he had traveled through several deserted villages, and that the Indians had killed a family by the name of Cooley. "The people at Indian Key are very much frightened," wrote Smith. "They are under arms and expecting attack daily." He also wrote that the sailors aboard the Carysfort Reef Lightship were ". . . alarmed for their safety."[11]

On July 23, 1836, the Indians made their first attack on a light station. They destroyed the buildings on the light station at Cape Florida, near the entrance to Biscayne Bay; they set fire to the light tower, killed the assistant keeper, and seriously wounded the keeper. When the Indian attack put the Cape Florida Lighthouse out of commission, the Carysfort Lightship became more important than ever— it was now the sole navigational aid between Key West and Saint Augustine, a distance of 475 nautical miles.[12]

It was a coincidence of history that Whalton, the captain of the lightship, found himself stationed on Carysfort Reef; his wife's (Feliciata Isabela Bucciani) parents were among the original settlers of New Smyrna, Florida. The HMS *Carysfort*, in 1767, protected the colonists' ships from the Barbary pirates as they sailed from Minorca.[13]

Whalton maintained a home in Key West for his family, and when he returned there for supplies he often brought his wife and children back with him to stay on the lightship. Whalton had his family aboard the *Florida* on June 26, 1837, when Whalton and four crewmen rowed ashore to a landing on Key Largo, which the men called Garden Cove. There they cultivated a vegetable garden to supplement the ship's food supplies from Key West, and cut wood from the surrounding hammock. It was a beautiful and peaceful place. Because there had been no recent Indian attacks in the Keys, Captain Whalton did not anticipate trouble—he had no way of knowing that the Indians had been waiting, perhaps for days, for the men from the lightship to come to Garden Cove. A correspondent from the *Pensacola Gazette*, who interviewed survivors of the attack, wrote the following report:

> . . . as soon as the men landed . . . Capt. Whalton and one of his men were shot dead—the other three made their escape, two of which were wounded, one on the left side, the other in the arm. The Indians, after taking scalps, stripping the bodies entirely naked and stabbing them in several places, even cutting off Capt. Whalton's finger to get his ring, retreated to the bush. The wreckers, or several of them, deserve much credit. In the afternoon of the same day they resolved to go on shore at the risk of their own lives to get the bodies, and Capt. Cold of the Schooner *Pee Dee*, Capt. English onboard the sloop *Brilliant* with their crews, ventured and got the remains, which were brought to this place [Indian Key] the next day, and as decently interred as circumstances would permit. The distressed family also came down and remained one night, and took the Mail Packet for Key West.[14]

This sudden, brutal attack on the men from the lightship caused the settlers on Indian Key to send an urgent plea to the government for help—to supply arms and a properly-manned government cutter stationed near Indian Key. The petitioners declared that the attack, together with the ". . . innumerable fires made by the Indians all around us, have caused the inhabitants very serious alarm and constant apprehension of danger."[15]

Indian campfires could be seen all along the coast, from Cape Sable on the southwest tip of the Florida mainland, throughout the Keys, and northeast to Jupiter Inlet, over 220 miles from Key West. The Indians, however, made no other attacks on the settlements in the Keys until 1840. Before dawn on the morning of August 7, the Indians attacked Indian Key, massacred several inhabitants, and burned the buildings on the island.[16]

Indian Key had once been considered a possible lighthouse site. In 1851 Captain M. D. Ricker, familiar with the island's location, thought a lighthouse erected there would be more effective than the lightship. Ricker, commanding the *John Hoven* out of Portsmouth, New Hampshire, engaged in coastal trade and made annual voyages past the Keys. He believed "the lights on this reef should be so close together, that no ship should stand in for the Florida shore without seeing a light. I am aware that this would be a death-blow to the wrecking fraternity but . . . ship owners, and the interest of the commercial community generally would be benefited, and the wreckers can find other business." Ricker stated, "If it were possible to build a light on [Carysfort] reef, I know of no place where a light would be more beneficial."[17]

Captain W. Rollins agreed. Rollins commanded the U.S. mail steamer *Isabel* and made twenty voyages a year to Havana from Charleston. He called the Carysfort Lightship "a poor thing . . . cannot depend on it at all." Records show the lightship displayed two flashing white lights, forty and thirty feet above sea level, visible at a distance of only twelve miles.

The captain of the U.S. mail steamer *Union*, Thomas S. Budd, considered the navigational lighting along the Keys so inadequate he decided to avoid that area completely. In his opinion, the Carysfort Lightship "shows two miserable lights . . . sometimes floating inside [the] reef." He never saw the lights outside the reef unless the weather was clear. In Budd's opinion, the lightship did more harm than good.[18]

Another critic of the existing lights in the Keys was Lieutenant David Dixon Porter, who commanded the privately owned mail steamer *Georgia*. Porter, the third of ten children of Commodore David Porter, knew the Florida Straits well. He first cruised the area with his father when he was ten years old. As a young man, serving as an officer in the Mexican navy, he was aboard the *Esmeralda* as it sailed off Key West and the Cuban coast in search of Spanish vessels. Porter, familiar with the lighted aids in the Bahamas and Cuba, was not impressed with the Florida aids. He declared the lights from the Carysfort Lightship:

> . . . are scarcely discernible from the outer ridge of Carysfort reef, which is from four to five miles distant. On two occasions I have passed it at night, when the lights were either very dim or not

lighted; and I am informed that a brisk trade in oil is carried on with the wreckers on the reef . . . five vessels have gone ashore on or about Carysfort reef since I have been navigating this route, all of them a total loss, and no doubt all of them deceived by the light-boat, and sailing directions which inform the mariner that the lights can be seen twelve miles.[19]

In January 1851 Porter wrote Congress, "There is, at this moment, $2,800,000 invested in twelve [mail] steamships; eight of these vessels pass all the lights from Cape Hatteras as far as Charleston or Savannah and then proceed to New Orleans, keeping the coast on [star]-board as far as Carysfort reef and the Tortugas." Porter, however, did not sail the *Georgia* along the Keys; instead he plotted a course from Carysfort Reef to Cuba's Morro Light. He considered the Morro Lighthouse far superior to most of the other lights on the coasts of the United States. Porter felt that the Spanish paid "great attention to the subject of Light-houses, and all of their lights are of the very first order." From the Morro Light, Porter set his course to the mouth of the Mississippi.[20]

Congress wanted to know why so many of the lighthouses and lightships in the United States were inadequate and below European standards. The answer turned out to be one of administration. When Albert Gallatin became the secretary of the Treasury in 1802, he assumed the work of lighthouse administration. While he was in charge, Winslow Lewis, an unemployed ship captain, developed (the terms "borrowed" and "copied" have also been used) a type of lamp that was much more effective than the "spider lamps" then employed in the lighthouses. He offered to sell his patent to the government. In 1812, at the urging of Gallatin, Congress appropriated $60,000 to purchase Lewis's patent for a "reflecting and magnifying lantern; and to contract with him . . . for fitting up and keeping in repair, any and all of the lighthouses in the United States or territories thereof, upon the approved plan of the reflecting and magnifying lanterns." In three years Lewis had refitted all forty-nine of the country's lighthouses with his lamp and reflector system. This decision by Congress postponed the installation of Fresnel lenses, to the detriment of U.S. lighthouses.

As the number of lighthouses and other navigational aids grew with the expansion of commerce, the government delegated the administrative work to the fifth auditor of the Treasury. In 1820 Stephen Pleasonton held this position. At the time of his appointment, the United States maintained fifty-five lighthouses at a total cost of $244,000 a year. By 1835 Pleasonton had built an additional 146 lighthouses, and the expenditure for constructing them was $382,000. The number of lighthouses had more than doubled by 1852, and there were forty-two lightships. Unfortunately, though the number of navigational aids increased, Pleasonton continued to run his office much as he had in 1820. Although he was honest and hardworking, he prided himself on the economy with which he discharged his duties, not on the efficiency of the navigational aids. Pleasonton had little, if any, knowledge of the sea or the needs of mariners. He paid scant attention to the thousands of complaints about the poor conditions and the insufficiency of the lighted aids from individual seamen, commercial shipping companies, insurance companies, and foreign commerce. Government inspecting officers found many lightships poorly constructed, and rigged with anchors so inadequate that a storm could easily blow the vessels off station. Inspectors also reported that crews sometimes left their lightships unattended for days or weeks at a time. Politics often played an important part in the selection of keepers before 1852; as a result, many keepers were lax and even derelict in their duties.[21]

Pleasonton, because of his lack of maritime knowledge, relied heavily on Winslow Lewis's technical advice. During Pleasonton's administration Lewis continued to maintain the lights, and to bid on and receive contracts for all newly-built lighthouses. Pleasonton may have prevented the modernization of American lighthouses because of his friendship with Lewis.

In 1822 the French physicist Augustin Fresnel revolutionized the ability to magnify and concentrate the beam of light emitted by lamps. Europe was quick to adopt the Fresnel lens for almost all their lighthouses, yet while Pleasonton was fully aware of the outstanding performance of the Fresnel lens, it was not until 1830 that he wrote to France to find out about the availability and cost of the lens. When he discovered the prices—$5,000 for a first-order lens, $2,000 for a third-order lens—he decided that no matter how good they were, they were too expensive, especially since his friend and unofficial advisor, Winslow Lewis, could supply and install his own system so cheaply. Critics of Lewis commented that he would work for nothing rather than give up his business. I. W. P. Lewis, a civil engineer and Winslow Lewis' nephew, challenged his uncle's knowledge of lighthouses and accused him of copying the Winslow reflector from the South Stack Lighthouse in Holyhead, England.[22]

The increasing complaints and hints of scandal forced Congress to act. A Congressional committee appointed to investigate the light-house situation presented a 751-page report that led to a new law creating a nine-member Light House Board established on October 9, 1852. The board immediately began installing Fresnel lenses in all new and existing lighthouses. It also issued an annual *Light List*, describing the position of each light, its physical appearance, and the light's characteristic. The board also published "Notice to Mariners," which described any newly-established lights and also changes in existing ones.

In 1848, before the investigation and reorganization of the light-house administration began, Congress had approved funds for the construction of a lighthouse on Carysfort Reef. The board decreed that the lightship *Florida* was to remain on station until the completion of the lighthouse. The government chose I. W. P. Lewis to design the screwpile structure. Alexander Mitchell, who invented the screwpile, assigned his patent to Lewis in 1844, and the U.S. letters of patent were issued in 1845.[23]

A foundry in Philadelphia received the contract to manufacture all the wrought iron parts for the lighthouse. The foundry completely assembled the tower to make sure all the pieces met specifications and fit together perfectly, and then disassembled the tower and shipped it—with all the needed tools and trained workmen—by schooner to the reef site. Engineers designed the prefabricated parts in sizes that would enable them to be moved and assembled efficiently on the reef and manufactured plates and sections that could be bolted together quickly. Plans called for the cast-iron fittings to hold the skeleton together by friction until workmen could erect the shell and make adjustments.[24]

The workmen, who had already assembled and disassembled the

tower at the foundry, expected no difficulties. However, constructing the tower on a submarine site proved much more difficult than erecting it on land. The site on the outermost bank of Carysfort Reef was four and a half feet below the water's surface. Captain Howard Stansbury, U.S. Army Corps of Topographical Engineers, had expected the coral to be solid and planned to screw the foundation piles deep into the reef, but the coral was not solid. When borings were made it was discovered that only the exterior crust was solid; below the crust was a softer mass of calcareous sand. Stansbury realized that the screwpiles bored through the crust would have insufficient bearings, so he designed large cast-iron disks (called foot plates) with holes in the center. The foundation screwpiles were passed through the center holes in the plates and driven ten feet into the sand, until a collar attached to the piles rested on the disks. The disks proved to be a successful innovation; however, lack of funds delayed the completion of the lighthouse.[25]

When construction resumed, Major Thomas B. Linnard was the engineer in charge; however, Linnard died before the tower was completed. The U.S. Army of Topographic Engineers sent thirty-five year old Lieutenant George Gordon Meade to take Linnard's place. Meade's grandfather had been a wealthy Philadelphia merchant and an ardent patriot who contributed generously from his private fortune to the revolutionary cause of the colonies. His father, Richard Worsam Meade, was a naval agent for the United States, stationed in Cadiz, Spain, when George was born. The Meades led an affluent and socially prominent life until Richard loaned the U.S. government large sums of money that the government neglected to repay. Almost destitute, the Meade family returned to Washington, D.C. Meade's parents could not afford to send him to a private university, so George applied to the U.S. Military Academy. Although he said he "did not admire" West Point or want a military career, he graduated nineteenth out of fifty-six members of the class of 1835. As a brevet second lieutenant of the Third Artillery, the army sent him to Florida at the outbreak of the Seminole War. Meade contracted yellow fever while he was in Florida, and in 1836 he resigned from the Army.

As a civilian Meade became a survey engineer for railroads, and later the government hired him to establish the boundary between the

United States and Texas. These jobs were not particularly profitable. When he married Margaretta Sergeant in 1840, Meade decided to reenlist. He joined the U.S. Army Corps of Topographical Engineers and was assigned to assist in designing and constructing lighthouses for the Delaware Bay, as well as in surveying and charting the Florida Reefs. The knowledge he gained from the waters off the Keys, combined with his experience in screwpile lighthouse construction, made him the obvious choice to complete the Carysfort Reef Lighthouse.[26]

Richard Bache, Meade's biographer, met him for the first time before Meade undertook the Carysfort project. Bache wrote, "He wore his hair down to the nape of his neck ... and that being the fashion, did not, of course, attract my attention; but what did attract and fix it was the new experience to me of a man with long ringlets, looking as to his head as a cavalier of the time of Charles I. He was, in a word, a dandy ... without being particularly good looking in face and figure ... he was tall and slender and graceful with an air of highest breeding."[27]

After becoming better acquainted with Meade and watching him work, Bache concluded that Meade's dandified looks were misleading, and that he was a man who became totally involved and dedicated to every job assigned to him.

Meade expected to complete the lighthouse on Carysfort Reef within a year after he arrived, but the Congressional investigation delayed appropriations. Meade barraged the government with requests for funds. When the final appropriations arrived, he made up for lost time and completed the lighthouse as scheduled.

On July 31, 1852, Meade wrote to the newly formed Light House Board describing the structure. The 112-foot Carysfort Reef Lighthouse was:

> ... composed of a framework of 9 iron piles, occupying the center and angular points of an octagon of 50 feet diameter and tapering from 50 feet at the base to 19 feet at the top. The dwelling house is the frustum of a cone, the sides having the same inclination as the Piles. The floor is 33 feet above the low water, and the house of two stories is 20 feet high. From the top of the house to the Lantern is a Cylindrical Tower for a stairway 38 feet high. The whole structure

is painted Red—except the Piles which are Black—and the doors and windows of the dwelling and roof of the Lantern which are white.[28]

To supply the keepers with fresh water, tanks suspended within the tower framework held a total of 3500 gallons of water collected from the roof. Meade also supplied the keepers with additional casks for six hundred gallons. Inside the lantern, men installed curtains of ordinary ticking, which they could draw across the lantern's glass during the day to protect the lens from sunlight.

Meade directed the keepers—although it was not their official duty—to board all wrecks or distressed vessels and to "... succor them as far as it is in [their] power either by piloting or the supplying of sustenance or materials of any kind on hand." For these purposes, as well as for general transportation, Meade proposed that the lighthouse be equipped with two boats with oars, and one sailboat of twelve tons.[29]

The Carysfort Reef Lighthouse began operating on March 10, 1852, and the Light House Board discharged the 225-ton lightship *Florida*, with Captain Wellington in command. Records indicate that a former captain of the *Florida*, Charles M. Johnson, received the lightkeeper's appointment.

The Board supplied the light with eighteen lamps, arranged with eleven in one circle and seven in the other. Instead of a Fresnel lens, the board shipped a catoptric apparatus, which reflected the light by means of mirrors. The Fresnel lens originally intended for the lighthouse had been shipped to the customs house in New York for storage until it could be installed. It remained there for over nine months; then, for some inexplicable reason, it was sold to the highest bidder. When it came time to put the light into operation, Meade installed the twenty-one-inch-diameter reflectors for the lamps until the board could purchase another Fresnel lens. This substitution, even though a temporary one, greatly disturbed Meade, for it meant that not only would the light be seen from a shorter distance, but the characteristic would be fixed rather than revolving. The light on the Cape Florida Lighthouse, only forty miles northeast, was a fixed light, and Meade feared that vessels might mistake one light for the other. He insisted that a revolving light with a Fresnel lens be installed at Carysfort as soon as possible.

Even as he suggested these changes, Meade knew it would take time for the Light House Board to act. He made the best of the situation and reported that he had improved the light by using additional reflectors and placing them more effectively. He also bought the best oil available for the lamps "without reference to price." As for the keepers, he reported, "Intelligent and faithful persons have been placed in charge, with strict orders . . . to keep the lights in their most efficient condition at all times . . . I have reason to believe these orders are obeyed and thus the apparatus from proper adjustment, good oil, and attention on the part of the keepers is in reality more efficient than under other conditions it would be."[30]

Three years later in 1855 the Light House Board installed a first-order Fresnel lens at Carysfort, changing the light's characteristic from fixed to flashing.

George W. Parsons was fascinated by the light and the lighthouse. Parsons, who lived near the Miami River, traveled in South Florida and the Keys from 1873 to 1876. Parsons kept a diary during this period, and in it he describes his sail with a friend to Carysfort Reef Lighthouse in February 1875. Captain Edward Bell, the head keeper, invited them aboard. He helped them secure their sailboat and then assisted them up to the landing platform, which was about twenty feet above the water. From there the men climbed:

> . . . iron stairs into the first room, a large one. . . . Here we see the oil tanks and one immense water tank holding two thousand gallons of water, much more, of course, than would be needed for these men, the [purpose] being to supply any vessel that may be short of the article. Here is the place where the cooking and eating are done. Going up a half dozen steps we are in the hall, as it is called, with three very pleasant rooms adjoining, all opening onto the balcony, which extends in a circle around the outside. Here is the Promenade where the spy glass is used, and where we spent a great deal of our time gazing far out into the Gulf and down into the waters below at the purple- and indigo-colored fish, and other curiosities of the reef.[31]

Parsons wrote that Bell presented them with a treat:

[He] brought out the *New York Herald* and [*New York*] *Times* . . .
only four or five days old, which he had received that very day from
the SS *City of New York* . . . the Captain being so kind as to run in as
near as possible and drop overboard to the keeper who was in his
small boat, the package carefully done up so as not to be injured by
accidentally falling in the water. On a pleasant day the head keeper
often runs out in his little boat a hundred yards or so when he sees
the right steamer coming and receives any number of papers, those
on board well knowing what he wants. . . . We eagerly devoured the
news.

The steam ships heading south charted a course that ran close to
shore, enabling them to pick up the slight southerly coastal current
and skirt the edge of the Gulf Stream with its swift flow in the opposite direction. Parsons notes that this course brought the vessels,
". . . sometimes within two hundred yards or less of the lighthouse . . . steaming north the [vessels] keep well out into the Gulf, or
Straits as this part of the stream is called, to feel the full force of the
current."

Half an hour before sunset, Bell, with his lighting lamp (called a
lucerne), and followed by the assistant keeper, ascended the tower to
perform their nightly ritual.

. . . we followed the keeper up the winding stairs into the room just
beneath the lantern. As we go up the few steps to the narrow platform between the lens and outside windows we are requested to be
careful and not touch the glass, a precaution we are careful to observe, especially when the keepers themselves are required to don a
loose blouse of some soft material to keep any buttons from contact
with the glass. We now commence a study of a first-order light. . . .

Parsons read a name stamped out on a small plaque on the lens:
"Henry Lepaute." It is the name of the company that built the lens in
Paris in 1857 and sold it to the Light House Board for $22,000.

Proposed lighthouse for Carysfort Reef designed by Winslow Lewis. The Light House Board rejected this plan and selected I. W. P. Lewis, the nephew and severe critic of Winslow Lewis, to design the iron pile structure. (NATIONAL ARCHIVES)

. . . we were much interested to see how the lamp is supplied continually with oil by the system . . . kept in motion by a pendant
weight, the oil being forced into the lamp incessantly, running over
into the reservoir below. Four wicks constituted the light, and these
took an immense chimney to cover them. The outside wick being
four and one half inches in diameter circular in form. . . . At pre-
cisely sunset, Cap B. and the first assistant, with their Lucernes (no
matches allowed) . . . ignite the wick in four different places.

Keepers had to follow specific instructions for every detail of the
lighting. When there are multiple burner wicks, the central, or number one wick, is first lit with the lucerne and immediately lowered to
the lowest point at which it will burn. Then numbers two, three, and
four are lit and lowered to prevent smoking the apparatus. At first the
wicks are kept low and the chimney high. As the wicks steadily burn,
the keeper raises them to their proper heights and lowers the chimney.
The clear white flame will then burn steady and bright.[32]

While Bell attached the smoke stack and set the oil feeder in motion, Parsons watched and states, "the second assistant winds up the
heavy, twenty-pound weight that [rotates] the lenses machinery, like
clock work, a system . . . beautiful to see, and now the light is lit and is
shining a distance of 16¼ nautical miles, flash visible 18½."

The dome-shaped first-order lens Parsons describes as "about ten
feet high and consist[ing] of the upper and lower prisms, throwing the
light down and up to the flame, and thus concentrated it is magnified
to the distance, maintained by the lens. It is like looking into one immense kaleidoscope to be under the lens and see the gorgeous colors
and tints reflected by the prisms as the lens slowly revolves from left
to right."

The light's characteristic was flashing, one in which the total duration of light in a period is shorter than the total duration of darkness,
and the appearances of light (flashes) are usually of equal duration.
Parsons observed that the flashes were caused by "an equal division
being made by means of the brass framework into which the prisms
and lenses are fitted."

"God with us" is the motto on the pedestal near the tracks of the revolving machinery that rotates the lens. When Parsons asked Bell

about the saying, Bell replied, "Indeed we need Him badly enough out here sometimes . . . when the hurricane comes down upon us and this whole thing totters and shakes as though it were about to fall."

Before sunrise the next morning, Parsons climbed the long staircase to the lantern to see "the 'Gleam doused' in sailor parlance. . . . The big lamp was extinguished like any ordinary one, cover placed over the lens and curtains hung to the windows."

Parsons did not, however, record the many details attended to by the keeper to ready the light for the evening's lighting. Duties included cleaning the lamps, burners, and chimney; trimming and renewing the wick in the burners; filling the lamp reservoir; and cleaning the illuminating apparatus.

During the day, the keepers cleaned the floors of the lantern, the tower, and the stairs, being careful not to raise any soot or dust, even though they already had covered the lens and lamps to protect them.

Keepers also updated two sets of daily records: watch records and light-station journals. The watch records were factual and included the date, condition of the light, weather, and water temperature. The journals contained much of the same information, but also included a record of maintenance work done on the lighthouse and the light. Keepers sometimes wrote detailed descriptions of the weather and daily events, and from these you can get a true feeling of what life was like on a lighthouse.

The early journals and watch records for Carysfort Reef Lighthouse, as well as the correspondence of the Light House Board and other records from 1852 to 1900, were on file with the Commerce Department. In 1921 a fire in the building destroyed many of these records.[33]

The first extant journal for the Carysfort Reef Light Station was started February 4, 1881. Captain Edward Bell, who welcomed Parsons and his friend aboard in 1875, was still the head keeper at this time, and he had been on Carysfort for twelve years. A veteran keeper, Bell had previously served on the Key West, Sand Key, and Sombrero Key lights. In 1881 his assistant, L. C. Warner, had just received a promotion from second to first assistant keeper. When the log opens a storm is brewing, and Bell describes its development: "The wind is east by south and very scully, the barometer 29.74." During the night, the sea gains momentum with waves breaking on the reef. The weather stays stormy, and for the next few days the wind continues "to blow a very fresh breeze." A heavy sea rolls onto the reef. On February 11, the storm begins to let up, and Bell decides to go ashore for supplies.

The lighthouse boat hung from davits on the landing platform above the water. Bell and Warner stowed the needed equipment aboard, rigged the sail, reefed it down, and were lowering the boat when one of the davits snapped, sending the boat and Bell crashing into the sea. Bell managed to swim to the platform ladder, and he and Warner tried to retrieve the boat. He wrote, "All we could do, because there was a good deal of sea running, was to try and get her upright again. When we failed in this, we had to tie her up as well as we could."

Without a boat the keepers were marooned. The keeper on leave had taken the second boat, and would not return for some time. The keepers flew the American flag upside down from the light tower to signal for help. Bell wrote in the log, "We hoisted the ensign on the lighthouse to get some assistance from someone on shore or from a passing vessel. The wreckers seem to have all gone northward. The boat is pretty badly used up, but she may still be repaired if we do not lose her altogether." The men stayed busy while awaiting some response to their distress signal; they kept the light, and when time permitted they tried to save the boat. Warner recorded in the journal that they rigged a chain to the broken davit and attached the other end to the boat. The powerful surge of the sea broke the chain. "The boat is bottom up. We took rope and put it under her by diving down and taking two turns around the boat, making it very secure, and then attaching it to the davit. We finally got her hoisted up out of the water at 12:30. In the afternoon we finally hoisted the boat up as high as she could be taken and secured her as best we could. The keeper took down the flag. The boat is nearly a complete wreck. We have nothing in the house in the shape of ropes or tackles."[34]

On February 13, help came in an unexpected way. The lighthouse tender *Alice*, bringing supplies from Key West, arrived ahead of schedule. Aboard were Mr. and Mrs. Harry Warner Magill, the new keeper and his wife. Bell returned to Key West on the tender, promising to see that the *Alice* would bring another boat.

Magill, born in Pennsylvania, served in the U.S. Army before joining the Lighthouse Service. He was familiar with Carysfort, having served on the light as first assistant keeper for three months before becoming head keeper of the Dry Tortugas Light on Garden Key.

On August 14, 1881, F. A. Brost replaced Magill. A Floridian who previously served on both the Carysfort Reef and Alligator Reef lights, Brost kept a lively log, describing the good weather as well as the bad. He once noted, "The weather was clear and bright all night, the stars brilliant, and I could see the light from Fowey Rocks Lighthouse all night." Boats often stopped at the light for water, and Brost recorded the events: "Schooner *Eugene* reported to this station in want of water. . . . Capt. Charles S. Baker of the Schooner *Rapid* boarded this station in want of water and provisions. I exchanged, with the consent of both assistants, a barrel of flour, a little pork, and about one quart of vinegar for different kinds of fruit."

On some occasions the keepers boarded passing vessels to post letters, pick up newspapers, or just talk and find out what was going on in other parts of the world. In the journals Brost makes no mention of current events, birthdays, or even holidays, but by sticking cutouts from magazines and food wrappers between the pages, Brost brings some color and a personal touch to the logs. His journals also reveal how much time the men spent maintaining the lighthouse.

In 1882 the men scaled and painted the iron structure, repaired the gallery railing, attached new fastenings on the iron ladder leading to the water, built a new landing platform, and repaired two of the lamp burners. The following year the keepers painted their quarters, made various repairs to the lighting equipment, and renovated the revolving machinery for the lens. In 1884 the men installed new mineral-oil lamps made at the Lighthouse Service Depot on Staten Island, New York.[35]

Martin Weatherford became keeper in 1885, and his entries in the journals reveal quite a different personality. Weatherford limited his terse notations to date, weather, direction of the wind, barometer readings, and temperature. He makes no mention of the new stairway and landing the keepers built, or the fact that they cut manholes into each of the water tanks so they could be cleaned. John Hubband, the lighthouse inspector, no less concise than Weatherford, once noted in the journal, "Delivered half-year's rations and exchanged libraries."[36]

Libraries originated when the Light House Board recognized the necessity of "doing something to satisfy the intellectual requirement of the keepers and their families." The library included both a case and the books. Each case, two feet high, two feet wide, and eight inches deep, could hold about forty volumes. This container, made of shellacked white pine and strengthened with heavy brass trimmings, had doors with a bolt and lock on the front. On the sides of the case hinged handles were attached. "The cases," wrote the board, "made a rather neat appearance when set upright on a table. . . . When locked, the library cases can stand rough handling." The books offered what the board considered "a proper admixture of historic, scientific, and poetic matter, with some good novels. . . . Preference is given in their distribution to those light stations most distant from towns and villages." Every three months an inspector would deliver a new set of books and collect the old ones, which he would later pass on to another station.[37]

Carysfort Reef was an isolated station. The keepers could obtain some supplies from Key Largo, but most came from Key West. The libraries provided welcome diversion for many men separated from family and friends for months at a time. However, some keepers did not mind the isolation, and several men took advantage of the situation to study.

Keeper William Hunt Harris had attended Mt. Lebanon University in New Orleans, but did not graduate. At twenty, he went to Key West and accepted the position of second assistant keeper at Carysfort Reef Light Station. Harris arrived aboard the station in 1889 with his law books in hand, and whenever he was free from lighthouse duties he studied law. After three months on Carysfort he transferred to the Northwest Passage Light, where he continued studying. The following year Hunt was practicing law in the circuit court, and later in the Florida Supreme Court.[38]

Shortly after Harris left Carysfort Reef Station, the Light House Board made an important addition to the light—three red sector panels. Because of the lighthouse's location, ships could pass on the deep ocean side of the reefs. (Vessels with a shallower draft could also use

Hawks Channel, which ran between the reefs and the shoals just off the islands.) A mariner in Hawks Channel or running oceanside of the reefs at night often found it difficult to know exactly where the line of reefs lay. To remedy this, panels of red glass were installed inside the lantern in exact positions so that when the white light flashed in those sectors it would show as red over the reefs. The flashing white light identified the position of the light, and the flashing red sectors identified the position of the reefs. If a mariner could see a flashing red light, he knew immediately that his vessel was too close to the reefs and in danger.[39]

The red sectors, although a great improvement at night, could not prevent ships from running aground during the day. Carysfort Reef, no matter how well marked during the night or day, still claimed ships under the command of unwary captains or caught in storms. Keeper Francis McNulty stuck a copy of the following shipwreck report between the pages of the light station journal in 1894:

At about 6:30 o'clock A.M. British steamship *Moonstone* from Portland, Maine, United States, bound to Tampeco, Mexico, wrecked near this light in clear daylight. Wind from south southeast, clear dry weather. The vessel was first seen from the light on August 14 at about 4:30 A.M., and struck the reef at about 6:30 A.M. The crew consisted of a captain, mates, engineers, cooks, stewards, and seamen of whom all were saved and are now in Key West. Every assistance in my power was rendered to those aboard the wreck. The vessel will not prove a total loss.

McNulty was born in England in 1835. After he joined the Lighthouse Service, he served at two light stations in Florida and at American Shoal and Rebecca Shoal lights in the Keys. As second assistant keeper he received a salary of $490 a year; first assistant keepers received $520, and head keepers, $820. Although there were some exceptions, the salaries paid by the Lighthouse Service remained constant from 1852 to 1900. In the United States in 1890, the average annual income of farm laborers was $233; teachers, $256; coal miners, $406; and ministers, $794. To earn these wages people worked an average of ten hours a day, six days a week. Keepers usually spent two months on the light and then had a month of shore leave.[40]

This was still the work schedule when Clement Brooks arrived at Carysfort Reef Light in 1925 to serve as second assistant keeper. Fifty-five years after he first arrived at the light he recalled that he had tried his "best to make myself at home and be contented." The keeper carried Brooks's "luggage up a small flight of stairs to my room, just like a big hotel." From his room Brooks could walk "out a door onto a circular bridge-type porch . . . that went clear around." There was an ocean view from every room in the keepers' house. Looking thirty feet below, Brooks could see the "breakers dashing over the coral reefs." It took Brooks a while to get used to living in a circular dwelling. He wrote:

> On the west side of the main room was the kitchen table. We used it for reading. A checkered tablecloth, blue and white, covered it and in the center a large size Holy Bible. On each side of the table was a captain's chair. Very comfortable . . . against the wall was a double . . . door library . . . next to it a two-burner oil stove . . . then the big iron double doors to the outside . . . usually open . . . next a clothesline that led to a swing shelf cooler for eats back of a storage closet for groceries. One thing I liked about the lighthouse, there was never a dull moment . . . you know that great big ocean never is without a storm. I remember one summer it hailed large lumps . . . really got cold. I put my Pea jacket on and walked to our lower bridge. When I got to the windward side I opened my jacket. I could lay on the wind. When you can lay against a strong wind, that's the tail end of a typhoon. I believe it was.[41]

Brooks especially liked to fish from the landing platform and meet the local fishermen who often came over to chat. The keepers occasionally invited anglers aboard. Such was the case in 1927 when Charles Brookfield and a friend were fishing near the light. "Come aboard," called Captain Pierce, the keeper, and motioned for them to bring their boat into the "parlor," a small opening between the reefs. Brookfield thoroughly enjoyed his introduction to life at a light station. He later recalled, "I realized for the first time what it meant to be

isolated for two months with only one companion and without refrig-
eration or fresh food. I was impressed with the cleanliness of the
dwelling. Everything of metal was bright and shining, especially the
brass fuel measuring containers, which must have required a great
deal of polishing in such a salty location."

The next time Brookfield and his friends visited the lighthouse they
brought newspapers, magazines, and fresh meat and vegetables. "In
response to our boat horn" said Brookfield, "the men came running
down the stairway, and we discovered as we drew closer that they
were not the same crew as before." The keeper was Captain Jenks and
his first assistant was Harry Baldwin, both from Key West. The keepers invited the men to stay for dinner and share the bounty. When the
visitors prepared to depart after dinner Captain Jenks asked, "Aren't
you having engine trouble?" He insisted that Brookfield try to start up
the engine. The engine ran smoothly, but Captain Jenks shook his
head and said, "It's missing and you are in distress." Slowly it dawned
on Brookfield that the regulations requiring visitors to leave ended
with the words ". . . except in cases of distress." Brookfield seized the
opportunity to watch the keepers operate the light and to investigate
the rumor that Carysfort Reef Light was haunted. Brookfield later
recalled:

> The big Fresnel magnifying lens, higher than my head, was
> mounted on a pedestal in the middle of the glass-enclosed room,
> surrounded on the outside by the upper gallery. First the keepers
> removed the curtains hanging inside the room that protected the
> lens from the rays of the sun, which was just about to set. Tenta-
> tively, I pushed the lens lightly with one finger and was amazed to
> find that even such a slight pressure made it revolve on its smooth
> bearings. The keeper next prepared the lamps for lighting, and I
> watched as the kerosene fuel was preheated in a tube to provide the
> gas for the mantle.[42]

The incandescent oil vapor system (i.o.v.), described by Brookfield,
replaced oil wick lamps in 1913. Next Brookfield observed the keeper
wind the clockworks that provided the mechanical power to turn the
lens. "It took 45 minutes for them to run down, whereupon a bell

warned the keepers to wind them up again. The lamp was gleaming and turning on its pedestal. Three flashes and a blank in succession, identifying Carysfort Reef to mariners. Fowey Rocks, forty miles to the north, flashed twice. Captain Jenks sat in his chair by the door opening onto the gallery, starting the first watch. The rest of us descended the winding stairway to the dwelling."

Stretched out on a mattress on the lower floor of the quarters, Brookfield said he had hardly closed his eyes "when a loud groan shook the room and startled me awake. I sat up thinking it may have been a dream. Then another groan came and I knew it was real." Brookfield took a flashlight and climbed the stairway "around and around to the beacon where the captain sat reading, the cool night air coming in through the open door while the big lens slowly revolved." After some trivial conversation, Brookfield asked the keeper about the strange moans. Jenks, not in the least surprised by the question, replied, "That's old Captain Johnson. You know, he died aboard this light, and he still comes around at night and groans." This answer was not particularly reassuring or satisfying for Brookfield, so he came up with his own theory, "I solved the mystery of the moans—I believe. Under the hot sun, the tower's iron walls expand; in the cool of darkness, they contract. Shrinking, they make sounds startlingly human. My theory may not be true, but I have clung to it ever since."[43]

Moan it might, but the Carysfort Reef Lighthouse has withstood raging storms and hurricanes, including the 1935 hurricane when the barometric pressure at the light was 29.68 inches. Keepers clocked the east-northeast wind at eighty miles per hour and reported that the light rocked so badly one of the keepers was seasick.

The U.S. Coast Guard manned the Carysfort Lighthouse from 1939 until its automation in 1960. During World War II, with the light blacked out, the station functioned as a watchtower for enemy submarines, and the Coast Guard reported many sightings. In 1942 a German submarine torpedoed the *Benwood*, a three-hundred-foot freighter built in England in 1910. The torpedoed freighter tried to make port, but a friendly ship unexpectedly rammed the freighter, causing its cargo of ammunition to explode. The *Benwood* sank in thirty to fifty feet of water near Carysfort Reef, where its remains still lie.[44]

This 1899 Light House Library measured twenty-four inches wide, twenty-six inches high, and ten inches deep. It was constructed of one-inch white pine with tongue and groove joints and brass hardware. A list of the books in the library was attached on the inside of the the door with brass nails. (PHOTOGRAPHY BY DEBBI RICCI, PLYMOUTH LIGHTHOUSE, DUXBURY, MAINE)

Once the Seventh Coast Guard District Aids to Navigation (ATON) automated the light it deteriorated considerably, damaged by nature and vandals. Rust soon covered the pie-slice stairways and ladders, and the glass in the portholes and in the windows enclosing the light were broken, cracked, or missing. Rain seeped in through dozens of cracks and holes, causing more rust and erosion. The rotating mechanism was no longer used, and in 1962 the Aids to Navigation Team (ANT) removed the original lens. The Historical Association of Southern Florida Museum acquired the lens from the Coast Guard and placed it on display in Miami. Personnel from ANT have replaced the lens with a solar-powered Vega VRB-25 rotating optic. Its characteristic is a regularly repeated, easily identifiable sixty-second group of three flashes.[45]

At night mariners can see the Carysfort light at a distance of fifteen nautical miles; however, mariners have other ways of determining position. Private yachts and all commercial vessels use LORAN (Long Range Navigation), and most recently GPS (Global Positioning System). These systems practically eliminate the need for lighthouses. Nevertheless, even with the navigational aid of a lighthouse and the most modern technology, the living coral reefs in the Keys, especially in the Carysfort Light area, have sustained enormous damage from ships that have run aground.

In August 1984 the *Wellwood* plowed into Molasses Reef, one of the most beautiful reefs in John Pennekamp Coral Reef State Park. The *Wellwood* was the largest vessel to have run aground in the sanctuary. The vessel sustained relatively little damage, but it left a twenty-thousand-square-foot gouge in the reef. The damage to the coral is still evident.

Molasses Reef suffered further damage in December 1986, when a 215-foot Panamanian freighter owned by Mini Laurel, Inc., rammed the reef. The owners were fined $525,000 because of the damage to the coral.

In October 1989 the 155-foot *Alec Owen Maitland* grounded one and a half miles south of Carysfort Reef, causing serious reef damage. Then on November 10, a Greek cargo ship, the 470-foot *Elpis*, struck a reef to the southwest of the light. People in the Keys and throughout the country were shocked and dismayed by these preventable accidents. As a result, many urged that legislation be passed to create a ten-mile buffer zone between the shipping lanes and the vulnerable reefs—the only living reefs off the continental United States.

Since the 1980s, there has been growing scientific interest in the coral reefs of the Florida Keys and the protection of the entire Keys's marine ecosystem, including sea grass meadows and fringing mangroves. Though Carysfort Reef Lighthouse marks the reef well by day and night, boat groundings continue to occur.

On November 16, 1990, President Bush signed a bill creating a thirty-five-hundred-square-mile Florida Keys National Marine Sanctuary, stretching from Biscayne National Park to the Dry Tortugas, including both the Atlantic and Gulf of Mexico sides. "Ironically," observed Robert Halley, H. L. Vacher, and Eugene Shinn, authors of

Clement Brooks proudly poses in his lighthouse keeper's uniform. The uniforms were first issued in 1884. By 1885 sixteen hundred employees were in uniform. (PHOTOGRAPH COURTESY OF CLEMENT BROOKS)

Geology and Hydrogeology of the Florida Keys, "the major shipping lanes in the Straits of Florida were moved away (seaward) from the Florida Keys—not for the protection of shipping, but for the protection of the reefs.[46]

The passage of the 1990 bill reflects changing attitudes about the environment—especially marine environment and coral reefs in particular. The number of shipping losses on the Florida reefs was so large by the mid-1800s, that in 1850 the Coast Survey sent scientist

Louis Agassiz to the Florida Keys to conduct the first American study of coral growth. The purpose of the study was to determine "... whether the growth of coral reefs can be prevented ... which are so unfavorable to the safety of navigation." After spending almost a year on a boat mapping the reefs and identifying coral, Agassiz replied, "The sooner a system of lighthouses and signals is established along the whole reef, the better."[47]

As the twentieth century comes to a close, the lighthouses fulfill not only their original purpose as navigational aids, but also protect endangered coral and the marine life dependent on it by marking the location of the reefs.

There are currently plans for the historic Carysfort Reef Lighthouse to serve as a marine research center under the direction of the National Oceanic and Atmospheric Administration (NOAA). As such, it would be the world's first permanent scientific laboratory over a living coral reef.

"This is an ideal location for marine scientists," says Alison Fahrer, President of the Pennekamp Coral Reef Institute, Inc. "Carysfort Lighthouse, six miles at sea, provides easy access to both shallow and deep reefs." The institute is a private, non-profit corporation formed in 1984 to support the preservation and care of the Florida Keys's reefs. As of 1998, it continues to seek donations for the construction of the laboratory, which requires $500,000 for completion. The laboratory's goal is to help support long-term coral reef research programs that will aid in the understanding of coral reef ecosystems, their protection, and utilization.

Qualified scientists will be able to apply to NOAA to use the facility (for a fee) and submit project specifications, which will be reviewed by NOAA scientists. "Basic laboratory facilities will be available, but any sophisticated equipment will have to be supplied and brought in by the project's scientists," says Fahrer. The lower level of the renovated lighthouse will house storage tanks for freshwater and wastewater and will have areas for electrical and mechanical equipment. According to Fahrer, there will be "a dry laboratory with air conditioning, as well as fresh running seawater twenty-four hours a day. The second level will offer spartan living conditions for two to four people, with modest cooking and bathing facilities." Fahrer notes that

Keeper "Captain" Jenks (right) and Second Assistant Keeper Hall on Carys-fort Reef Lighthouse in 1927, when Charles Brookfield paid them a visit and solved the mystery of the moans. (PHOTOGRAPH COURTESY OF CHARLES BROOKFIELD)

the creative new use of the lighthouse will not end with the laboratory facilities. "A complete weather station will be established in the light-house that will transmit weather conditions at Carysfort locally, statewide, and to area shipping."[48]

The recording of wind direction and velocity, barometric pressure,

Carysfort Reef Lighthouse when the Coast Guard manned the station. The light is now automatically operated, and it is the oldest functioning lighthouse of its kind in the United States. (U.S. COAST GUARD OFFICIAL PHOTO)

and air and water temperature was once the job of the lighthouse keepers, and they noted the information in their stations' watch books. These records, particularly water temperatures, could be valuable to modern scientists studying global warming. One research geologist, Robert B. Halley, says, "These long-term records would be excellent for comparison to modern temperatures." Halley, who is with the

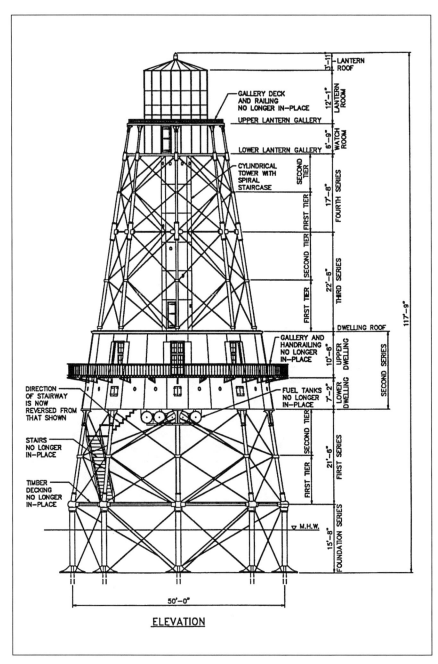

The 1994 overall refurbishing plan for Carysfort Lighthouse. (U.S. COAST GUARD, SEVENTH DISTRICT)

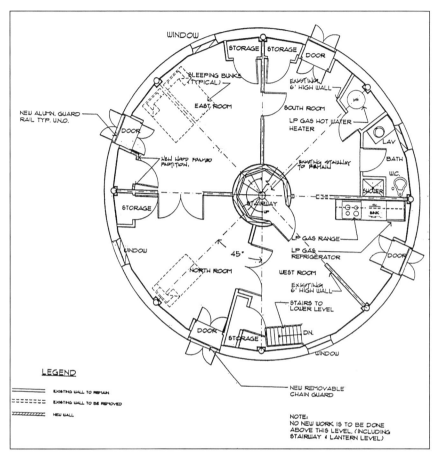

Floor plan for the new upper-level living quarters for the proposed offshore marine research facility on Carysfort Lighthouse. (POST, BUCKLEY, SCHUH, & JERNIGAN, INC.)

Center for Coastal and Regional Marine Studies, has recently located records from the lighthouses at the Dry Tortugas, Key West, Carysfort Reef, and Fowey Rocks; he is still searching for more.

The information gained from the weather station and the projects undertaken at the Carysfort Marine Laboratory (CML) will be invaluable. The Rosenstiel School of Marine and Atmospheric Science in Miami lists a few types of research that could best, and maybe only, be done in a permanent reef facility: long-term studies of reef dynamics, behavioral studies of reef animals, and coral spawning research.

George Gordon Meade Easby, great-grandson of the man in charge of completing the construction of Carysfort Reef Lighthouse, examines the first-order Fresnel lens at the top of the lighthouse. The glass behind Easby creates the red sector of the light, warning mariners of the nearby reefs. The first Fresnel lens installed is on display at the museum of the Historical Association of Southern Florida in Miami. (PHOTOGRAPH BY PHIL FOLEY)

"Over time," states Dr. Samuel Snedaker, a professor at the Rosenstiel School, "the researchers working at the CML would necessarily generate an intensive database that could serve as a baseline to quantify and document changes due to unusual or extreme events such as hurricanes or oil spills."[49]

The researchers and scientists will bring life to the light tower that has stood empty for so many years. Perhaps as those before them have done, the scientists will climb to the upper level of the lighthouse and experience the panoramic view. In the daytime, looking eastward, they will see ships plowing through the dark blue waters of the Gulf Stream. Toward the west, the dark green band of Key Largo, six miles away, will seem to float above the light green, shallow waters offshore. From high above the weblike iron-pilings, the acres of staghorn and elkhorn coral growing just under the water's surface will be visible. On clear nights, those aboard the lighthouse will see a sky full of brilliant stars and the bright guiding light of Fowey Rocks Lighthouse, and maybe even hear the noise that alarmingly sounds like the moaning ghost of old Captain Johnson.

The notes for this chapter begin on page 281.

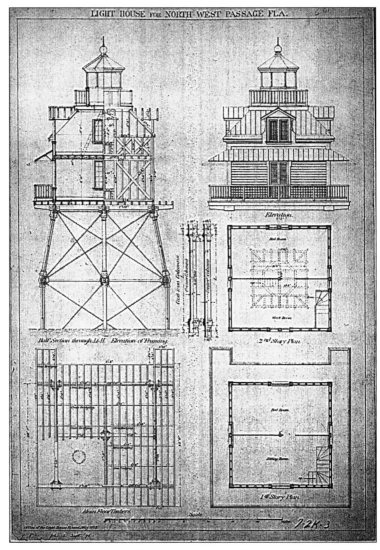

Original drawings for the new Northwest Passage Lighthouse to replace the original one built in 1855. (NATIONAL ARCHIVES)

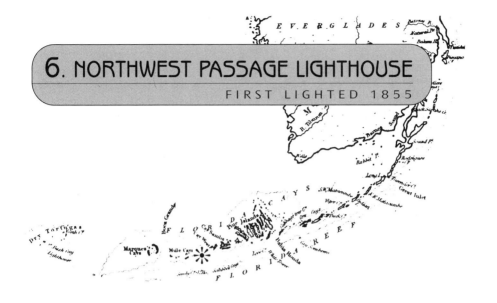

6. NORTHWEST PASSAGE LIGHTHOUSE

FIRST LIGHTED 1855

There is one lighthouse in the Keys that has slipped from the memory of mariners and into the realm of mystery and legend—the Northwest Passage Lighthouse. In 1970 the Association of the American Institute of Architects declared the lighthouse a Florida landmark. Twenty-eight years later, the only evidence of its existence is the skeletal remains of the iron screwpile foundation. Yet the menacing looking blackened forms, sticking up from the clear blue-green waters, continue to serve as an unofficial day mark for those using the channel. Current charts verify the last remaining trace of the forgotten lighthouse with the simple notation "Platform (in ruins)."[1]

The epitaph gives little indication of the life experienced by those who built and manned the Northwest Passage Light. There are few extant records, and people familiar with the lighthouse are fewer still. Tales abound, and some in their retelling have become romantic substitutes for the history that may be forever lost.

When a house on pilings still existed above the now ruined platform, locals called it the "Pilot House." People supposed that the wooden house sheltered harbor pilots as they waited to board incoming ships and guide them into Key West harbor. It may have served this purpose, for pilots continue to guide vessels through the channel,

A passing steamer delivers newspapers to a lightship. There are no extant drawings for the Key West Lightboat that marked the Northwest Passage, but the vessel would have been similar to the one shown in this illustration for Harper's Weekly *in September 1867.* (MONROE COUNTY PUBLIC LIBRARY)

but the Light House Board built the structure primarily as a lighted navigational aid and to house the keepers who manned the light.

In the 1930s when Ernest Hemingway lived in Key West, a story circulated that the structure was his stilt house where he escaped to write. At that time the light had been discontinued for years, and many people did not realize that the picturesque building had ever been a lighthouse. It might be supposed that a structure built so close to the historically busy harbor of Key West would have an abundance of easily available facts and memories to document its existence, but there is scant information about this lighthouse, which guided vessels between the Gulf of Mexico and Key West for forty-two years.

The 1842 edition of the *American Coast Pilot* describes the navigable Northwest channel: "There is a passage through Key West from the Florida Stream, into the Bay of Mexico, for vessels drawing 12 feet at

low water. This passage is about 6 miles in extent, and vessels by passing through it save the danger and delay of going round the Dry Tortugas. . . . Good pilots can be obtained at Key West to carry vessels
through."[2]

The channel offered the only navigable route in the area. Rocky
reefs and banks, covered with barely a foot of water, lie to the north of
the island of Key West, and shoal waters extend to the west. In the
daytime and in good weather, mariners could identify the passage by
the darker blue color of the water, but locating the entrance when approaching from the gulf side, particularly at night, was not only almost impossible, but also dangerous. As commerce increased among
the gulf ports, Key West, and Cuba, it became important to mark the
channel with navigational aids. On March 3, 1837, Congress appropriated $10,000 for placing a lightship at the Northwest Passage and
$800 for buoys at Northwest Passage and Key West Harbor.[3]

The lightship (sometimes referred to in official reports as the Key
West Lightboat) was stationed about seven miles north and west from
Key West, marking the offshore end of the channel.

The design of lightships posed interesting naval architectural challenges. For the efficiency of the light and for the comfort of the crew,
vessels had to be steady; rolling and pitching needed to be controlled.
The Lighthouse Service expected shipwrights to build sound and
sturdy vessels. Most lightships were well-built and durable—twelve
remained in service for fifty years, and one for sixty-seven years. Before 1877 builders used both white and live oak for lightboat construction. (After 1877 yellow pine was used, when available, and later,
steel.) Some of the larger lightships stationed off the coast topped two
hundred tons and carried a complement of fifteen officers and men.
Only a captain and three seamen manned the 145-ton lightship at
Northwest Passage, since the size of the passage required a smaller
ship, and thus, a smaller crew.

Once the lightship and buoys were in place, the number of vessels
using this expedient route continued to grow. Pilotage was much in
demand. According to an 1840 report, Jeremiah Cottrell, the first captain assigned to the Northwest Passage Lightship, was "taking every
vessel that comes that way to the detriment of other pilots." On rare
occasions keepers did guide vessels to Key West when local knowl-

edge of the reefs was essential for the safety of the vessel, but piloting was not a side occupation that was encouraged. As a result of the report, Cottrell's superiors forbade him to act as pilot.[4]

One of the crewmen serving under Cottrell was John O'Brien. O'Brien carried out his duties satisfactorily, but when Cottrell discovered he was only fifteen years old he sent him home for being underage. This was not a rare occurrence. On one lightship an inspector discovered that the captain and crew had left in charge a fourteen-year-old, who did not possess the strength to hoist the lantern to the masthead. O'Brien would not have had any difficulty in hoisting the Northwest Passage lightship's lamp to the top of the mast—it was quite small. The single light's fixed, white characteristic could be seen twelve miles at night.

In his report of October 9, 1838, superintendent of lights Adam Gordon stated, "it is a useful but feeble light, owing to the construction of its lamp. I have recommended to the department to substitute a larger lamp with reflectors, showing more lights, &c. and have hopes it will soon be improved."

Gordon was one of the first lawyers to settle in Key West, and he became the local collector of customs. Collectors of customs served as direct representatives of Stephen Pleasonton, the government official in charge of navigational aids. Pleasonton gave customs collectors the title "superintendents of lights." Even though Gordon's duties included hiring, firing, and paying light keepers; selecting lighthouse sites; supervision of contractors who built or repaired navigational aids; and inspecting lighthouses, he could only spend up to $100 without seeking Pleasonton's approval. Because of this there was little Gordon could do to improve the lightship other than make recommendations. Pleasonton took no action, and mariners filed sporadic complaints about the light over the next seventeen years.[5]

Many seamen considered duty aboard lightboats to be dangerous, uncomfortable, and monotonous. Every day at sunrise, after lowering the lantern, the crew breakfasted and then prepared the lantern for the evening lighting. The ship, just as a lighthouse, had to be kept in spotless condition. The men spent many hours cleaning and maintaining the vessel, but there was still much free time. After exhibiting the light at sunset, the crew went on rotating watches, leaving time for those not on watch to play cards, write letters, read books from the lighthouse library, and sleep. Shore leave depended on the weather. During stormy seasons the entire crew remained aboard, but at other times the men took turns ashore. In addition to being able to maintain the light properly, crewmen needed to have seamanship skills; it was essential that the vessel be kept on station at all times.[6]

Moored as it was near the entrance of the channel, the Northwest Passage Lightship was almost surrounded by shallows, a particularly precarious position to be in during strong northerly winds. From June through September, late afternoon and evening thunderstorms are customary for ten to fourteen days a month. During the torrential downpours, visibility can be briefly restricted to near zero. Although gale force winds are infrequent, they occur during tropical cyclones, thunderstorms, and strong cold fronts. Hurricanes, originating in the west Caribbean and moving north, are the most potentially destructive of the storms. The hurricane season begins in June and lasts through November.[7]

The Northwest Passage Lightship weathered its share of storms. Alexander L. Patterson was captain in October 1841 when gale force south winds that had been building at sea for days swirled into the area and blew for two days without stopping. The men must have worked continuously to keep the ship on station. In early September 1842 another hurricane clobbered Key West and the surrounding area. The whipping winds attacked the lightship for four days and nights.

Captain Henry Benners, who came aboard the lightship in March at a salary of $700 year, luckily missed that blow. When he arrived, the ship needed hauling. On September 26, 1843, Adam Gordon reported, "The light-ship at the northwest bar has been brought in [to Key West] for repairs; and, on examining her copper, it was found so defective as to require new, which has been supplied; and she is moored today—having been thoroughly recaulked, recoppered, and repaired."[8]

In 1844 Benners experienced his first hurricane aboard the lightship. The storm, traveling north from Cuba, blasted the area on October 4 and 5, and the hurricane-force winds blew half of Sand Key away. Unbelievably, the Northwest Passage Lightship reported no damage and remained on station. One of the most devastating hurricanes to hit the Keys occurred on October 11 and 12, 1846. Stephen Mallory was collector of customs and superintendent of lights at the time. He reported to Pleasonton: "During the storm the lightship at Northwest Passage broke adrift from her moorings, but as her heavy chains kept her head into the wind and sea, she backed astern and drifted sixty miles to sea, safely. . . . The lightship is now being moored (October 21st) at her station."[9]

Mariners continued to complain about the ineffectiveness of the vessel's navigational light. One report, appearing in *Hunt's Merchants' Magazine*, expressed the view that, although the light was faithfully kept, the power was "by no means what it ought to be . . . the lightship is old and the light they attempt to show is miserable."[10]

Before the completion of the screwpile lighthouse on Sand Key, the Light House Board reported that the lightship stationed off the island had been "removed from her station and sold during the last summer before this board was organized." The board felt it was important to have a lightship stationed off Sand Key until the lighthouse was in operation, and suggested transferring the Northwest Passage Lightship to Sand Key. The lighthouse superintendent, Samuel J. Douglass, informed the board that the Northwest Passage Lightship was hardly worth repairing, and needed to be replaced. This, of course, raised budgetary problems.

The board recognized that the Sand Key Lighthouse would soon be operational, and therefore a lightship stationed off the island might not be necessary. The board also realized that Northwest Passage needed a new lightship or "some other means employed to mark this important channel . . . the present one being very defective." The pros and cons of establishing a lighthouse rather than maintaining a lightship were considered by the board: "The necessity for a mark, the inefficiency of the one formed by the light-vessel, its great annual expense and rapid decay, on the one side; and . . . the durability, efficiency, and comparative economy of the light-house proposed, on the other."[11]

On March 3, 1853, Congress appropriated $12,000 for a lighthouse built on iron piles to take the place of the lightship at Northwest Passage. Plans took time to implement, and in the meantime the board decided to have the lightship repaired and "restored to her position."

Though the ship's condition was better than had been first thought, the board decided to proceed with plans for a lighthouse to mark the channel.

In June 1852, Samuel Douglass first examined the Northwest Passage area to select an appropriate site. He made another survey a year later, and then chose the location for the lighthouse. The board approved the plans and estimates for the Northwest Passage Light on July 30, 1853.[12]

A Philadelphia firm built both the wooden house and the iron pile foundation and shipped them to Key West early in May 1854. The lighthouse should have been erected without any difficulty, but work was postponed because of an outbreak of yellow fever in Key West, the most serious health crisis the people there had ever experienced. In the 1820s, during the early settlement of the island, there were deadly recurrences of the fever, and in 1826 the residents virtually abandoned the island. Sometimes called "Key West Fever," this acute infectious disease occurred during the summer, but not necessarily every year. Those arriving on the island during "the sickly season" felt they were taking an enormous risk, and even longtime inhabitants were fearful.[13]

The Light House Board reported that the mechanics who came to Key West during the outbreak returned immediately to Philadelphia. Another working party arrived in October, but, according to the board, construction was often suspended for days at a time, "in consequence of the boisterous character of the season and the exposed position of the work."

The engineers, working on a submarine site, needed calm waters in order to accomplish the difficult task of setting the wrought iron piles for the structure's foundation in exact positions. The five piles had to be driven into the coral formation through cast-iron disks four feet in diameter. Once in place, twelve-inch yellow pine spars formed the second tier of the foundation, on which the keepers' house was secured. The frame building contained living quarters for the keepers, with the illuminating apparatus and lantern set above the galvanized iron, fireproof roof.[14]

It took almost six months to complete the lighthouse, the board reported, "notwithstanding the unremitting efforts of the superintendent in charge, and those under him." The board bought a fifth-order Fresnel lens, which had an inside diameter of almost fifteen inches and a height of seventeen inches. A former keeper of the Key West Light, William Richardson, obtained a transfer to the Northwest Passage Light, and he lit the lamps for the first time on the evening of March 5, 1855. The superintendent of lights, John T. Baldwin, said the light "was visible over 275 degrees of the horizon, with an available range of ten miles beyond the bar."[15]

For the first ten years, the well-constructed lighthouse needed nothing more than routine maintenance to keep it in good condition. The only major repairs made were to the roof, which leaked considerably. But after many more years of severe storms, such as the hurricane of 1865, Superintendent Charles Howe reported that the station was beginning to show the effects of the climate and needed a general overhauling. In 1869 Howe oversaw the repair and repainting of the wrought iron piles and the replacement of a number of the lantern's glass panes. He noted that the roof continued to be unsatisfactory and that the wooden house was rotting.[16]

Almost every year between 1870 and 1876 inspectors reiterated the need to scale and paint the lower braces, and emphasized that the lighthouse needed extensive repairs. In 1877 superintendent Frank A. Wicker wrote, "As the structure is not a suitable one for this station it is thought better, and in the end, more economical, to erect a new one of the latest and most approved construction." The Light House Board requested an appropriation for $20,000—Congress turned it down. In 1878 Wicker reported that the woodwork of the dwelling, as well as its supports, were rotten, and it would cost $6,000 to repair the structure properly. Congress approved the more modest request. With funds in hand, the board proceeded, not to repair the house, but to have it replaced.[17]

During construction, Wicker had a temporary masthead light erected nearby, and the old keepers' house and pine spars were removed from the iron pile foundation. A landing deck was constructed on the first set of pilings, with a second set of iron braces providing support for house. A ladder extended from the water to the deck and to the first floor of the house.

The keepers' new wooden house was a gracefully designed, square, two-story building. A porch with an overhanging roof ran along the perimeter of the first story, extending beyond the roof on two sides and at the front of the house. This allowed ample space for the keepers to work the winches, as well as raise and lower materials and supplies. The keepers also used the extended porch to raise their small boats to a safe level in event of high storm waves. The first floor of the house contained the principal keeper's quarters and areas for general use, and an interior winding stairway led to the assistant keepers' rooms on the second story. The many windows in the house offered uninterrupted views of the surrounding clear blue waters, beige shoals, and dark green mangrove islands.

The lantern was placed in the top section of the roof, surrounded by a gallery and balustrade. A new, larger fourth-order lens replaced the fifth-order Fresnel. Wicker noted, "The increased height of the light above sea-level and the higher order of illuminating apparatus have rendered the light much more effective than the old one." The light, forty-seven feet above sea level, was exhibited for the first time on June 30, 1879.[18]

The next improvement to the light came in 1882, when a tender delivered new mineral oil (kerosene) lamps to the station. Kerosene had long been considered too dangerous to use as an illuminant; in 1875 the board had hesitated "to endanger lives of employees and valuable property by placing mineral oil at . . . points from which keepers could not escape in case of accident." The board first introduced the new fuel to lighthouses with fourth-order (and smaller) lenses, and by 1885, after separate houses were built for kerosene storage, all lighthouses in the United States used kerosene. To further improve navigation in the channel, the board decided to establish range lights on the bar and install red sectors on the Northwest Passage Light. The positions of the red sectors, to warn mariners of the shoal areas off the channel, were laid out in 1892. The light's characteristic officially changed from a fixed white light to a fixed white light with red sectors on April 30, 1893.[19]

The lighthouse was in good condition as it began its service in the 1900s with improvements such as a new oil room built on the lower platform near the cisterns. The board also improved channel navigation by having range lights erected in the channel entrance, and by building a square beacon at the turning point into Key West Harbor. The beacon showed a fixed, red lens–lantern light, thirty-three feet above mean high water. In 1901 the Northwest Passage Light had only two keepers, George H. Gibson and his assistant, Oratio C. Carey. The board increased their salary "since they now have the responsibility of taking care of the Northwest Bar Beacon also." With this raise the keeper earned $624 a year, and his assistant $480.[20]

The hurricane of 1909 produced 111- to 130-mile-per-hour winds and a nine- to twelve-foot storm surge. The waves caused major damage to some of the braces in the lighthouse foundation, and the keepers could make only temporary repairs. In February 1911 inspector Henry B. Haskins urged replacing both braces and gutters before the next hurricane season, but the work party did not arrive until August 9. Fortunately, there had been no storms. Once work commenced on the foundation pilings, Haskins discovered seriously damaged girders, which supported the oil room and the cisterns. When Haskins proposed that hog chains be used to relieve the girders of some of the weight, the commissioner realized the need for immediate action and sent Haskins a telegram approving the additional repairs and expenses.[21]

Once the station was in good order, W. C. Dibrell, the next inspector, was eager to improve the light itself. In January 1913 he proposed changing the characteristic of the light from fixed to flashing, as well as increasing its intensity by substituting a thirty-five-millimeter incandescent oil vapor (i.o.v.) lamp for the kerosene. Dibrell justified his suggestions by noting the number of vessels using the Northwest Passage. He reported:

> One large steamer, *Olivette* (1,678 gross tonnage), makes semi-weekly trips between Key West and Port Tampa, and one smaller steamer (343 gross tonnage) makes weekly trips between here and San Carlos Bay, both via Northwest Passage. In addition to these, the channel is used by many small sailing vessels, a few other small steamers, and occasionally by large freight steamers when light. If funds were ever provided for deepening the channel, as seems probable, this route will be made use of by many more vessels bound into or out of the Gulf.[22]

The 1878 Northwest Passage Lighthouse built to replace the 1855 original. After the light was discontinued, the house became a popular destination for picnicking, romancing, and dreaming. But the unattended lighthouse was often vandalized, and in 1971 it burned. Only the skeletal remains of foundation piles attest to the lighthouse's former existence. (NATIONAL ARCHIVES)

The Northwest Channel was not dredged, but the future of the lighthouse soon changed. In May, Dibrell again wrote the commissioner: "Serious consideration has of late been given to the advisability of changing Northwest Passage to an unwatched acetylene light, and I am now of the opinion that this is the proper solution." He proposed installing an AGA complex flasher (the American Gas Accumulator Company of Philadelphia was the maker of the acetylene equipment) and a group of three one-cubic-foot burners. Dibrell also suggested a change in the characteristic of the light—from fixed white to group flashing—and that candlepower be increased. A sun-valve control for turning the light on and off was also proposed by Dibrell. The valve, which would respond mechanically to temperature, would close with the sun's heat, cutting off the light. After sunset the valve would open, allowing the fuel to ignite. The Bureau of Lighthouses approved Dibrell's proposals on May 4, 1913.[23]

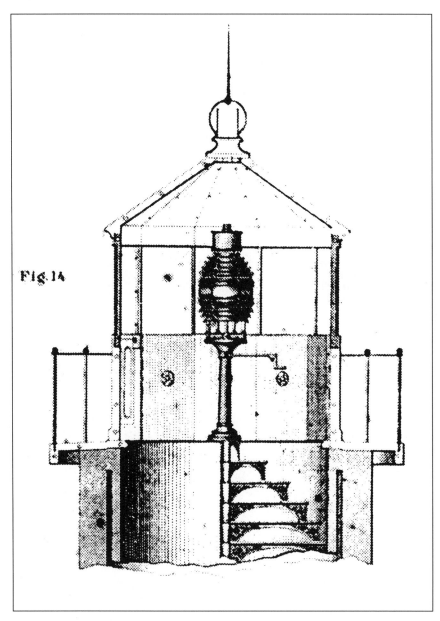

Drawing of a fourth-order Fresnel lens showing vertical section of a fourth-order lantern and tower mounting. The lens was about two feet, four inches tall, with an inside diameter of a little over nineteen inches. The Light House Board changed the Northwest Passage lens from fifth order to fourth order when the second lighthouse was completed in 1879. (NATIONAL ARCHIVES)

CP-1

The Light House Board was particularly proud of the distinctive architectural design of the Fowey Rocks Lighthouse. Today, a rotating 190-millimeter lantern has replaced the original Fresnel lens. The new optic is powered by solar panels. (U.S. Coast Guard Official Photo)

CP-2

Recognized as South Florida's oldest standing structure, many people familiar with the Cape Florida light have always known it as a red-brick tower. The texture and color of the old bricks have been much admired, and attempting to match the bricks to replace the damaged ones was a challenging and expensive job. There was some opposition when the tower was eventually painted white, its original color. (U.S. Coast Guard Official Photo)

It took contractors and volunteers eight years to restore the Cape Florida Lighthouse. It is now a privately maintained navigational aid; the Florida Department of Environmental Protection, Division of Recreation and Parks, manages the 415-acre Bill Baggs Cape Florida State Recreation Area where the light station is located. The station and the park are open for the public to benefit from and enjoy. (Florida Division of Tourism)

CP-3

Carysfort Reef Lighthouse, in 1998, is the oldest functioning screwpile lighthouse in the United States. (U.S. Coast Guard Official Photo)

CP-4

Alligator Reef Lighthouse has been called one of the finest iron, sea-swept lighthouse structures in the world. The graceful, tapering, white, octagonal skeleton tower rises 136 feet above the sea. Located on the outer line of reefs off Lower Matecumbe Key, it marks some of the best fishing, diving, and snorkeling opportunities in the Keys. Alligator Reef Lighthouse sits on a reef where more species of fish have been found than in almost any other dive area in the Keys. (Photograph by Larry Lipsky)

CP-5

Sombrero Key Lighthouse is said to be the most important lighthouse built by General Meade. The brown, octagonal, pyramidal skeleton tower stands 142 feet above water on the outer line of reef south of Boot Key. It is the tallest of the reef lights. (U.S. Coast Guard Official Photo)

CP-6

American Shoal Lighthouse may appear stark when seen on a sunny day, but the dark brown superstructure with its white, cylindrical center stairwell is easily identifiable, especially against the tropical blue sky and sea. (U.S. Coast Guard Official Photo)

CP-7

CP-8

The Sand Key Lighthouse is located on a coral reef that is sometimes covered with a sandy island. The island has taken on many different shapes over the years—when it exists it has been an alluring place for birds and boats. This photograph was taken before a disastrous fire roared through the 109-foot lighthouse. The stairwell and the keepers' house, both badly damaged in the fire, have been eliminated. (Florida Division of Tourism)

The Dry Tortugas Harbor Light at Fort Jefferson in 1998. In 1935, the government proclaimed Fort Jefferson a national monument. In 1992, the fort and the light tower became part of the Dry Tortugas National Park. (Photograph by BM2 Ray Potter, Aids to Navigation Team, Key West, Florida)

CP-9

CP-10

A Coast Guard helicopter delivering the new Vega VRB-25 rotating beacon to the Dry Tortugas Lighthouse on Loggerhead Key. (Photograph by PA1 Jeff Hall, Seventh Coast Guard District)

CP-11

Neither the Sand Key Lighthouse nor the most modern navigational systems can prevent human error. The 660-foot freighter Contship Houston *went up on Maryland Shoal twelve miles southeast of Key West on February 3, 1997, heavily damaging the coral. (Photograph by PA1 Jeff Hall, Seventh Coast Guard District)*

25 USA

COAST GUARD

AMERICAN SHOALS, FLORIDA

CP-12

In 1990, the American Shoal (not Shoals) Lighthouse was honored by the United States Postal Service in their American Lighthouses postage stamp series issued on April 26. The design (by Howard Koslow) accurately depicts the lighthouse, but the artist included a U.S. Coast Guard cutter passing nearby the tower. This would, of course, be impossible, since the water surrounding the American Shoal submarine site averages a depth of about five feet, and the 210-foor cutter draws at least fourteen feet. (Stamp design © 1990 U.S. Postal Service. Reproduced with permission. All rights reserved.)

The keepers remained on duty until the installation of the new acetylene equipment. In September 1913 fire broke out on the platform. John Peterson, who received his appointment as keeper in 1911, wrote to the inspector in Key West:

I have to inform you that I left NW Passage Light Station at 11 AM Sept 9, 1913, for the purpose of trimming and filling the NW Bar Beacon on the completion of which I proceeded to Key West for the purpose of obtaining necessary supply, leaving the light unattended. On Sept. 20, 1913 the tender *Magnolia* bound out for the NW Passage and I took passage out. When I neared the station, I found the lower platform on fire, whereupon one of the seamen of the *Magnolia* came to my assistance and we both boarded the light, found lower platform burned and the remains of the dinghy still burning. The oars, sail, mast and dinghy are a total loss. After hard work, we succeeded in extinguishing the flames.[24]

After investigating the fire, William Demeritt, superintendent of the district, found that the flames did not damage the dwelling or any permanent parts of the structure. The origin of the fire could not be determined. "It must have been started," wrote Demeritt to the commissioner, "during the absence of the Keeper, for it is evident that with the breeze that was blowing the entire structure would have been destroyed within a few hours." Demeritt was of the opinion that:

some fishermen, knowing that the Keeper was not present, spent the night on the platform, and while smoking dropped fire between its dry yellow pine cracks. The damage amounts to $64.00. . . . The dinghy was purchased nearly nine years ago and cost $35.00; its equipment was worth $9.00, and the material in the platform $20.00. As this platform offered an excellent loafing place for boatmen, it was to have been removed as soon as the new . . . light was established and the position of Keeper of this station abolished. As it is not considered that the damage was caused through any fault of the Keeper, it is recommended that no action be taken against him.[25]

In 1913 W. C. Dibrell proposed using a fourth-order Fresnel lens with an incandescent oil vapor lamp for the Northwest Passage Light, similar to the one photographed. Note the clockwork system in the stand below the lens. This rotated the bull's-eye lenses to produce a flashing effect. (U.S. COAST GUARD PHOTO, NATIONAL ARCHIVES)

By October 1913 the Bureau of Lighthouses automated the light. The last men to tend the Northwest Passage Light were John Peterson, keeper, and his assistant, John M. Lopez. For the next eight years the sun valve unfailingly turned the Northwest Passage Light off as the sun rose and on as the sun set. To those using the channel, the group occulting light characteristic was a familiar nightly aid. There were other navigational aids marking the channel as well—lighted and unlighted buoys, and two sets of ranges. On May 26, 1921, Demeritt proposed discontinuing the light since the channel and approach were marked with other aids. The estimated savings was $1,600, plus an annual maintenance savings of $250. Demeritt recommended that the "tower be left for the present as a day mark." The bureau decommissioned the light on June 30, 1921.[26]

To further mark the Northwest Passage, Demeritt had lighted turning ranges and inner ranges erected between 1923 and 1926, which guided vessels through the deepest part of the channel. Jetties were later constructed along the east and west sides of the gulf entrance to restrain the currents and help protect the channel from shoaling.

The old lighthouse continued as a day mark. It looked somehow magical, sitting isolated above the turquoise waters where no house was expected to be. It was a romantic sight, a place for dreaming. Its charming architecture and shady porches often lured boaters aboard, and as they approached double-crested cormorants and laughing gulls perched on rails and roof would rise in noisy confusion and fly away. Some who visited the house picnicked, some fished from the deck for the silver barracuda that slowly circled in the shallows, some explored the house. Too many people covered the walls with graffiti and took mementos from the old building. A charred depression in the floor of one of the rooms, evidence of a charcoal fire, was a black warning of what was to come.

On August 30, 1971, word spread through Key West that the Pilot's House was aflame. The rumor turned out to be true, and the fire destroyed the Northwest Passage Lighthouse.[27]

The channel continues to be a popular sea route for recreational boats and shallow-draft commercial fishing vessels, and the Coast Guard often reposition buoys and add new ones to mark the shifting, deeper channel. Because of the currents, the gulf end of the passage continues to move westward, and recently only the outer part of the east jetty showed above low water. The centerline controlling depth was twelve feet in 1996, but there is continual shoaling inside the channel, and the annual *Atlantic Coast Pilot* keeps mariners up to date.

The weathered and vandalized Northwest Passage keepers' house in 1971, forty-nine years after the Bureau of Lighthouses decommissioned the light and one year before the house was destroyed by fire. (FLORIDA STATE ARCHIVES)

Today few people remember or even know about the Northwest Passage Lighthouse. Still, there is one reminder—the last line of the channel's description in the *Atlantic Coast Pilot* captures a bit of history: "The pilings and skeletal structure of a former lighthouse are about 0.3 mile southwestward of the south end of the west jetty."[28]

The notes for this chapter begin on page 284.

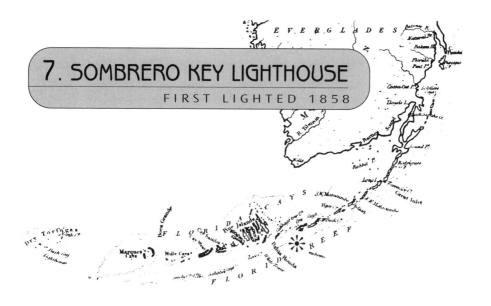

7. SOMBRERO KEY LIGHTHOUSE
FIRST LIGHTED 1858

From a distance, the racing fleet resembled giant white birds with their wings outspread. Indeed, their sails were set "wing and wing." More sailboats than ever before had entered the annual Sombrero Cup Race, and the competition was exhilarating for spectators and participants. The day was perfect for fast sailing, with an eighteen- to twenty-knot wind, but little sea. Crews adjusted whisker poles and sheets, trying to perfectly set their sails and keep them full during the downwind leg of the course. Ahead was their mark, the Sombrero Key Lighthouse, so tall that it did not appear to get any closer for a long while. The iron pile lighthouse, built on submerged coral reefs and surrounded by water, presented the competitors with a navigational problem. Aboard each sailboat, the skipper and crew were mentally calculating how much water their boat drew and how close they could cut the mark without running up on the reef. If they could outguess the shoals they could save seconds, even minutes.

With Sombrero Key Lighthouse looming over them, most of the boats rounded the mark safely. Wings were folded and crews set sails for a fast reach. A few boats miscalculated and went up on the reef, but eventually they were able to work free, losing nothing more than time. Finally, the last boat rounded the mark and sailed toward the finish line. Since the advent of its annual boat race in the 1980s, Som-

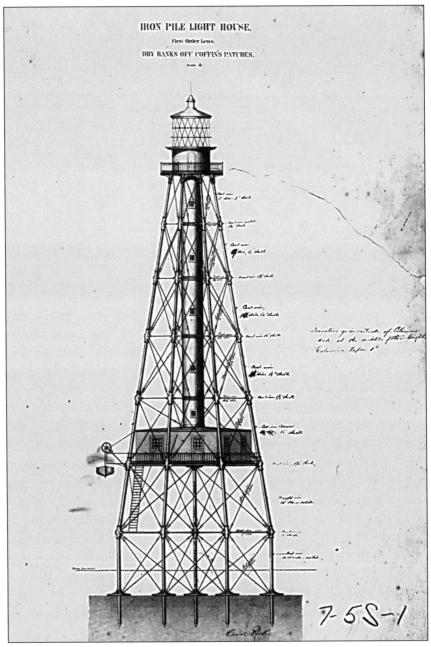

Original drawing for the Sombrero Key Lighthouse. This is the tallest of the iron pile lighthouses built in the Florida Keys and the last to be built by George Gordon Meade. (NATIONAL ARCHIVES)

brero Reef Lighthouse has fulfilled a function its builders never anticipated.

The iron framework of the 160-foot light tower looks almost delicate from afar, but the open-skeleton design is structurally strong, offering little resistance to the high winds and crashing waves generated by fierce storms and hurricanes. Storms have caused many shipwrecks, but a significant number of vessels grounded on the reefs in the vicinity of Sombrero Key even in calm weather. In 1856 an agent for the Boston underwriters at Key West reported that seventy-one vessels were in distress on the reefs and that the value of these ships and their cargoes was $4,484,600. "Notwithstanding all that has been done and is still being done by the government to light, buoy, and mark this coast, still we have an uncommon number of wrecks," wrote the agent. "Almost every week some unaccountable one occurs. Not a few, I fear, were, if not intentional, very careless; and not until an example is made of some of them, will the wrecks be less frequent, or the expenses be reduced."[1]

A great deal of money could be made in wreck and salvage—both honestly and dishonestly. Certainly there were times when wreckers set aside a part of salvaged cargo for themselves. The temptation must have been great, for opportunities were readily available; the salvagers had to remove cargo from vessels to float them off the reefs. Sometimes they had to jettison cargo to save time. Attempting salvage efforts during storms resulted in the destruction of many stranded vessels before all the cargo was removed. To make an accurate accounting of the cargo was often impossible.

There were also dishonest ship owners and captains. Judge William Marvin, who heard the salvage cases in the admiralty court in Key West wrote, "Nearly half the losses at sea may be ascribed to ignorance, incapacity, and carelessness of the masters and crews. Add to these the frauds of the masters and ship-owners, and it is possible, that half the ship-wrecks that occur ... may be fairly ascribed to causes other than perils of the sea. The existing system of marine insurance, undoubtedly, conduces to the production of many voluntary ship-wrecks."[2]

With the advent of steam vessels, many an unprofitable sailing vessel ended up on the reefs. Nevertheless, many vessels wrecked because there were insufficient navigational aids marking this dangerous shipping passage. After completing the Carysfort Reef and the Sand Key lighthouses, George Gordon Meade wrote to the Light House Board suggesting the establishment of a lighthouse somewhere on the reefs off Vaca Key. Although thoroughly familiar with iron screwpile construction, Meade did not automatically assume that this was the only type of construction suitable for the Florida reefs. The Sombrero Key Lighthouse might have been a masonry structure if Meade had not considered economic factors. In 1854 he wrote to the board again, reminding them of his proposed masonry tower and of his belief that this type of lighthouse would be stable. He went on to say, "I do not believe the force of the sea on this reef can injure such [masonry] structures, if properly erected on suitably selected sites . . . but to accomplish this result would require a great outlay of money. The structures on Bell and Skerryvore rocks, coast of Scotland cost respectively $300,000 and $400,000. Neither of these structures was as large as the one required [at Sombrero Key] . . . and both were within a short distance of all the resources of Great Britain."[3]

Meade also considered an iron structure built on a masonry foundation to be another option. At the time, engineers knew little about the effects of salt air and salt water on wrought iron. Meade's particular concern was for the metal parts exposed at low tide and then submerged at high tide. On the other hand, laying the first course for a masonry foundation would require "the bottom to be leveled and all loose material removed . . . and the construction of a cofferdam or the use of the diving bell . . . such a foundation would require an expenditure of not less than $100,000."

Meade's final opinion was that a wrought iron structure, such as the ones already built at Carysfort and Sand Key, would be the most economical and practical. Wrought iron was a fairly malleable, yet tough, material. To form structures such as the skeletal one proposed for the light tower, engineers designed castings with flanges, making it possible to bolt the component parts together. The manufacturer could prefabricate and erect the structure at the foundry, then dismantle it for shipping and reassemble it at the lighthouse site.[4]

At that time, metallurgists in America and Europe were conducting experiments to determine the effects of weather and seawater on various types of iron. The Light House Board made a thorough study of the results of these tests before beginning the construction of the third iron pile lighthouse on the Florida reefs. Meade concluded that ". . . the iron piles, if made sufficiently massive, are not so perishable, and if properly protected, will probably last longer, or as long as the superstructure."

Meade needed to determine what diameter would be "sufficiently massive" for the iron piles. He concluded: "For the sake of security, and to allow for what is believed to be the increased action at the alternately wet and dry part . . . [and] after having calculated the diameter of the pile necessary for strength and stability, we have only to add one inch to that quantity for every one hundred years it is desirable it should last before being reduced to the proportions required for mere stability." Meade wanted the structure to be economically feasible, but he also wanted it to last.[5]

There was one other important consideration—to find a method of protecting the metal itself. The application of massive amounts of zinc to the foundation pilings at Carysfort Reef Lighthouse had been done only a few years before, and it was too soon for Meade to assess the results. The process of galvanizing iron was fairly new, the first patent being granted in England in 1838. Yet, an experiment in France demonstrated that galvanized iron exposed to the sea for over fifteen years showed no effects of corrosion. A company in Philadelphia galvanized iron by heating the metal until it was red hot and then immersing it in fluid zinc. This process differed from the English method, in which the iron was first given an acid bath before being dipped in the liquid zinc. Taking this into account, Meade submitted drawings of the iron pile foundation to the Philadelphia company for an estimate. He reported to the Light House Board that an additional appropriation of $10,000 would cover the cost of galvanizing "all wrought iron exposed to the sea."[6]

The site for the new iron pile light was Meade's next consideration. Using the small schooner from the Sand Key Lighthouse, he sailed into an area of reefs about fifty miles northeast of Key West. He wanted to establish the light in a protected area halfway between the Sand Key and Carysfort Reef lights. Meade first explored an area of reef with a well-deserved ominous name—"Coffin's Patches." (On modern navigational charts, the apostrophe has been dropped.) This area of isolated and detached shoals is about eight nautical miles east-northeast of Sombrero Key, and three nautical miles south of Crawl Key. Pillar coral grows across two acres of sea bottom in this area, and the shoals are covered with eight to fourteen feet of water, separated by narrow channels eighteen to twenty-four feet deep.

Meade also examined (and at first recommended) Turtle Shoal, just north of Coffins Patches. Star coral predominates in the area around this extensive shoal, which still contains ballast stones and other evidence from many wrecks. Modern charts designate the area as West Turtle Shoal and East Turtle Shoal. Meade was not able to make a thorough investigation of the reef, "owing to the tempestuous weather encountered, and the insufficiency of the vessel. . . ."[7]

After further investigation, Meade selected a site first charted and named Cayo Sombrero by the Spanish. English topographer George Gauld accurately charted the area in the 1760s, and an 1837 chart describes the area as broken and irregular in breadth and depth with patches of coral rocks, some under and some above water. Since parts of this area were so shallow they were exposed at times of low water, the reef was also called "Dry Bank."[8]

In 1852 the U.S. Army Coast Survey erected a day beacon on the shoal, consisting of a thirty-six-foot pole topped with a barrel painted red and white. The Light House Board referred to the area either as "Coffin's Patches" or "Sombrero Shoal." In 1857 the board noted: "The most important lighthouse structures underway in this district are the Dry Bank lighthouse (near Coffin's Patches) . . . and the first class masonry tower at Dry Tortugas."[9]

Meade wanted the same type of construction for the Sombrero Key Lighthouse that had been used for the Carysfort Reef Lighthouse. He recommended a disk-pile structure because he wanted to use as few pilings as possible so as not to obstruct the free flow of water, especially when waves built up on the reef, and he also believed that the disk principle provided a greater bearing surface for each piling.

Difficulties did not arise during construction, but with the financing. Meade could not build the foundation on schedule "owing to the failure of the necessary appropriation." No matter how economical Meade tried to be, Congress never appropriated enough money to meet construction expenses. Meade submitted a detailed and carefully prepared budget, and he calculated to the penny what the lighthouse would cost. I. P. Morris and Company of Philadelphia manufactured the iron parts for the structure, and Meade included all the costs for assembly and disassembly of the parts at the foundry. He included the weight of materials affecting shipping costs and estimated the funds needed for the pay, subsistence, and transportation of a construction crew from Philadelphia to Duck Key, the island chosen for construction headquarters. He itemized the expenses for everything from the Fresnel lens to the necessary furniture. In addition, Meade wanted to provide for any contingencies and added another ten percent, justifying the amount by reminding the board, "One disaster, such as the loss of a vessel freighted with materials required to sail over 1,400 miles, and through part of her voyage the Florida gulf [stream], as dangerous as any navigation in the world, might of itself swallow up the whole contingency, and such a catastrophe is by no mean[s] improbable." Meade's total estimate came to $118,405.60. As it turned out, he needed the contingency fund.[10]

On August 29, 1856, a hurricane hit the Florida Keys. Property was destroyed and many lives were lost. The Light House Board reported that the storm had so badly damaged the temporary work at "Coffin's Patches" that it was beyond repair. Meade began construction again in 1857. Soon the scaffolding could be seen ten miles at sea, and as the tower took shape during the year it became a day mark for vessels sailing along the Keys.[11]

Meade predicted that the nine twelve-inch pilings would last two hundred years. Plans called for placing the pilings at the angles of an octagon, fifty-six feet in diameter, with one piling in the center. Each piling was driven through the center hole of an iron disk that was eight feet in diameter. The pilings, sunk ten feet into the coral, could each support an estimated weight of sixty-four tons. When the foundation piles were set, six sections of pilings with horizontal bracings were added on top of them. The keepers' house, supported within the second section of pilings, was a thirty-five-foot square. The house was constructed with one-quarter-inch boiler iron, and it had four rooms with wooden interior walls. A ladder, which could be raised and lowered, led from the water to the lower platform. An open stairway led

George Gordon Meade, circa 1856, as a captain. Meade was sent by the U.S. Army of Topographical Engineers to complete the work on Carysfort Reef Lighthouse. Later he was in charge of the construction of Sand Key and Sombrero Key lighthouses and Rebecca Shoal Beacon. (MILITARY ORDER OF THE LOYAL LEGION WAR MUSEUM, PHILADELPHIA, PA)

to the keepers' quarters, and an enclosed circular stairway with 133 steps led to the light. The tower tapered from fifty-six feet wide at the base to fifteen feet at the top.[12]

The Light House Board decided that the light would have a fixed characteristic since the Sand Key and Carysfort Reef lights were revolving. Henry Lepaute of Paris manufactured the first-order lens and sold it to the board for $20,000. The Scottish lighthouse engineer

Alan Stevenson, who built the Skerryvore Lighthouse, greatly admired the large lens, almost eight feet high and six feet wide at its focal point. "Nothing can be more beautiful," he said, "than an entire apparatus for a fixed light of the first order." The glass prisms in the lens both refracted and concentrated light rays, the central belt of refractors forming a cylinder six feet in diameter and thirty inches high. Below this central belt were six rings of glass, and above it was "a crown of thirteen rings of glass, forming by their union a hollow cage composed of polished glass . . . I know of no other work of art more beautiful or creditable to the boldness, ardor, intelligence, and zeal of the artist," wrote Stevenson.[13]

On March 17, 1858, the light on Sombrero Key Lighthouse beamed for the first time through its powerful lens. Sombrero Lighthouse cost $153,158.81—considerably more than Meade estimated, but less than a masonry structure. The Light House Board asked Meade to design and oversee the construction of a beacon on Rebecca Shoal, between Key West and the Dry Tortugas.[14]

By 1858, the lighted navigational aids in South Florida consisted of harbor lights at Key West and on Garden Key in the Dry Tortugas, and five seacoast lights: Cape Florida, Carysfort Reef, Sombrero Key, Sand Key, and the Dry Tortugas light on Loggerhead Key. An article appearing in *Hunts' Merchant's Magazine* commented: "The increase in the number of beacons, reef signals, buoys, and light-houses . . . does not seem to lessen the number of accidents to vessels passing through the Florida Straits, but there is no doubt that the average number of accidents to the amount of shipping is less than in former years when the lights and signals did not exist."[15]

Joseph Bethel secured the appointment as head keeper on the completed lighthouse, previously serving on the Garden Key Light in the Dry Tortugas. Bethel was born in the Bahamas, and his wife, Nicholosa, was the daughter of Michael and Barbara Mabrity, who had both been keepers of the lighthouse at Key West. The Bethels had five children, and Bethel maintained a home in Key West for his family. Bethel had numerous assistant keepers during the twenty-one years he kept the light on Sombrero Key, and a variety of good and bad experiences. During the Civil War, funds were available for keeping the light lit, but little else. By the war's end, the light structure required major repair. The iron foundation braces needed new clamps, and the keepers made plans to completely scrape and paint the iron-work. The keepers took care of the routine maintenance; the district office handled major repairs and construction.[16]

The Light House Board specifically defined the keepers' duties, but sometimes questions arose concerning the keepers' role in helping vessels in distress. In September 1872, Adolphus Seymour, acting head keeper while Bethel was on leave, recorded the following incident: "A strong breeze from the east southeast . . . a brigantine with signals for a pilot or distress signals passed about 8:40 in the morning beating to windward . . . she hove to and then headed into shore. At 10:30 the wind began to moderate. No wreckers were in sight and none of the shore boats appeared to be coming out to her. I lowered the boat and sent the two assistants to give whatever information the boat required and render whatever assistance was in their power."

The assistant keepers at that time were Hiram S. Seymour and Robert H. Saunders. The vessel in distress was the British brigantine *Rapid*, whose captain signaled for a harbor pilot because he thought he was off Key West. The keepers could barely persuade him other-wise—they finally convinced him that he was off Vaca Key and that the lighthouse was the Sombrero Key and not the Sand Key light. Re-alizing his mistake, the captain offered them $150 if they would pilot him to Key West, and they made an agreement. Assistant Seymour acted as pilot, sending the other assistant, Saunders, with the boat back to the lighthouse. Seymour safely guided the vessel to Key West and returned to the lighthouse. Rather chagrined, Seymour reported to the keeper that J. F. Marrero, agent for the brigantine, invalidated the offer of $150 made by the captain and offered only $60—"an offer I had to accept, for there was no alternative."[17]

All keepers were familiar with the safe passages through the reefs and southwestward through Hawk Channel. Not only did most of them have family in Key West, but they also sailed there to pick up their pay. In late July 1873 Richard White, who obtained the first as-sistant keeper's job on Sombrero four months earlier, left Sombrero for Key West to collect his quarterly allowance. He did not intend to be gone long and took the lighthouse sailboat. The keeper recorded the following tragic event:

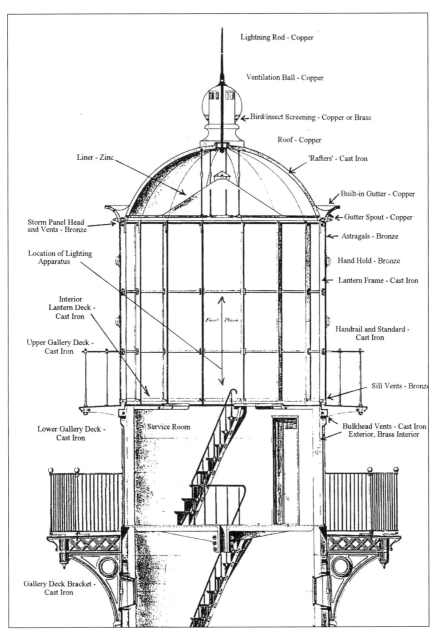

Lightning Rod - Copper

Ventilation Ball - Copper

Bird/insect Screening - Copper or Brass

Roof - Copper

Liner - Zinc

'Rafters' - Cast Iron

Built-in Gutter - Copper

Gutter Spout - Copper

Storm Panel Head
and Vents - Bronze

Astragals - Bronze

Location of Lighting
Apparatus

Hand Hold - Bronze

Lantern Frame - Cast Iron

Interior
Lantern Deck -
Cast Iron

Handrail and Standard -
Cast Iron

Upper Gallery Deck -
Cast Iron

Sill Vents - Bronze

Lower Gallery Deck -
Cast Iron

Service Room

Bulkhead Vents - Cast Iron
Exterior, Brass Interior

Gallery Deck Bracket -
Cast Iron

A diagram of a typical first-order lantern, similar to the one on Sombrero Key Lighthouse. (DIAGRAM BASED ON UNITED STATES LIGHT HOUSE SERVICE DRAWING IN THE *HISTORIC LIGHTHOUSE PRESERVATION HANDBOOK*; NATIONAL ARCHIVES.)

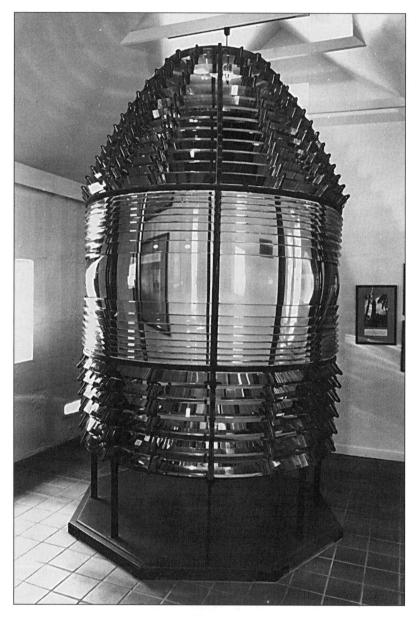

This first-order Fresnel lens, manufactured by Henry Lepaute of Paris, was purchased by the Light House Board for $20,000. It was installed on Sombrero Key Lighthouse in 1858. In 1982 the lens was removed and is now on display at the Key West Lighthouse Museum. (HISTORIC FLORIDA KEYS PRESERVA-TION BOARD)

We saw nothing more of him or the boat until August 6th at 10:00 A.M. We discovered the boat was coming from Hogg Key. It was blowing fresh and began to be getting squally. At 10:30 we saw the boat when it was struck by a squall and instantly capsized. After a few minutes, the squall passed over. We saw the man floating on the collapsed boom and the sail of the boat. The boat was capsized, still floating a few yards away from him. He was very visible, for at the time of the accident he was not over one and a half miles from the lighthouse. The tide set in toward us, till we could distinctly see his features and could he have assisted the spar that bore him up by swimming in the least he would have most assuredly reached the house. The tide turned against him and swept him in a west-southwest direction about four miles from us. This was about 3:30 P.M. at which time we lost sight of him altogether . . . as soon as the boat capsized we hoisted the ensign from the top of the tower to attract the attention of three little turtlers or spongers that were cruising about outside Knight's Key, but no one came on that day. On the following day we hoisted the ensign again in distress to draw attention to any of the vessels that might pass. At 4:00 P.M. the steamer *Clyde*, Captain Kennedy finally hove to and sent his boat and crew to whom I imparted the news and also delivered letters relative to the casualty to the official in Key West. The steamer happened to be one of the regular line of packets plying between New York and Galveston via Key West. . . . August 14, Mr. Babcock, chief engineer of the Light House Department of the district, having heard of the calamity and on his passing seeing that we were not as yet supplied with a boat to take either my assistant or myself on shore in case of any emergency . . . very kindly came and brought a good and sufficient boat and left a man, an old light-house keeper, Mr. William Bates, to assist me.[18]

Bates, born in England in the 1830s, previously served on the Dry Tortugas light at Garden Key and on the Sand Key light. Both of these lights were located on a bit of land, and the keepers were not as removed from other people as were the men at Sombrero or Carysfort. Without a boat the keepers were totally isolated on their stations.

Meade had recommended that the lighthouses on the reefs be supplied with "two boats with oars and one sailboat of 12 tons."[19]

In 1879 when Joseph Bethel, the veteran head keeper of Sombrero, became ill, his assistant, Jefferson, used the station's only boat to take him to Key West. In the log book the other assistant keeper recorded: "Mr. Bethel took sick and he was so bad he had to give up and leave off duty . . . he groaned so for three days I had to send Mr. Jefferson to Key West with him. I remain alone at the lighthouse station waiting for the boat to return." The assistant keeper spent thirteen days and nights alone before Jefferson returned.[20]

Unlike many lighthouses that were family stations, the men on the reef lights seldom had their families with them. Many were lonely and they found it difficult at times to adjust to the other men on the station. In such close quarters, personalities sometimes conflicted. Josiah Butts, an assistant keeper on Sombrero from 1873 to 1875, finally quit his job after problems with drinking and arguments with Keeper Adolphus Seymour. Fredrick DeCourcy, an assistant during the same period, also resigned because of disagreements with the keeper. Thomas Cassidy believed that he failed to qualify as second assistant keeper at Sombrero in 1876 because the keeper did not like him. Cassidy later returned as assistant keeper on Sombrero and served without complaints against him on two other Florida lighthouses.[21]

Rudolph Reike, keeper at Sombrero Key Light from 1893 to 1904, realized he had difficulty in getting along with the men and he preferred to be alone. Reike emigrated from Hamburg, Germany, with his wife and daughter in the late 1860s, brought to Key West by salvagers after their ship was wrecked there. The Reikes decided to remain. Soon after they settled, Reike's wife died of smallpox, and the nuns at the Convent of Mary Immaculate in Key West assumed care of Reike's daughter. After his wife's death, Reike obtained a position as keeper and served on Carysfort Reef Light, as well as on Sombrero.[22]

Serving on the reef lights provided the isolation from society Reike desired and also gave him the mental and physical challenges he wanted. Reike, however, was not popular with the men who served with him. Nevertheless, Samuel Lowe remained with him on Sombrero for three years, and George Wilson was his assistant for five years.

Reike first arrived at Sombrero Key Lighthouse on August 13, 1893. Michael Eickhoff, also from Germany, was first assistant keeper. The second assistant, Miguel Fabal, had been born in Spain in 1874. Reike performed his duties as keeper well, but he did not socialize with his assistants or with the crews from boats that anchored by the lighthouse and came aboard to visit. Reike seldom spoke. Most keepers looked forward to the conversations and the opportunity to exchange stories and news; these were welcomed breaks in an otherwise routine schedule.

There was one occasion, however, when Reike longed for a ship to stop. Fabal had taken the lighthouse boat to Key West, leaving Reike and Eickhoff alone on the light. Reike recorded the events that followed in the light station journal: "Dead the 18th [October] at 6:45 A.M. First Assistant Michael Eickhoff. I came down the stairs of the watch [room] and went down to the platform to see what he was doing and I found him dead. I set the American Ensign at once, upside down on top on the lantern tower. Weather cloudy." Reike, not wanting there to be any question of foul play, kept the body in the living quarters that night. No vessels sailed by that day or the next. Reike finally moved the body out on the platform. On October 21, the schooner *Champion* hove to and Captain R. Pearson came aboard the light to find out why the keeper was displaying the distress signal. Reike wrote, "The Captain found the corpse on the platform in bad condition. Buried the corpse in the sea at 11:50 A.M."[23]

Death on the lighthouses was not an unusual tragedy, but only one other keeper had died on Sombrero, Martin Weatherford. Weatherford served on Alligator Reef and Carysfort Reef before transferring to Sombrero in 1889. He died on the light May 7, 1891.[24]

During the time Reike was keeper, the Light House Board made an important addition to the light. Red glass was installed inside the lantern panes at precise angles to the lamp, which would appear red over the reefs and dangerous waters when light from the lamp shone through. The board did nothing more to improve the light until 1912, when they replaced the oil-wick lamps with an incandescent oil vapor (i.o.v.) system to illuminate the light.[25]

Sombrero Key Lighthouse sometime in the late 1950s, when the Coast Guard still manned the light. The light was automated in 1960, at which time the Coast Guard Aid to Navigation Team (ANT) removed the Fresnel lens. The lens is now on display at the Key West Lighthouse Museum. (U.S. COAST GUARD OFFICIAL PHOTO)

Tucked between the pages of the log describing the new i.o.v. installation was a list of groceries that were needed by the lighthouse, left by John Watkins, the keeper: "Milk, 36 cans; potatoes, 2 bushels; butter, 8 pounds; prunes, 6 pounds; apples, 2 packages; onions, 20 pounds; white beans, 4 quarts; applesauce, 2 quarts; black beans, 3 quarts; black pepper, 2 cans; grits, 6 quarts; raisins, 4 packages; sugar, 50 pounds; crisco, 10 pounds; garlic; pickled shoulder, 3; roast beef, one case; eggs, one-half case; salt beef, one-half barrel; tomatoes, one case; hams, 3; vanilla, 2 bottles; pork, 20 pounds; tea, one pound; crushed oats, 5 packs; syrup, one gallon."

The grocery list offers a more personal glimpse into the keepers' lives than the journal itself. Through the years, only the handwriting in the journal seems to change as new men take over the ritual of record keeping. Only on an official notice inserted between the pages in December 1920 is Christmas mentioned. The lighthouse inspector brought printed greetings to the men stationed at Sombrero. The form reads: "My dear Sirs, I write to extend to you my earnest wishes for a glad Christmas and a happy and useful new year. I am confident that the work of the public service committed to your hands will be well done in the year about to open and I thank you for the past good work that makes this confidence possible." There was no Christmas bonus for the past good work, nor was any expected.[26]

When Coast Guardsmen replaced the civilian keepers on Sombrero Key in 1939, the lighthouse duties and routine did not change. The men continued to polish brass and scrape and paint the ironwork. Reports of hurricanes take up little more space in the logs than the reports of clear sunny weather. World War II is not mentioned at all, nor was the death of Seaman Willis Parker.

The fatal accident occurred in August 1959. Boatswain's mate Furman Williamson was alone on Sombrero. One man was on extended leave, and Seaman Willis Parker, the other Coast Guardsman stationed at the light, had taken a special work crew back to Key West in the lighthouse's launch. Just before dark, the sea began to build when Williamson saw the launch returning. Williamson went down to the lower platform to help raise the launch to the dock platform. To accomplish this, a block and tackle needed to be attached to a line that ran from the rings fore and aft on the launch. Williamson lowered the block with its huge hook. Parker grabbed it, but before he was able to attach the hook to the line, a wave lifted the boat up and forced it away from the lighthouse. Parker instinctively held onto the block as the wave swept his boat away, and he was still holding on when the block swung and smashed his head into a piling. He dropped into the sea. Williamson, watching in horror and unable to prevent the accident, quickly threw Parker a life ring. Parker grabbed the ring and seemed to be all right, but then he went under the waves and the life ring floated away.

Williamson, without any help aboard the lighthouse and without a boat, could do nothing but get to the phone and call for help. It was dark when the rescue operations got under way. Charter boats and the Coast Guard cutter began to search the area. Coast Guard rescue planes and helicopters dropped flares. Someone finally spotted the launch; it had drifted northward in the Gulf Stream. Parker's brother came from Homestead, a town south of Miami, to aid in the search. He found the body the next afternoon.[27]

There have been other bad experiences on the light, but no other fatalities. The Coast Guardsmen stationed on the light during hurricane Donna in 1960 experienced a two-day ordeal. The winds were recorded at 166 to 200 miles per hour, and the seas around the light were twelve to twenty-five feet high. The waves ripped off the lower platform of the lighthouse, but did not damage the living quarters, forty feet above normal sea level. Seas swept away the fuel tanks and workshop on the lower level, but the men managed to save their eighteen-foot launch and keep the light burning throughout the hurricane. As soon as it was possible to go out to the lighthouse, a charter boat rescued the men and brought them to Vaca Cut. As the men approached the cut they could see that the only thing left standing was the first floor of a two-story building. Once ashore, the Coast Guardsmen swore they would never go back to the light and proceeded to get drunk.[28]

Of course, the men did return to duty on Sombrero Key, but their assignment was soon over—in 1960 the Coast Guard automated the light. In 1982 the Coast Guard Aid to Navigation Team (ANT) removed the jewel-like polished glass Fresnel lens. It is now on display at the Key West Lighthouse Museum.

Lights called "flash tube arrays" were experimentally used, but this new type of lighting proved unreliable and was replaced by three-hundred-millimeter lamps powered by solar-charged batteries. Later ANT personnel installed a solar-powered 190-millimeter rotating optic.[29]

By 1997 the Coast Guard's Aid to Navigation Branch (ATON) used the VRB-25, twelve-volt rotating beacon for Sombrero Light. This optic has only one moving part: a sealed bearing guaranteed for twenty years. It has a six-bulb switcher that uses tungsten halogen lamps, which have a life of about two thousand hours each, so theoretically, ANT only has to service the optic every 2.7 years. This, of course, does not include visits to the light if it malfunctions. The manufacturers of the optic, Vega Industries Limited, Porirua, New Zealand, claim that the optic does not fail as often as a classical light. "The beacon was designed specifically for solar powering," explains Chief Richard "Beau" Lewis, ATON. He describes the Fresnel lens system as using "six lens panels arranged symmetrically on a rotating carousel, which rotate around a stationary lamp."[30]

The Sombrero lighthouse is structurally in good condition, according to Chief Charlie Pantelakos, ANT, Key West. "Sometime in 1998," he reports, "Sombrero Lighthouse will be scraped and painted by contractors using the latest techniques for both preserving the iron-piling structure and protecting the environment." After accomplishing this extensive task, the Coast Guard's visits to Sombrero Key Lighthouse will be rare. Today there are more people under the iron pile structure than were ever on it. Boats are usually anchored off Sombrero Reef with divers overboard exploring the staghorn and elkhorn coral. On the south side of the lighthouse, coral formations reach out toward the Gulf Stream like giant fingers. Coral grows ten to fifteen feet above the sand and there are fifty- to sixty-foot drop-offs on the ocean side. Tropical fish are always plentiful, especially rock beauties, jewel fish, and barracuda that slowly patrol along the light's foundation. In March after a good blow, fishermen come to the area for mackerel. In November sailboats head for the light during the Sombrero Cup Race.[31]

At night, Sombrero's group of five flashing lights every sixty seconds is an essential navigational aid. It is the tallest of the Reef Lights, and the last lighthouse built by George Gordon Meade. Those who see Sombrero Key Light may, for a moment, wonder about the man who worked so hard for this light's establishment, a man who is still remembered as a soldier but has been forgotten as a builder of lighthouses.[32]

The notes for this chapter begin on page 285.

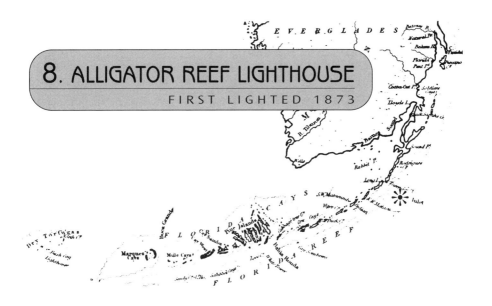

8. ALLIGATOR REEF LIGHTHOUSE
FIRST LIGHTED 1873

The USS *Alligator* was wrecked neither by storms nor pirates. Instead, the *Alligator*'s tragic end came on the Florida reefs during the night of November 19, 1822, when the schooner went hard aground on the southwest part of a hazardous stretch of coral known as Carysford Reef.

The day before, the *Alligator* had sailed from Matanzas, Cuba, en route to Norfolk, Virginia, escorting the brigantine *Anna Maria* and several other vessels recaptured from pirates. Lieutenant John M. Dale, in command of the *Alligator*, received information that pirates would make an attempt to take some of the vessels; he was anxious to keep the convoy together.

Peyton Henley, the acting sailing master, later appeared before the Court of Inquiry held aboard the U.S. Frigate *Guerriere* at Norfolk, Virginia, to explain the loss of the *Alligator*. "During the afternoon the *Anna Maria* fell considerable to leeward . . ." Dale testified. "We steered a North by East course until about ten P.M. . . . and afterward continued through the night to make short tacks in the hope of keeping the Convoy in company." In the morning, lookouts could see only two of the ships. By the evening of November 19, they had lost sight of them all.[1]

Henley described what happened next. "At half past nine o'clock

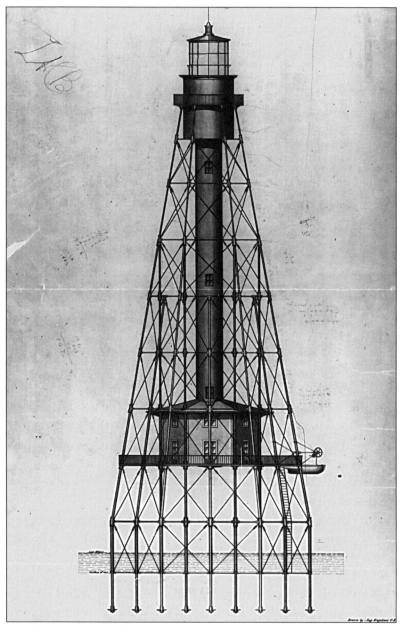

Original drawing for Alligator Reef Lighthouse. The Light House Board requested Congressional appropriations for this lighthouse in 1857, but building did not begin until 1871. The lighthouse was completed in 1873 at a cost of $185,000. (NATIONAL ARCHIVES)

we were . . . going about five knots when the vessel struck on Matacumbee Reef, being a part of Carysford, we had kept the Lead going every half hour from dark, but got no bottom at forty-five fathoms." No amount of effort, curses, or prayers by officers or crew could dislodge the schooner. Lieutenant Dale later reported to the Navy Department, "After remaining by her three days, using every exertion to get her off, but to no purpose, and expecting any moment that she would go to pieces, I was forced . . . to come to the resolution of abandoning her and making an encampment on one of the Keys."[2]

In the early morning of November 21, a wrecker sailed near the reef. The *Alligator* engaged the vessel to stand by and take on board the most valuable articles. A few hours later the crew sighted a brigantine to westward. "We fired several signal guns," testified Henley, "and sent a boat to her, she soon came near us and proved to be the *Anna Maria*."[3]

The threats of pirate activity along the Florida Keys persuaded Lieutenant Dale to sink his ship. Not wanting to leave anything the pirates could use, he ordered all government property, including cannons, transferred to the *Anna Maria*. This was difficult, heartbreaking work for a crew already saddened by the recent death of their former captain, William H. Allen.[4]

The Navy had given Allen command of the *Alligator* for the purpose of capturing the pirates that had been harassing vessels and plundering wrecks all along the Florida coast for years. The United States government determined to end these illegal attacks on domestic and foreign shipping. The USS *Alligator*, built in the Boston Navy Yard in 1820, weighed 177 tons and measured eighty-six feet long, with a draft of a little over eleven feet. The twelve-gun schooner's first assignment was to intercept ships involved in illegal slave trading. During 1821, the *Alligator* captured several slave ships off the west coast of Africa. The Navy expected the schooner's speed and firepower to be equally effective against the pirates.[5]

Allen sailed the *Alligator* southward from New York intercepting all unknown vessels just off the coast along the way to identify their hailing port and the purpose of their voyage. He did not encounter any pirates. Then, while the *Alligator* was anchored off Matanzas, Cuba, two men came aboard to tell Allen that pirates had seized their ship.

The USS Alligator *in the West Indies, November 9, 1822, by Welsh-born artist Irwin John Beva, who was a keen naval historian. Lieutenant William Howard Allen, commanding the* Alligator, *was mortally wounded as his forces routed the pirates in this naval engagement east of Matanzas, Cuba.* (The Mariners Museum)

They had come to Matanzas to raise the money demanded for the release of their vessels, cargoes, and crews. Allen ordered his men to weigh anchor, and the *Alligator* set sail to search for the captured vessels.

On the morning of November 9, 1822, Allen sighted two brigs, five schooners, and a ship in the Bay of Lajuapo. Allen's men cast off in the *Alligator's* launches, with Allen taking the lead. Seeing them approach, one of the schooners got under way. In the light wind the pirates used their long sweeps (oars) to move the eighty-ton schooner. As Allen, Captain Freeman of the marines, and twelve men in the lead launch pulled to within hailing distance, the pirates opened fire with a long, pivoting eighteen-pounder and four other guns. Allen and his men pulled alongside and boarded the schooner. There was a desperate battle, and before the rest of the men from the *Alligator* arrived, the pirates took to their boats or jumped overboard.

As Allen urged his men on, he was struck by two musket balls. The surgeon of the *Alligator* later wrote a friend, "He continued giving orders and conversing with Mr. Dale and the rest of us, until a few minutes before his death, with a degree of cheerfulness that was little to be expected from a man in his condition."[6]

Two of the pirate schooners had escaped, but Allen's crew captured the two brigs, the ship, and the other schooners. Four of the *Alligator*'s crew were killed and three wounded. Fourteen pirates were killed and several drowned. It was a remarkable victory, and Allen's name became a Naval war cry.

Fourteen days after the tragic death of Lieutenant Allen, the schooner's crew set fire to the *Alligator* fore and aft. The vessel blew up and sank. Lieutenant Dale wrote, "I shall ever sincerely lament the unfortunate affair." Today only piles of rock ballast and some pieces of the schooner's hull timber remain scattered along the reef renamed "Alligator."[7]

On December 9, 1822, after the death of Lieutenant Allen, President Monroe sent a special message to Congress: "Recent information of the multiplied outrages and depredations which have been committed on our seaman and commerce by the pirates in the West Indies and Gulf of Mexico, exemplified by the death of a very meritorious officer, seems to call for some prompt and decisive measures on the part of the Government." Monroe then requested the formation of a special Naval squadron to operate against such piracy.[8]

Congress appropriated $160,000 for the squadron and sent Commodore David Porter to the Keys to organize and command it. Porter settled in Cayo Hueso (Key West) and renamed it Allentown in honor of his friend and fellow officer. The West Indies Squadron consisted of eight schooners, five towing barges, and, to pull the barges, the old New York ferryboat *Sea Gull*, the first steam-powered vessel used by the U.S. Navy. The small barges, each carrying twenty men and a cannon, made it possible to seek out and engage the pirates in the Keys, who used shallow-draft vessels to pass through the narrow cuts and anchor behind mangrove islets along the shores. Here they would dismast the vessels and wait within the thick mangroves for unsuspecting ships sailing in the deeper offshore waters. But the effective barge fleet, known as the Mosquito Patrol, and the schooners slowly brought a halt to the rampant piracy.

Although the threat of piracy had been removed, the reefs remained a constant danger to shipping. The *Florida Herald*, a newspaper published in Saint Augustine, reported on June 2, 1846, "The mail packet *Stranger* on her way from Key West to this port, reported a large ship . . . ashore on Alligator Reef. This is an extremely dangerous point of navigation, which is not indicated by any light. The current of the Gulf Stream sweeps directly upon this reef . . . and it is a very easy thing for even the most prudent navigator, with his lead line constantly going, to find himself suddenly on the rocks."

In 1852, Lieutenant James Totten, with the U.S. Army Coast Survey, erected fifteen day markers along the reefs indicating dangerous points, including Alligator Reef. Totten designed the beacons himself, using an iron shaft 36 feet high erected upon an iron-screw foundation and topped with a large barrel painted black. These day beacons were visible for two to three miles with the naked eye and six to ten miles with a small telescope.

In 1857 the coastal surveyors replaced the black barrels with hoop-iron latticework cylinders. They erected the new day markers four to six miles from the seaward shores of the Keys and within a half mile of the Gulf Stream's edge. The depth of the water around these markers did not exceed four feet. To make sure that navigators would not mistake one beacon for another, each showed a different letter, as well as a unique combination of red, white, and black colors on the vanes, cylinders, and shafts. The marker on Alligator Reef had a black shaft, a white cylinder, and the letter C painted on a red vane. Even with these additional navigational aids, 618 ships were wrecked along the Keys from 1848 through 1858 with a loss of cargo valued at approximately $22,000,000.[9]

It was not until 1857 that the Light House Board recommended an iron pile lighthouse to mark Alligator Reef in order for the "entire extent of this dangerous coast and reef . . . [to be as] perfectly lighted as it is believed any capable and intelligent mariner could desire. In a distance of three hundred miles there will then be Dry Tortugas, Sand Key, Dry Bank, Alligator Reef, Carysfort Reef, Cape Florida, and Jupiter Inlet seacoast lights."[10]

The original estimate for building a light on Alligator Reef was $130,000. Congress did not make the appropriation. The government was well aware of the number of wrecks and groundings in the area, but there were other problems and needs that took precedence. The Civil War was looming, and Florida, which as a territory had embraced statehood in 1845, seceded in 1861. The Light House Board could not attempt erecting a lighthouse on Alligator Reef during the war. The board made requests for the light again in 1867 and 1868, but later reported, "The rebellion prevented any steps being taken between 1861 and 1865, and since that time, other works of pressing necessity on the southern coast claimed the particular attention of Congress and the Board."[11]

In 1868 and in 1869, the Light House Board renewed its efforts to fund a navigational aid. The board described Alligator Reef as forming "a kind of elbow or turning point for vessels passing either way through the Florida Pass. The unlighted area causes . . . the navigator to grope his way through . . . [while] having to contend against strong and irregular currents, which are greatly influenced by the prevailing winds, by tides, and by the general character and state of the weather." The complaints of shipping companies and the urgings of the Light House Board finally resulted in an appropriation from Congress on July 15, 1870. The board could not predict a completion date for Alligator Light, although engineers were familiar with the necessary construction techniques. Building progress, the board said, depended on the condition of the wind and sea, "to say nothing of the health of the mechanics and laborers in such a climate."[12]

As headquarters for the project, contractors selected eleven-acre Indian Key, four miles from the proposed lighthouse and about three-fourths of a mile southeast of Lower Matecumbe Key.

Indian Key has a rich history. Excavated artifacts indicate that Indians have been inhabiting or visiting the island since about 1200 B.C. In the early sixteenth century, when shipwrecks often occurred on the reefs, Indian Key became one of the Calusa Indians' salvage centers. They also captured and killed many shipwrecked French and Spanish sailors. Spanish charts first identified the island as "Matanza," suggesting "slaughter." A 1722 chart called it "Matana," meaning "massacre." In 1775, historian Bernard Romans recorded that Calusa

Wrecker from Key West, illustration for New Monthly Magazine. *When one wrecker saw the completion of the Alligator Reef Lighthouse he commented, "I wish those d—d lights was sunk below the sea!"* (MONROE COUNTY PUBLIC LIBRARY)

Indians had captured and killed a crew of 300 or more men from a wrecked French vessel. By the early 1800s, however, only a few fishermen and turtlers lived on Indian Key. [13]

In 1825 wrecker Jacob Housman envisioned the island as a salvage center. Housman, a man of questionable moral scruples but unquestioned ambition and ability, had discovered the Keys and the wrecking business when his vessel struck a reef sometime in the early 1820s. While ship carpenters repaired his schooner in Key West, Housman quickly saw the moneymaking possibilities in the salvaging business and decided to remain. Key West wreckers, however, did not welcome him, and Housman's reputation worsened after the way he handled the salvage of the French brig *Revenge* in 1825.[14]

Aboard his schooner *William Henry*, Housman discovered the *Revenge* on a reef off Elliot Key, north of Key Largo. The officers and crew had abandoned the brig. After boarding the vessel, Housman ordered his crew to remove the cargo and load it on the *William Henry*. Instead of returning to Key West with the salvaged goods, however, he continued north to Saint Augustine. Without the authorization of either the master or the owner of the *Revenge*, he then settled his salvage claim through arbitration.

The *Pensacola Gazette* reported the proceedings on December 8, 1825. "The jury of five citizens have allowed [Housman] ninety-five percent for salvage. The French consul . . . thinking this a most shameful proceeding has employed consul . . . and will have the question of salvage tried in [Superior] Court." Wreckers and merchants in Key West accused Housman of robbing the *Revenge*. Housman retorted that he had decided to take the salvage to Saint Augustine to avoid the dishonesty in Key West. The French consul appealed the decision before the Superior Court in St. Augustine, which reduced Housman's salvage award by thirty percent.

In 1830 Housman began to acquire property on Indian Key, which would serve as a home as well as a wrecking base. Workmen built storage warehouses for salvaged goods, laid out streets, and raised wharves that extended out into deep water. The new inhabitants built houses, a grocery store, a post office, and eventually a hotel with a dance hall. They cut large cisterns into the coral rock for storing rainwater.

Housman, like the Calusa Indians before him, recognized Indian Key's strategic location. Nearby were two of the most notoriously dangerous reefs—Alligator and Carysfort. Wreckers departing from Indian Key were almost guaranteed to be the first to reach any disabled vessels that had wrecked along the upper Keys. According to one report, during the last nine months of 1834 and the first three months of 1835, seventeen vessels wrecked on reefs within forty miles of Indian Key, and ten of these wrecked within fifteen miles of the island.

Housman also used his political connections to liberate Indian Key from Key West control. In 1836, the Florida Territorial Legislative Council created a new county, designating Indian Key as the county seat and partially fulfilling Housman's goal. They named the county for Captain Francis L. Dade, who had been massacred along with his entire company during one of the first incidents of the Second Seminole War in 1835.

Housman and his wrecking fleet continued to monopolize the lucrative salvaging business from Big Pine Key to Biscayne Bay. In November 1836, the *Ajax* went aground on Carysfort Reef. Housman, aboard the *Sarah Isabella*, was one of the wreckers involved in removing cargo from the merchantman in an attempt to refloat the vessel. During the presentation of the salvage case in Key West, the captain of the *Ajax* accused Housman of stealing cargo. The court found Housman guilty and forfeited his share of the salvage award. After a similar case in 1838, the court revoked Housman's wrecking license.[15]

Financial problems forced Housman to mortgage property on Indian Key in 1840. The sudden demise of Housman's island empire came on August 7, 1840, when Indians attacked the island and looted and burned the buildings. Housman and his wife barely escaped, then moved to Key West, where Housman secured work as a crewman aboard a wrecker. On May 1, 1841, the forty-one-year-old Housman was attempting to board a grounded vessel in rough seas. He apparently slipped and was crushed to death between the wrecking vessel and the disabled boat. His body was buried on Indian Key but later was disinterred.[16]

By the time Indian Key became the headquarters for the men constructing Alligator Reef Lighthouse, there was little evidence of Housman's ambitions for the island; even the boundary lines had been

Indian Key, the eleven-acre island four miles from Alligator Reef, was developed into an important wrecking center by Jacob Housman in the 1830s. In 1872 and 1873, the island served as construction headquarters for the men building Alligator Reef Lighthouse. (MONROE COUNTY PUBLIC LIBRARY)

changed, making Indian Key once more a part of Monroe County. The 1870 census recorded a population of forty-seven people on the island. Captain William H. Bethel and his wife Mary owned the island, and shipbuilding, rather than salvaging, was the main industry.[17]

While the locals built boats and farmed on neighboring islands, the contractors for Alligator Reef Light reported that their workers on Indian Key were constructing "a new wharf, quarters for mechanics and laborers." They built "a capacious cistern, a smithery, and a large shed for the iron-work and other materials for the lighthouse, whence it can be transported as wanted to the reef." They also built a fuel wharf and an adjoining coal storage building.[18]

Paulding Kemble, after forging the iron pile structure, shipped it from Cold Spring, New York, to Indian Key. The 1872 annual report of the Light House Board noted (by someone who was a realist) that raising the lighthouse would begin "as rapidly as the unfavorable circumstances attending all engineering operations along the Florida reefs will permit."

Once the contractor completed the essential construction work on Indian Key, materials and workers were sent to the designated area on the reef, a circle about fifty-six feet in diameter. After boring in various areas, engineers had found the coral most suitable for providing a solid base here at the northeast end of Alligator Reef, thirty yards from the already existing day beacon C. This would place the new light about two-hundred yards from the deep water of the Gulf Stream.

At this site, workmen first built a small landing jetty and a platform, sinking mangrove piles five feet into the coral. Although these were temporary structures, the piles had to withstand the heavy waves that built up on the reef. Once the men completed the platform, the real work began.

The coral reef was leveled to receive nine heavy cast-iron foundation disks. These had to be placed five feet under water, at the center and the outside corners of an octagon. The Light House Board reported the process: "By an ingenious system of gauges the disks were set in their positions, with their proper relative distances. The talent and perseverance of the assistant engineer . . . has nowhere been more conspicuously shown than of the placing of these disks upon which the whole structure depended; the difficulties of operation being enormously increased by the necessity of doing the work under water."[19]

The wrought iron foundation piles that passed through these disks were twenty-six feet long and twelve inches in diameter, with pointed lower ends. The men used a pile driver powered by a portable steam engine to drive the piles through the center holes of the disks and into the coral. The two-thousand-pound pile-driver hammer fell an average distance of eighteen feet, forcing the pile down into the coral from a half inch to one and a half inches each time. The workers drove the piles into the reef to a depth of ten feet. This laborious and dangerous work needed to be exact in every detail before the engineer could have the second series of pilings attached.

The Light House Board reported in their 1873 *Annual Report* that "great delays have occurred during the construction, owing to the exposed position of the lighthouse, the sea breaking heavily on the reefs at times, rendering landing on the platform of men and materials impracticable, sometimes for several days in succession." The engineer also had to postpone the work because of insufficient funds. Congress, after several months delay, finally appropriated an additional $25,000.

On November 25, 1873, the contractors completed the Alligator Reef Lighthouse. The final cost was $185,000. When the light was first exhibited, it flashed white every five seconds, with every sixth flash red. The focal plane of the light was 136 feet above sea level, giving a visibility of eighteen nautical miles. The light was a welcome sight for mariners, but perhaps not so welcomed by one wrecker, who bitterly lamented, "I wish those d—d lights was sunk below the sea."[20]

On June 17, 1874, Keeper George R. Billberry Jr. reported the first grounding after the light was exhibited. A storm had blown an English vessel loaded with timber up on the bank between nearby Crocker Reef and the lighthouse. A month later, an American bark with a cargo of sugar bound to New York from Jamaica ran aground on Little Conch Reef, northeast of Alligator Reef. Billberry wrote in the keepers' journal, "The wind was strong, many squalls . . . several wrecking schooners laying by the bark." The wreckers removed cargo for five days, working in high winds and seas, until the vessel was high enough in the water to float off the reef.

September storms brought other groundings. Billberry's report for September 13 and 14 reads, "Blowing a gale all night, heavy rain squalls, sea running very high and breaking heavy around this station . . . three masted schooner *Florence Rodgers* from Jamaica for New York loaded with logwood on shore close by Indian Key. She lost topmast and nearly all sails during gale."[21]

In 1876 Billberry was joined by William A. Bethel, first assistant, and Thomas A. Franklin, second assistant. The keeper described events of October 6 through 12 as follows:

Bethel discovered a full rigged brig on shore about 15 miles to the eastward of this station in the neighborhood of Pickles Reef— hoisted flag to call attention and ask for assistance. . . . About nine in the morning several wreckers got to the brig. Keeper went ashore to Indian Key. The night of the 10th and the morning of the 11th, rain. On the 11th, keeper ascertained while ashore that the wreck was a Spanish brig laden with logwood and mahogany. She struck the eastern side of Pickles Reef and after beating across the reef sunk inside, the water covering her deck so as to leave only the forecastle out of the water. Keeper could not ascertain the cause of the wreck or if the light had been seen. Thursday, the 12th . . . the cause of the wreck was that the Captain mistook this light for Carysfort and ran aground about 11:30 P.M. This light was very plainly seen all night. The Master and crew left the ship after she filled with water and were on their way to this station when they were picked up by a wrecker about daylight.[22]

On October 18, Billberry and his assistants began preparing for a hurricane:

> Blowing a gale all night. Sea running very high. Barometer 29.89.... October 19, Barometer still falling 29.03. Blowing a hurricane from the east. No land visible. Wind and sea increasing every minute. Bethel, being on watch, sounded the alarm bell. Found the damper pipe had slipped down over the chimney, raised it and secured it. This was caused by the shaking of the lantern and lenses. Revolving very uneven, sometimes 5 or 6 seconds fast, next 5 or 6 seconds slow.... 8:30 P.M. Wharf washed away. Barometer at 29.3.... 9:15 P.M. the after ring bolt of dinghy gone, hanging now by the lashings only. Could do nothing to secure her, it blowing fearfully hard and the sea running so high.... 9:30 Barometer 29.28.[23]

Billberry was in the act of passing more lashings around the boat when the high waves caught it and swept it away. Fortunately, Billberry did not go overboard. Three days later, a wrecker returned the boat—undamaged. Billberry noted in the journal, "Received from Capt. Albury the dinghy belonging to this station and gave him a receipt for it. The boat was picked up by the Carysfort Light Station."[24]

All of the keepers stationed on Alligator Reef Light experienced storms, high seas, and strong winds as well as the long, bright hot days and clear, starry nights. The men carried out many routine tasks, taking pride in the condition of their lighthouse. The keepers on board in 1893 must have been especially pleased when the Light House Board chose the Alligator Light to be one of two depicted in oil paintings for the board's exhibit at the World's Columbian Exposition held in Chicago. In describing Alligator Reef Lighthouse, the Board wrote, "This is one of the finest and most effective lights on the coast." The Board considered the light tower to be the most gracefully designed iron pile structures in the Keys.[25]

When the lighthouse needed any major repair, the crew of a lighthouse tender helped the keepers with the task. The tender *Arbutus* was called for assistance after the storm of June 16, 1906, damaged the lighthouse and blew down a number of day beacons in Hawks Channel. The *Arbutus* quickly arrived to help with repairs and returned after the storms in 1907 and 1909. In 1913, the tender delivered the new incandescent oil-vapor system to the lighthouse to replace the oil-wick lamps. The crew installed steel oil storage tanks for kerosene within the tower frame.

It was also in 1913 that the light tender *Mangrove* hauled the British steamer *Antaeus* off French Reef, northeast of Alligator Light, and later rendered assistance to the schooner *Igo*, which had bilged. Light tenders and light keepers often assisted vessels that were in trouble on the reefs, but in 1919, a different type of accident occurred, when a disabled seaplane crash-landed about ten miles from the light. The keepers witnessed the landing. Richard C. Richards, an assistant keeper, immediately launched the lighthouse's boat and went to the aid of the seaplane. The Bureau of Lighthouses, in its annual report, wrote that Richards "dived into shark-infested waters to locate the two men on the plane, then towed the plane about four miles when it was taken in tow by a naval boat."[26]

The most devastating storm endured by the Alligator Reef Light came on Labor Day in 1935. The barometric pressure dropped to 27.35 at the light and read 26.35 at Long Key twenty miles west-southwest. The wind from the north-northeast was recorded at 200 miles per hour. At fifty feet above normal water level, the metal doors that opened outward on the keepers' quarters were jammed inward by towering seas, while the interior wooden doors were ripped off their hinges. Keeper Jones A. Pervis recorded in the light station journal:

At 6:30 P.M. while Lighting the Lamp for the night the lantern glass began to break . . . and flying glass was a danger to life . . . the lens was completely wrecked, and other damage done by wind and water to the watch room, and property therein. The Row boat washed away about 8 P.M. The launch No. 34 was in fair condition at 9:30 P.M. this was the last time we were able to be outside until the next day. The platform landing was completely wrecked and launch No. 34 gone. This is the worst hurricane I have experienced

Form 396
DEPARTMENT OF COMMERCE
LIGHTHOUSE SERVICE

JOURNAL OF LIGHT STATION AT Alligator Reef
Jones A. Pervis, Keeper ▓▓▓▓▓▓▓▓ 1st assistant James O Duncan 2 assistant

1935 MONTH	DAY	STATE WORK PERFORMED BY KEEPERS REGARDING UPKEEP OF STATION, AND RECORD OF IMPORTANT EVENTS, WEATHER CONDITIONS, ETC.
September	1st	Quiet duty
	2	Securing against Tropical hurricanes. On the afternoon of the second day the Barometer began falling. normal Rating. 29-97 fell as low as 27-35 by 9.30.P.m. same day. 10.P.m. the Barometer began to rise, and on the third day of this month at one oclock P.m. the Barometer reading was 29-37 with very bad rainy weather strong wind from the south the second day, the wind was from the north east blowing a fresh Breeze and increased to gale force by 4 P.m. 6 P.m. was a regular hurricane. 6.30. P.m while lighting the Lamp for the night the Lantern Glass began to break, and sectors began to break flying glass was danger to life. I left the watch Room and hurried to living quarters, the doors began to break in, the keepers and second assistant room, was badly damaged, to doors and water soaked beds, and clothing. I managed to save doors in first assistant room, and the Kitchen. the Lens was completely wrecked, and other damage done by wind and water to the watch Room and Property there in. The Row boat washed away about 8.P.m. the Launch no 34 was in fair condition at 9.30.P.m. this was the last time we were able to be out side until the next day the platform Landing was completely wrecked and launch no 34 gone this is the worst hurricane I have experienced. during the Eleven years of service the Light will be out of commission ontil temporely repaired. Signed by Jones A Pervis Rating Keeper ...

Page from the 1935 keepers' journal kept at Alligator Reef Light Station. Keeper Jones A. Pervis wrote: "September 1, Quiet duty," . . . "September 2, Securing against tropical hurricane. . . ." (NATIONAL ARCHIVES) during the eleven years of service. The light will be out of commission until temporarily repaired.

The storm blew ballast from Long Key Viaduct on the first-level deck of the lighthouse. But true horror must have been experienced when the keepers saw a twenty-foot stormwave bearing down on the light. With destructive force, the tidal surge swept toward the town of Islamorada on Upper Matecumbe Key. Almost everything along the shore was wiped out except a tombstone known as "the littlest angel" and one wall of a grocery store. Four hundred and twenty-three people were killed in the Islamorada area. On October 3, Bob Combs, chief deputy sheriff of Tavernier, Key Largo, visited Alligator Reef Light and reported seeing broken panes of glass around the light 136 feet above the water. Throughout the keepers' quarters all the windows were broken except for one on the southeast side.[27]

In 1939 the winds of political change arrived when the Presidential Reorganizational Act incorporated the lighthouses into the Coast Guard. The government gave the keepers the option of remaining on duty as civilians or of joining the Coast Guard. By July 1, 1939, when the reorganization went into effect, most of the men who served on the lighthouses in the Keys had joined the Coast Guard.[28]

In the 1950s Coast Guardsman Dick Gooravin was serving on Alligator Reef Light Station. Later he recalled, "The water around the lighthouse on most days was calm and gin clear. You could see the formation of the reefs perfectly, the sandy spots in between, and the deep waters of the Gulf Stream just a few hundred yards away. When you looked down you would see all kinds of fish. There were always lots of barracudas cruising lazily around the lighthouse." A few hours before dinner the men would ask, "Well, what will it be, grouper, yellow-tail, snapper, or lobster?" The main course was always available. The men fished from the lower platform or dived into the water and speared what they wanted.[29]

The keepers' living quarters contained four bright and airy rooms, with large double doors instead of windows. Few insects reached the lighthouse and only occasionally, when a gentle wind blew from the west or northwest, would the mosquitoes become a nuisance. The men had a telephone, the crank type, mounted on the wall with a direct line to Homestead on the south point of mainland Florida. This hookup made Islamorada, on the nearest island, a long-distance call, which amused and sometimes annoyed the men stationed at the light.

Large water tanks hung beneath the living quarters. Every few years, the men scrubbed out the tanks and painted the insides with melted paraffin. When the work was completed, a Coast Guard tender arrived and filled the tanks with water. After the supply was exhausted, rainwater collected on the roof was funneled into the tanks.

The Coast Guardsmen's routine duties included four hours of work each day on the lighthouse structure, keeping records of weather and sea conditions, and maintaining the standing watch on the light. Gooravin took particular pride in polishing the brass. When he had the brass gleaming, he would take a book up to the shady side of the highest platform and read, relax, and enjoy the spectacular view.

The men also had to regularly clean the lantern roof. Birds, blinded by the light at night, often crashed into the iron pilings. Once, Gooravin recalled thousands of warblers rested on the lighthouse, covering almost every part of the structure. Exhausted from flying against adverse winds during migration, the birds took refuge on the iron perches.

Between the diversions of birds and storms, the men entertained themselves with kite flying, fishing, swimming, poker, and an occasional visitor. But for some Coast Guardsmen, life at Alligator Reef was too quiet, too confined; they requested transfer. Gooravin never did. He remained on the light from 1950 to 1953 and remembers those years as some of the happiest and most contented of his life. After Gooravin was discharged, he moved to Islamorada, where he enjoyed an islander's view of his favorite lighthouse.[30]

In 1960 Hurricane Donna hit the upper Keys. The storm was not as severe as the 1935 Labor Day hurricane, and people were better prepared, but the Coast Guardsmen on Alligator Reef Light still had a terrible experience. As the storm wave surged toward the lighthouse, the men climbed to the highest platform and lashed themselves to the iron structural braces to avoid being blown away. The steep, cresting waves hammered against the iron pilings, shaking the entire structure. The eye of the hurricane passed over nearby Duck Key between 2:00 and 2:30 A.M. When the hurricane finally swept past and the winds

began to subside, the men scanned the nearby land through binocu-
lars. They saw no movement and for a while thought they were the
only survivors. In fact, all of the residents were either still in shelters
or being fed and cared for inside the Methodist Church.

On the water, an unbelievable view surrounded the men on the
lighthouse. One Coast Guardsman describing the scene: "We looked
out and saw a sight we will never forget if we live a thousand years.
Scattered over the ocean, like croutons on a dish of soup, were derelict
small boats, pieces of boats, chairs, bedsteads, boxes, lumber, trash, rising and falling on a twelve foot sea that still ran frothy and gray."[31]

No one endured the hardship or terror of the 1965 hurricane aboard
the Alligator Reef Lighthouse—the light was automated in June 1963.
Since automation, the only ones to enjoy the spectacular view from the
highest platform are contractors who scale, scrape, and paint the iron
work, and men from the Aids to Navigation Team (ANT) who come
to check the light every three months. Today there is so much boating
activity around Alligator Reef that if the light isn't working properly
someone usually notifies the Coast Guard station in Islamorada right
away.

Chief Richard "Beau" Lewis, Seventh Coast Guard District, Aids to
Navigation (ATON), talks about a new device being tested for use on
Alligator Reef Light "that will monitor the Vega VRB-25 rotating
beacon and solar batteries." He has been working with Sea Air Land
Technologies, Inc. (SALT) of Marathon, Florida. "The company has
developed the means of measuring the amount of solar charge to the
batteries and the amount of draw," Chief Lewis explains. "This information will feed directly into a computer work station. By studying
the graph produced I can tell if the batteries are charging and if the
light is functioning properly." If this device is successful, Aids to Navigation will install it on all of the reef lights. The Coast Guard in
Miami will monitor the Fowey Rocks and Carysfort Reef lighthouses,
and the Key West station will monitor the other four.[32]

Eighty-six miles west of Alligator Reef Light, someone sitting at an
air-conditioned work station will read a computer printout and know
that all is well with the light. Alligator Reef Lighthouse will be flashing four four-second white lights that can be seen for sixteen miles at

The Vega VRB-25 is the rotating beacon now used by the Coast Guard on Alligator Reef Lighthouse. The optic is comprised of six Fresnel-type lens panels arranged symmetrically on a carousel, which rotates around a stationary lamp. The VRB-25 is designed specifically for solar powering and is fitted with a photoelectric sensor device that switches the lamp on at dusk. (PHOTOGRAPH BY BM2 RAY POTTER, ANT, KEY WEST, FLORIDA)

sea and sending red flashes over the reefs that hold the few remains of the USS *Alligator*.[33]

The notes for this chapter begin on page 287.

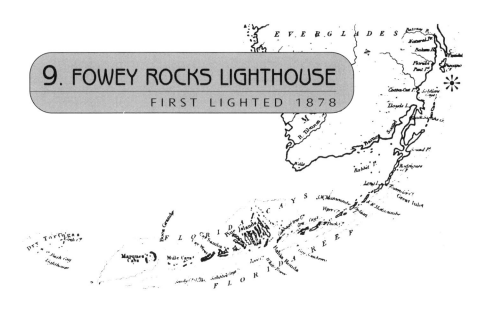

9. FOWEY ROCKS LIGHTHOUSE

FIRST LIGHTED 1878

In 1875 the Light House Board decided to cease operations at the lighthouse on Cape Florida. The brick tower would be left standing as a day mark, but the board no longer considered its light an effective navigational aid for marking the extreme northern point of the Florida Reef. Iron pile lighthouses, built in the water on the reefs, had proved so successful that the board now proposed building a new one to mark the dangerous reefs southeast of the Cape.

The site chosen for the new 110-foot lighthouse was named, as were so many reefs in the Keys, for a shipwreck. The HMS *Fowey*, a twenty-gun British warship commanded by Captain Francis William Drake, sank in this area in 1748. On January 6, 1875, the deed for the reef was obtained by the United States for lighthouse purposes from the state of Florida. Fowey Rocks was described on the deed as "a circular area having a radius of 235½ feet."[1]

The lighthouse on Fowey Rocks would be the fifth iron pile light constructed in the Keys. In February 1877 the Light House Board awarded the contract to manufacture the iron foundation to Paulding and Kemble of Cold Spring, New York. The board granted Pusey, Jones & Company of Wilmington, Delaware, the contract to build the tower on the foundation pilings. The company was to deliver all ma-

Original drawing for Fowey Rocks Lighthouse. The Light House Board was especially pleased with the architectural design of the tower and the keepers' house within the skeletal frame. (NATIONAL ARCHIVES)

terials by ship to the Florida site from Delaware and to complete the lighthouse thirteen weeks from the date of the contract.[2]

The builders chose Soldier Key, a small island four miles from the construction site, as the project's headquarters. Each day, lighters carrying the workers and all needed materials were towed by a steam launch to the platform work site. But before work on the lighthouse itself could begin, workmen constructed an eighty-foot-square platform on the reef to receive building materials. Local mangrove trees furnished the lumber for the platform pilings. The men shod the wooden piles with iron, hammered them into the coral, and secured the platform to the pilings about twelve feet above the water.

Next, divers leveled the reef for the light tower. The reef lay about five feet below water at low tide. Workmen then positioned the iron disks to receive the pilings. The first iron piling driven through the eyehole of a disk was the central one. After each blow of the pile driver, the men tested the angle of the piling with a plummet and corrected the slightest deviation from the vertical. They repeated the process for each piling until they had driven all of them eleven feet into the coral. After the pilings were in proper position, the men leveled the tops and attached sockets to receive horizontal girders and diagonal tie-rods. The first deck was put into place and completed during the summer of 1876.[3]

During the two months of the initial phase of the construction, the sea was calm and the weather excellent. Then bad weather set in, threatening a storm that might last for days and maroon the men at the work site. Launches that transported the workmen to the site often returned them back to Soldier Key at the first sign of bad weather. To allow the men to continue working when the seas were rough, the contractors provided the work crew with tents and provisions and had them remain on the platform.[4]

As luck would have it, during the first month the men lived and worked under these arrangements there was only one day of good weather. The seas crashed the precarious perch, while supply launches waited night and day for the seas to calm so food and additional building materials could be delivered. While at work, the men kept their minds occupied with the construction, but when building materials

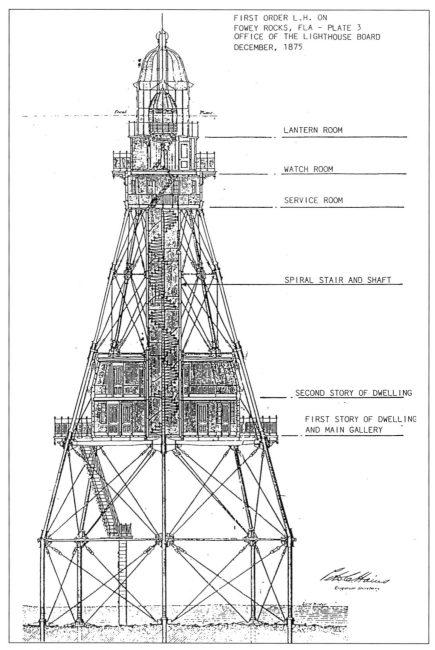

FIRST ORDER L.H. ON
FOWEY ROCKS, FLA – PLATE 3
OFFICE OF THE LIGHTHOUSE BOARD
DECEMBER, 1875

LANTERN ROOM

WATCH ROOM

SERVICE ROOM

SPIRAL STAIR AND SHAFT

SECOND STORY OF DWELLING

FIRST STORY OF DWELLING
AND MAIN GALLERY

A 1994 diagram showing various sections of Fowey Rocks Lighthouse, based on an 1875 Light House Board drawing. (TAYLOR ENGINEERING, INC., FOR U.S. COAST GUARD AID TO NAVIGATION, SEVENTH DISTRICT, MIAMI) were lacking, they sometimes sat idle for days, marooned on a small platform surrounded by a threatening sea.

One night a new and completely unexpected danger threatened from the ocean side when the men saw the running lights of the steamer *Arakanapka* headed in their direction. The lights from the ship appeared larger and larger; the men knew that if it continued on course it would demolish the platform. Just before the collision, only yards away from the watching men, the *Arakanapka* wrecked on Fowey Rocks.[5]

On March 16, 1877, the weather improved. During the next sixteen days, lighters delivered six loads of building materials and supplies for the men. By April 7 the second series of girders, sockets, and tension rods was in place. Work was going well, but before the lighthouse could be completed, the men once again watched in horror as another vessel approached directly toward them. Only moments before the *Carondelet* would have rammed the work platform, it ran aground on the reef. The *Carondelet* was more fortunate than the *Arakanapka*. After the crew jettisoned most of its cargo, the vessel floated off the reef. Those on shore quickly commandeered every local boat available and scooped up this unexpected bounty from the sea, while men on the light tower continued their work. After watching two ships run aground on the reef while building the lighthouse, they now fully appreciated the need for a navigational aid to guide vessels around Fowey Rocks.[6]

On April 30, 1878, workmen finished the two-story keepers' house. The octagonal, iron-sheeted house contained eight ample rooms with wooden interior walls. The sides of the lower story were vertical, but the walls of the upper story were angled inward, repeating the shape of the iron tower surrounding the house. For light and ventilation the architects had included windows on all eight sides of the watch room and in the iron cylinder enclosing the circular stairway leading between the keepers' quarters and the watch room. They used casement windows for the upper story of the keepers' house, with shuttered windows for the lower. For a homey touch and for daytime identification of the lighthouse, the house was painted white with green trim and shutters.[7]

Once the contractors completed the house, work began on the

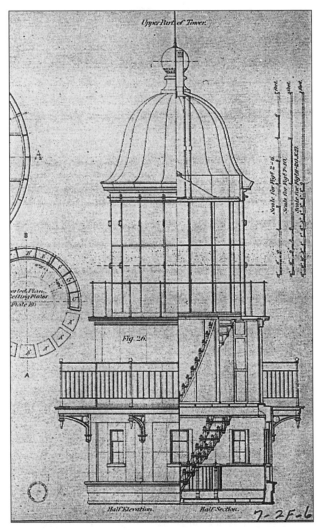

An 1875 drawing for the lantern, watch room, and watch room vestibule for Fowey Rocks Lighthouse. (NATIONAL ARCHIVES)

upper tower. Workers installed the spiral stairs that led from the service room to the lantern. Outside galleries with balustrades encircled the lantern, the service room, and the keepers' quarters. The beautifully crafted first-order lantern was designed with sixteen sides, providing a weatherproof room for the lens and lamps. Vertical and horizontal bronze bars (known as astragals and clamps) joined the glass panes. The copper roof of the lantern was topped with a copper ventilator ball and a lightning-conductor spindle. The ventilator ball served as the primary vent for the fumes and smoke created by the illuminant.

The company of Henry Lepaute of Paris, France, had built the first-order Fresnel lens in 1876. The Light House Board displayed the lens and lantern at one of the greatest exhibitions of the century—the 1876 Philadelphia Centennial. On May 25, 1878, workmen positioned the lens in its permanent home inside the lantern, and on June 15, the keeper lit the Fowey Rocks light for the first time.[8]

The Centennial display proved so popular that the board decided to prepare another exhibit for the 1892–1893 World's Columbian Exposition in Chicago. The exhibit included lenses, lamps, tools used by keepers, various types of buoys and models, as well as paintings and photographs of lighthouses and tenders. The board included a painting and a model of the Fowey Rocks Lighthouse at a scale of ¾-inch to the foot. Engineers had built the model to serve as a guide in planning future similar structures, using silver-plated and oxidized brass (to resemble iron). "The model attracted much attention," the Light House Board reported, "not only on account of its intrinsic merits, but because of its beauty and novelty." The watercolor of Fowey Rocks Lighthouse inspired the Board to proudly describe its tower as standing "in lonely grandeur with waves gently lapping its base, in the clear bright light of the subtropical day, with nothing in sight except a few vessels at varying distances, which aid in giving an idea of its height . . ." The Fowey Rocks Light, explained the Board, "cost about $163,015 to build . . . It consumes yearly about 2,225 gallons of mineral oil; and it is cared for by three keepers who receive each year $820, $510, and $490, respectively, for their services."[9]

John W. Frow, the first keeper of Fowey Rocks, had served on the Cape Florida Lighthouse until it was discontinued. He had been aboard less than three months when a hurricane struck the area with winds well over one hundred miles per hour. In the station journal, Frow recorded that as the winds increased on September 6, the keepers secured the lighthouse boat to an upper platform of the tower. At one o'clock on the morning of September 7, 1878, "there was a heavy hurricane blowing and increasing rapidly. The glass of the lantern

Jefferson B. Browne's first job after graduating from high school was as assistant keeper on Fowey Rocks Lighthouse. Browne later became a Supreme Court justice for the state of Florida. His book, Key West: The Old and the New, *is one of the most significant histories of the city.* (MONROE COUNTY PUBLIC LIBRARY)

leaked badly." All day and all night, Frow and his two assistants worked to keep things dry, mopping the lantern floor, wiping the lens, and keeping the lamps burning. Frow wrote, "Eastern door of dwelling so strained one of the panels is almost off and starting to tear the other off." The hurricane raged unabated for the next three days. The glass panels in the lantern were loose, "allowing the rain into the lantern constantly." On September 11 the barometer began to rise. "The gale broke and the wind came around to the southwest." Fowey Rocks Lighthouse had survived its first test by hurricane.[10]

One of the assistant keepers on duty during the hurricane was Jefferson Browne. Browne had just graduated from high school, and the keeper's job was his first. The work during the week of the hurricane and in the weeks afterward, while the men cleaned up and repaired the damaged lighthouse, was exhausting. When the lighthouse rou-

The Alicia, *bound for Havana, ran up on Ajax Reef off Fowey Rocks Lighthouse. The ship carried a varied cargo, including a complete iron bridge, pianos, soap powder, and casks of rum.* (MONROE COUNTY PUBLIC LIBRARY)

tine returned to normal, Browne found that he had quite a bit of free time to read his law books, which so absorbed him that he never took a day's vacation. After studying law in his spare time for fifteen months, Browne left the Lighthouse Service to attend the University of Iowa Law School. He obtained a law degree in less than two years and passed the bar examinations in both Iowa and Florida. In 1880 he was elected attorney for the town of Key West and for Monroe County. In 1916 voters elected him to the Florida Supreme Court, the highest judicial office in the state of Florida.[11]

The life of storms, wrecks, and lighthouse tending continued for head keeper John Frow and his father, Simeon Frow, who served as first assistant keeper at Fowey Rocks. The Frow family had a tradition of lightkeeping. Simeon's sons, John and Joseph, both served at various times on the same lights with him. The brothers were together at the Cape Florida light from 1869 until 1878. Simeon also had two daughters; one of them, Julia, married keeper Robert H. Thompson, who served with his father-in-law on Fowey Rocks Light in 1879 and 1880.

It was not unusual for the vocation of lightkeeper to be shared

Wreckers came from as far away as Key West to help remove cargo from the Alicia. *A squall moving through the area sank the steamer the day after it had been successfully refloated.* (MONROE COUNTY PUBLIC LIBRARY)

within a family. William Archer, head keeper on Fowey Rocks from 1895 until 1905, had been serving on Florida lights since 1881. His son, William Jr., served on the American Shoal Lighthouse. The names Curry, Albury, Bethel, Weatherford, Thompson, Russell, and Saunders, among others, appear repeatedly through the years on the lists of keepers in the Keys.[12]

Henry P. Weatherford was the head keeper at Fowey Rocks Lighthouse in 1905 when the *Alicia*, bound for Havana, ran up on Fowey Rocks. One of the witnesses, Mary Conrad, lived southwest of the light on Elliot Key. "I used to wake up at night," she wrote, "and see the fingers of the light in the sky and think what a blessing to all sailors, especially during storms." But she also remembered the wreck of the *Alicia*, whose cargo included a complete iron bridge, buggies, harnesses, cases of Edwin Clapp shoes for men, Queen Quality shoes for women, coffee, condensed milk, laces, plain and flowered linen, and cases of silverware and jewelry.[13]

Mary Conrad's brother Johnny, and their friend, Captain Fuller, were the first to reach the *Alicia*. Wreckers came all the way from Key

The Coast Guard is now displaying the first-order lens removed from the Fowey Rocks Light at the U.S. Coast Guard National Aids to Navigation School, Yorktown, VA. (PHOTOGRAPHY BY GAIL FULLER, CURATOR, U.S. COAST GUARD)

West to aid in the salvage. "The oddest thing about the salvage," wrote Conrad, "came from the soap suds. There were many cases of washing powder on the ship and the water became so soapy the men would not go into the hold." The captain of the *Alicia* paid the salvagers cargo instead of money for their work. Conrad recalled, "Johnny received a buggy with a patent leather dash board." Afterward, most of the men from Key West to Miami were wearing Edwin Clapp shoes, and Queen Quality shoes became the fashion for local women.

The *Alicia* was successfully refloated, but the next day a squall moved through the area and sank the ship, sending its remaining cargo of furniture, pianos, and casks of rum and wine to the bottom.

After the second salvage operation, many of the wreckers were quite tipsy when they returned to shore.[14]

In 1914 while a working party aboard Fowey Rocks Light was installing oil tanks for the new incandescent oil vapor (i.o.v.) system, the schooner *Alice B. Philips* went aground on the reef. Keeper Henry Weatherford and John Peterson, foreman of the working party, immediately went out to aid the disabled schooner. The Bureau of Lighthouses credited them with saving the vessel and all those aboard. The following year, Weatherford and Richard Palmer, second assistant keeper, rescued five people from the yacht *May Belle*, which sank immediately after the passengers were safely transferred to the lighthouse boat. Later, after rescuing the crew and passengers from the yacht *Inwood*, Weatherford and Palmer also towed the yacht to the lighthouse and repaired the vessel to keep it from sinking.[15]

Although wrecks and groundings continued, the number of ships that ran up on the reef diminished. Nevertheless, reporting disabled vessels or getting additional help if they needed it was impossible for the isolated keepers. The most they could do was fly the ensign upside down and hope a passing vessel would take notice and come to investigate. It was not until 1923 that keepers gained direct communication with the mainland via a submarine telephone cable. The Bureau of Lighthouses also improved the light in the mid-1930s by replacing the i.o.v. system with electricity. The electrical generators also allowed the keepers to operate a radio beacon, which workmen installed on top of the cupola.

The last keepers on the Fowey Rocks Light before its automation in 1974 were Coast Guardsmen. Later, Aids to Navigation (ATON) equipped the light with battery-powered automatic lamp changers. These improvements ensured the reliability of the unmanned light. Without keepers, the radio beacon was no longer functional and was removed.

Since automation, ATON personnel have experimented with various possible ways of charging the lighthouse batteries. A windmill generator introduced in 1975 proved unreliable and was replaced in 1982 with a flash-tube array with solar-powered batteries. Coast Guardsmen dismantled and removed the Fresnel lens, which was no longer needed, and moved it to a display at the U.S. Coast Guard's National Aids to Navigation School in Yorktown, Virginia.

The solar-powered batteries proved successful, but the flash-tube array lamps were not. In 1983 the Aids to Navigation Team (ANT) replaced them with a three-hundred-millimeter optic. This optic did not have the range the Coast Guard felt necessary for Fowey Rocks, however, and was replaced by a rotating, 190-millimeter optic. Lieutenant Commander J. V. O'Shea, Seventh Coast Guard District, ATON, observed that "the 190 provides a range of about sixteen miles. That is comparable to the old Fresnel lens, but it is much cheaper and requires less maintenance."[16]

In 1987 contractors scraped and painted the lighthouse and later removed the water tanks from the working platform beneath the keepers' house. The tanks were no longer needed, and ATON feared that high seas might tear them off and damage the foundation of the tower. A few years later, in 1992, Hurricane Andrew violently buffeted the lighthouse before slamming ashore to devastate South Miami. Surprisingly, Fowey Rocks Lighthouse survived, although the hurricane smashed every pane of the quarter-inch glass in the lantern room. The worst storm to hit Florida in thirty years, Andrew also damaged three other nearby navigation aids: Pacific Reef Light, Triumph Reef Light, and the Miami Radio Beacon (formerly on the Fowey Rocks Lighthouse).[17]

Concerned with the tower's structural soundness, its operational safety, and its historic value, a team of engineers and architects inspected the lighthouse in July 1994 to document needed repairs. They itemized twenty-seven repair tasks at an estimated cost of $403,700. Most important were the replacement of the lantern glass and the installation of two modern (Lexan) panels of red glass behind the north and south light sections needed to mark the reefs.

Their report indicated that "given its age and exposure, Fowey Rocks Lighthouse is in fair condition." Some corroded brackets in the galleries "require immediate replacement," and some rods in the foundation "exceed safety margins"; however, what was needed most to slow the lighthouse's deterioration included sandblasting and painting.[18]

Once the Coast Guard automated the Reef Lights, vandalism and

Fowey Rocks Lighthouse was called the "Eye of Miami" when it was manned by the Coast Guard; the men on duty in the tower could see if a boat was in distress and would radio for help. The radio beacon attached above the lantern was removed and placed in the entrance of Miami Harbor when the light was automated in 1972. (U.S. COAST GUARD OFFICIAL PHOTO)

deterioration caused more damage than any hurricane. In retrospect, one fully appreciates the importance of the routine jobs keepers performed, not only to keep the light burning, but to maintain the entire structure.

The Seventh Coast Guard District, ATON, has the responsibility of maintaining and improving these aids within a limited budget. In addition to the structural work required on Fowey Rocks Lighthouse, ATON has installed a totally new optical system, the Vega VRB-25. This rotating beacon improves the intensity of the light, yet is energy efficient. Powered by solar batteries and fitted with a photoelectric device (which switches the lamp on at dusk), Fowey Rocks still flashes a white, ten-second light, with red flashes over the coral reefs. Fowey Rocks Lighthouse is the first navigational light seen by ships approaching the city of Miami from the south. Neil Hurley, historian for the Florida Lighthouse Association, Inc., believes this is the basis for Fowey Rocks Lighthouse's popular nickname, "The Eye of Miami."[19]

The notes for this chapter begin on page 289.

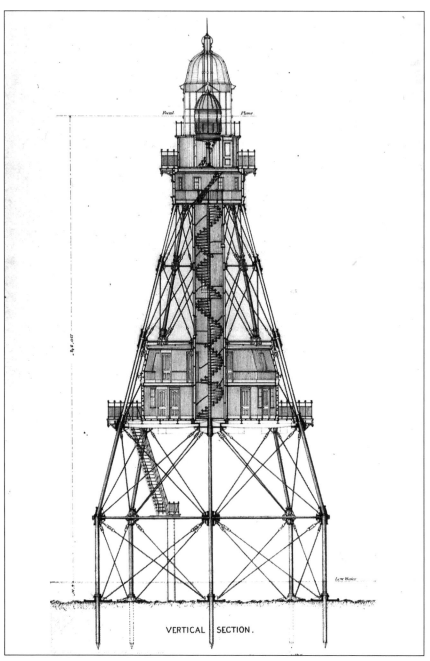

Focal Plane

Low Water

VERTICAL SECTION.

The American Shoal Lighthouse was the last iron pile lighthouse to be built on the Florida reefs. The architectural design is almost identical to the lighthouse built on Fowey Rocks. The light was first displayed on July 16, 1880. (NATIONAL ARCHIVES)

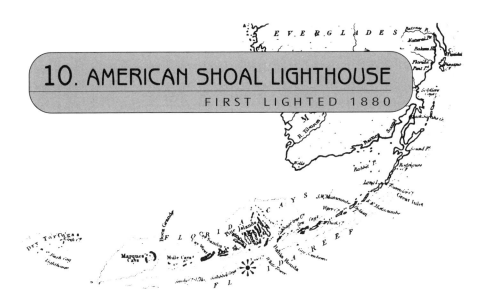

10. AMERICAN SHOAL LIGHTHOUSE

FIRST LIGHTED 1880

The American Shoal Lighthouse was the last iron pile light erected in the Florida Keys. It took the Light House Board many years of planning before establishing this lighthouse. The preliminary board of 1851 had an ambitious, long-range plan for marking the Florida Reefs from Cape Florida to the Dry Tortugas. By 1874 only three additional lighthouses were needed to mark this sea route: one on Fowey Rocks, to replace the light at Cape Florida; one in the vicinity of Looe Key, between Sand Key and Sombrero Key in the lower Keys; and one between Sand Key and the Dry Tortugas.

The Light House Board had already decided that the lighthouses on Fowey Rocks and in the lower Keys were to be similar iron screw-pile structures. In 1874 Congress granted the board's funding request for the Fowey Rocks Lighthouse but turned down the $100,000 appropriation needed for the lighthouse off the lower Keys.

The board, in explaining to Congress the reason for the Looe Key site, said, "The navigation of this portion of the gulf is always dangerous, particularly to vessels bound southward and westward because of the strong and variable currents near the reef, causing many wrecks and loss of property."[1]

Plans to mark the area with some type of beacon were not new. Ten years before, in a letter of February 17, 1845, Key West insurance underwriter John C. Holt had mentioned that a beacon was "to be put up at Loo Key."[2]

Looe Key, as it is spelled on contemporary charts, is a reef lying east-northeast of another reef area known as American Shoal. Once an islet, Looe Key now extends from shallow water to a depth of forty-five feet. The seaward side of the reef has narrow projections of thick coral growing in canyonlike formations. Although it is clearly visible in calm weather, Looe Key can be a dangerous area for vessels because of unpredictable currents. There is ample evidence of shipwrecks, including cast-iron ballast blocks and scattered and half-buried timbers from the HMS *Loo*, which sank in 1744 and gave the reef its name.

The *Loo* was a frigate of the Royal Navy carrying forty to forty-four guns. Launched about 1706, the frigate was named for an old seaport town on the coast of Cornwall. Captain Ashby Utting, the master of the *Loo*, commanded a fleet of ships guarding the South Carolina coast from Spanish privateers. The British Navy also ordered Utting to "cruize [sic] between Cape Florida and the northwest part of the Grand Bahamas" and to "diligently look out for the Enemy's ships passing through the Gulf of Florida for Europe," and use his "utmost endeavors, to take, sink, burn or destroy them."[3]

In February 1744 the *Loo* was cruising in the Florida Straits. Off Havana, the frigate captured the *Billander Betty*, which had been taken by the Spanish. Escorting the prize, Utting set a northeast by north course for South Carolina. The ships sailed for two nights. At 1:15 A.M. on the second morning, the *Loo* suddenly found herself in shallow water with breakers visible. Despite the helmsman's efforts to steer the *Loo* away from the reef, the *Loo*'s headsails caught as the vessel veered offwind, and the aft part of the ship struck the reef. Pounded by swells on the reefs, the frigate began to sink rapidly. The prize ship, *Billander Betty*, also struck the reef. Utting and the men from both ships eventually made Port Royal in small boats and a sloop the crew captured off the reefs. Court-martialed for the loss of the *Loo*, Utting was acquitted by a unanimous decision that neither Utting nor his officers contributed to the vessels being wrecked on the reef, "that the course the ship steered was a good one, and must have carried her through the Gulf of Florida, with all safety, had not some unusual current rendered the said course ineffectual."[4]

One hundred years after the wreck of the *Loo*, the unpredicatable currents in the area were still causing wrecks. One of these involved the *Mississippi*, which went up on the reef in 1840. Thirty-nine men from three wrecking vessels labored continuously from four o'clock in the afternoon until six o'clock the next morning to remove about thirty tons of cargo. They had to throw sixty tons of stone ballast overboard before they could tow the ship off the reef. The value of the salvage was $100,000. At the salvage claim hearing in Key West, Judge William Marvin awarded shares to the men averaging $188, the largest shares decreed by the court up to that time.[5]

A beacon on Looe Key might have prevented the grounding of the *Mississippi*. Such a marker would not only help navigators identify their position, but would also alert them to the effect of the current on their vessel. After the 1846 survey of the Florida reefs was completed, the surveyors designated particularly dangerous points on the reefs for day beacons. In 1850 they placed a thirty-eight-foot pole on Looe Key reef topped with a barrel painted black. Two years later, Lieutenant James Totten, U.S. Army, had an iron screwpile sunk into the reef at American Shoal while assisting the Coast Survey. The white pile was thirty-six feet high. Attached to the top of the piling was a red hoop-iron, latticework cylinder, with the letter B painted on a black vane beneath. The position of this beacon was latitude 24° 31' 24" north, longitude 81° 31' 16" west. Mariners could see the beacon two to three miles with the naked eye and six to ten miles with a telescope.

Captain Rollins of the *Isabel*, who passed along the reef four times a month, reported in 1852 that the beacon on American Shoal was most helpful. *Hunt's Merchants' Magazine and Commercial Review* described the beacon as being within a half mile of the Gulf Stream in four feet of water. Mariners could approach the day mark from seaward within a few hundred yards, but the magazine article cautioned:

> It would always be prudent, and particularly with very light winds, or in bad weather, to give it a good berth. In moderate weather, it often happens, especially after easterly gales, that the force and direction of the Gulf Stream sets across the reefs, and then vessels are imperceptibly carried amid its dangers, although the course steered should, if made good, carry them outside all danger. When a mas-

ter of a vessel finds one of these beacons to the eastward of him, he may be sure that he is between the reefs and Cays, and consequently surrounded by shoals and dangerous rocks.[6]

Improved charts of the Florida Keys were published after the 1846 survey. The charts and the day beacons erected in the 1850s aided navigation considerably. The day beacons, however, were of little value to vessels at night. Laden with assorted cargo, the bark *F. A. Everett* stranded on American Shoal in darkness during a storm. A schooner went to aid the bark, but the sea was so rough it was impossible to board. The next day several wrecking vessels arrived, and, according to later testimony, "One of the masters boarded the wreck with much difficulty and personal danger." When the weather moderated, the wreckers were able to save the cargo.[7]

Despite the groundings near American Shoal and the Light House Board's recommendation for a lighted aid at Looe Key, Congress took no action. The board repeated its request for an appropriation in 1876, stating that American Shoal rather than "Loo Key" was "more nearly the desired position." In asking for $75,000, the board stated, "This light-house should be erected without unnecessary delay; labor and materials being unusually low, the present is a very favorable opportunity for construction."[8]

The board continued its yearly plea until Congress appropriated $75,000 on June 20, 1878. The board already had a survey of the four submarine acres needed on American Shoal, which the governor transferred to the United States for lighthouse purposes. Engineers used plans almost identical to those for Fowey Rocks Lighthouse. Phoenix Iron Company of Trenton, New Jersey, secured the ironwork contract for $47,000. As for all other reef lights, the board required the company to assemble the parts completely to assure perfect fit before shipment to Key West.[9]

Although several islands lay closer to American Shoal, Key West, approximately nineteen miles west, became the project headquarters. The lighthouse depot was in Key West, and the town offered good accommodations for the working crew, as well as services and supplies. The contractors immediately had a scow built to transport the men and materials to the site northwest of Day Beacon B. Workers first constructed a platform at the site using piles made with mangrove wood, and shod the bottom ends with iron. After a steam engine helped drive the piles into the coral, the men secured a wooden platform across the tops. Divers then leveled the five-foot deep coral reef to receive the foundation pilings for the light tower. All was then in readiness for the building to begin.

The contractors shipped the iron structure from the New Jersey foundry in late 1879. Construction followed the same steps used at Fowey Rocks. Unlike the miserable weather encountered during the erection of Fowey Rocks Light, the winter of 1879–1880 was mild; the builders were unhampered by high seas or winds. The only mishap was in funding; Congress had to appropriate an additional $50,000 before the lighthouse could be completed.[10]

The foundation pilings were set, as for all the lights on the reef, ten feet into the coral. The keepers' house duplicated the one at Fowey Rocks, except that it was painted brown instead of white. The enclosure for the spiral staircase connecting the house to the lantern was painted white, and the lantern was black. Though Fowey Rocks and American Shoal lights were almost identical in design, their colors made them appear quite different. The distinguishing colors were important; although the distance between the two lighthouses was almost one hundred miles, the Light House Board knew navigators could make mistakes. Hadn't the captain of the *Rapid* mistaken the Sombrero Lighthouse for the Sand Key Light and run aground, and didn't a Spanish brig wreck on Alligator Reef when the captain mistook that light for Carysfort Reef Lighthouse? To further distinguish the American Shoal light, the board designated its white flashing light. Twenty miles southwest, Sand Key Lighthouse showed a fixed white light, and at about the same distance northeast Sombrero Key's light was also a steady glow.

Henry Lepaute of Paris had manufactured American Shoal's first-order Fresnel lens in 1874. The glass used in the lens was quite hard and scratch resistant, yet had to be handled with care as it would chip and fracture easily. The jewel-like lens had twenty-four panels. There were eighteen hand-polished glass prisms above the central drum of the lens, with eight prisms in each panel below. The central drum contained seventeen elements in each of the twenty-four panels. Flashes

The "Black List to whom no Wrecking License will be issued with reason of forfeiture" was found loose among the court records of wrecking cases. Of the thirty-nine men salvaging the SS Mississippi that went aground near American Shoal in 1840, eighteen are on this list. (EAST POINT GEORGIA REPOSITORY NATIONAL ARCHIVES) were produced by the entire apparatus revolving around the lamp, one revolution every two minutes.

A clockwork mechanism turned the lens on what was called "ball-raceways" with "v" grooves. The lens rested on thirty-nine ball bearings, each one and a half inches in diameter, which rolled in the grooves. The clockwork formed the pedestal for the lens. The cord that wound the clock ran from the base down through the watch room floor to the weight and back again. The "weight box" housed this arrangement. After winding, the clock ran for four and a half hours, but the keepers wound it more frequently.[11]

The lantern formed the top of the lighthouse. It had been manufactured up north, shipped in sections to Key West, then hauled to the work site. After workmen completed the fifth section of the tower and the enclosed spiral staircase, they raised the lantern, section by section, then assembled and secured it. The lantern room, which protected the lens from the elements, was a little over twelve feet in diameter and had glass walls nine feet, nine inches high. Forty-eight curved glass plates formed the cylindrical walls. The plates, called storm panes, were joined by iron bars forming three tiers. Each horizontal section held sixteen plates, creating an aesthetic yet structurally strong pattern. During the day, keepers drew inside curtains across the panes to protect the lens from sunlight. The copper-roofed, iron lantern dome was surmounted with a ventilator ball through which air could pass. On top of the ball vent was a lightning-conductor spindle.

An outside iron gallery with a balustrade encircled the lantern room. Handholds were built into the vertical iron bars of the lantern, allowing the keepers to clean the storm panes without the risk of blowing away in the strong wind. Keepers would have blown away if they had not been able to hold fast. Beneath the lantern room was the service room, where the clockwork for rotating the lens was located. The men used this room to clean and fill the lamps for the night. Eight windows in the service room provided light and ventilation. There were also three large windows about twenty inches by four feet, five inches in the stair cylinder between the keepers' quarters and the lantern. Bell wires for calling relief keepers led from the service room to the bottom of these stairs.[12]

With the lens and lantern in place, American Shoal Lighthouse was ready for service. William Bates, head keeper, lit the light for the first time on July 15, 1880. Bates had come to the Keys from England and married a woman from Florida. At his first assignment on Garden Key Lighthouse in the Dry Tortugas in 1860, he drew a salary of $300 a year. He later served on the Sand Key and Sombrero Key lighthouses before being transferred to American Shoal.

The other keepers had also previously served on iron pile lights. For the first assistant keeper, Key Wester Dudley Richardson, the transfer from Alligator Reef Light meant a promotion and a $10-a-year raise in salary. The second assistant keeper, Henry Johnson, came to Florida from the Bahamas. He had served on Sombrero Key Light before coming to American Shoal.[13]

The keepers' duties varied little from those at other lighthouses in the United States. In the Florida Keys, there were no fog signals—no whistles, trumpets, sirens, or bells were needed. The men also did not have to contend with snow and ice. Otherwise the routine remained the same as explained in the keepers' "bible," *Directions to Lightkeepers, Showing Them How to Perform Their Duties.* This manual gave meticulous directions on how to clean lamps and burners, trim and renew wicks, fill the lamp reservoirs, and check and maintain the revolving machinery.

The Light House Board expected all areas of the lantern to be scrupulously clean at all times. Keepers washed the storm panes inside and out to allow the greatest amount of light transmission. Every component of the lens required daily dusting with a feather brush to remove surface dust and then cleaning with spirits of wine (vinegar). Once a year, keepers polished the lens with rouge. (Sometimes called "jeweler's rouge," it is a polishing powder made from a finely ground preparation of terric oxide.)

In the evening, the keeper on duty would ascend to the lantern room and check the wind direction. Adjustable vents in the lantern room allowed the right amount of draft into the room. At the top of the lantern, the wind passing horizontally through the ball vent created a vacuum, pulling the draft from the lower vents across the storm panes and up to the top of the lantern room. This prevented the glass from fogging. It also created a draft in the metal vent tube, attached to the glass chimney of the lamp, that drew fumes from the oil-burning lamp up the tube to the ball and out of the lantern room. In case of strong winds, the manual instructed keepers that "the leeward venti-lators alone must be opened, and only so much of them as is necessary to allow the lights to burn bright, steady, and clear." An hour after sunrise, the keeper extinguished the light and readied the lamps for the next lighting at one hour before sunset. All preparations for the coming evening were to be finished by 10:00 A.M.[14]

By 1910 successful experiments with the incandescent oil vapor (i.o.v.) system prompted its installation in forty-four lighthouses in the United States. The Bureau of Lighthouses made plans to install the system in its stations as rapidly as possible. In 1912 i.o.v. replaced the kerosene-oil wick lamps in use at American Shoal Light. Equip-ment for the i.o.v. system included the lamp; one high pressure tank with connections to the lamp; a spirit lamp for the initial heating of the vaporizing chamber; and the implements required to clean, adjust, and repair the various parts. The i.o.v. lamp used kerosene that was forced, under pressure, into a vaporizing chamber. When the kerosene struck the hot walls of the chamber, it vaporized. The vapor then passed through a series of small holes where it was ignited by a Bun-sen burner, heating an overhead mantle that gave off a bright light. The illuminating power of the light was many times greater than that achieved with the use of an ordinary kerosene wick lamp. Red panes of glass, secured to the inside of the lantern frames at certain angles (68° to 90°; 115° to 130°; 242° to 263°), created zones of red lights over the reefs. With the introduction of i.o.v., the intensity of both the white and red flashes increased: the white flashes were equal to 250,000 can-dlepower and the red flashes 64,000 candlepower. In addition, the once arduous tasks of keeping wicks trimmed and burners cleaned were now things of the past.[15]

Other innovations helped keepers to pass the lonely night watch hours. When radio broadcasting was introduced in 1921, with trans-mitters established throughout the United States, a tremendous de-mand was created for receivers. Radio proved particularly important to keepers at isolated light stations. After the hurricane in Miami in 1927, the family of a keeper asked that the news of their safety be broadcast so that the husband stationed at a lighthouse "could have his anxiety relieved." Radio allowed keepers to receive advance storm

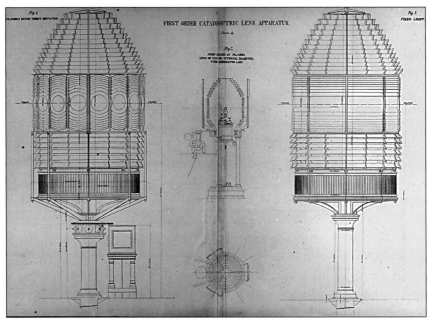

The first-order Fresnel lens on the left shows the bull's-eye lenses at the center focus, which, as the lens revolved, caused the light to flash. The smooth glass at the center focus on the lens on the right emitted a steady light. The illustration at the center shows how the fixed lens could be used with outside rotating panels; the panels blocked the emission of light at intervals, causing a flashing effect. Rotation was achieved through a clockwork system that was mechanically operated by a weight hanging in a tube; the tube went up through the watch room and connected to a steel drum and gears to the lens or outer rotating panel housing (illustration to the right of the apparatus containing bull's-eye lenses). The weight was wound up periodically by the keeper. (NATIONAL ARCHIVES)

warnings as well as news of the outside world. Many of the keepers listened to Sunday broadcasts of church services. Knowing this, a Key West woman in 1931 donated radio sets for the light stations at American Shoal, Sombrero Key, Alligator Reef, and Carysfort Reef as Christmas presents. The Atwater-Kent Number 82 sets, complete with batteries and antennae, were delivered to the light stations by the tender *Ivy*. The keepers also had the services of a library provided by the Lighthouse Service.[16]

Light Keepers always had to keep the glass in the lantern clean to allow the greatest amount of light transmission. Handholds were built into the vertical iron bars of the lantern for the keepers to grip while they were cleaning the storm panes. The handholds were essential, for sometimes the wind was so strong that the keepers would have been blown away if they had not been able to hold fast. (THE BETTMANN ARCHIVE)

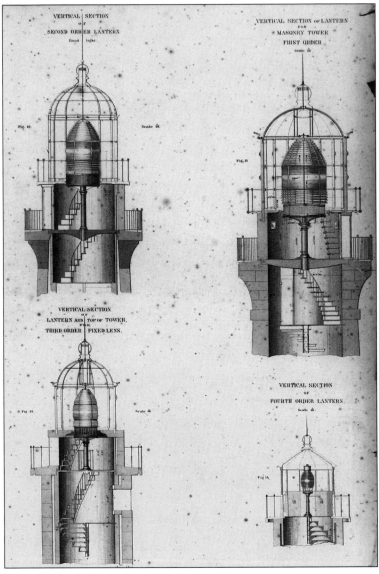

First-order through fourth-order lenses showing vertical sections of lanterns and tower mountings. The first-order lens was the largest, six feet wide and ten to twelve feet tall; the smallest was the sixth order. Usually the fourth, fifth, and sixth orders were used for channel navigational lights, while lights of the third order were either major harbor or minor coastal lights. First-order and second-order lenses were generally used on primary or major seacoast lights. (NATIONAL ARCHIVES)

On duty, the men took four-hour work shifts, the same routine that was followed on ships of the U.S. Navy. When the Coast Guard took over the duties of the civilian light keepers, their men were already well adapted to this work routine. The Coast Guardsmen usually served on the light for six months, but some enjoyed the duty so much they requested reassignment.

The Coast Guard automated American Shoal Light in June 1963. After the Coast Guardsmen left, there was no one aboard the tower to continually examine the structure for rust or corrosion or to maintain the iron piles. The Coast Guard changed the batteries and lamps when needed but hired private contractors to scrape, paint, and repair the structure. A Coast Guardsman from the Aids to Navigation Team (ANT) arrived periodically to inspect the lighthouse. In 1964 Patti Altland described the work crew repairing American Shoal Light for the *Key West Citizen*:

> [They] came into our establishment on Friday nights on their way home to Miami for weekends. They were a jovial but motley group. They were often grizzled with a good growth of whiskers. Some-times their clothes were soaked through from the salty sea spray in a rough crossing from American Shoal to Cudjoe Key. Some of these men had been underwater treasure divers who had sought the gold and valuable artifacts from wrecks of the sixteenth century Spanish galleons lying at the bottom of the ocean off Florida's At-lantic coast and all along the Keys. The task they were now on was that of checking and stabilizing the wrought iron structure of the American Shoal Lighthouse. This was just as adventuresome and arduous as treasure diving had been. From the very start the weather had been against them . . . high winds and frequent ground swells caused numerous delays.[17]

The Civil Engineering branch of the Coast Guard is now responsi-ble for structural repairs made to the tower. If any part needs to be re-placed, the engineers can work from copies of the original blueprints to duplicate it. The American Shoal Lighthouse remains sound, but the keepers' house is in disrepair and all of the automated lighthouses have been vandalized. One Coast Guard inspection report revealed that in addition to vandalism, "termites have taken their toll over the years in the interior of the dwelling place and the light remains infested."[18]

Workmen made extensive repairs to the lighthouse as a result of the Coast Guard's plan to use American Shoal, as well as Sombrero Key and Alligator Reef lighthouses, as a radar/visual station during the Mariel refugee exodus from Cuba in 1980. Chief Warrant Officer Gregory Holman, project officer, reported that crews exterminated the termites and covered the floor of the keepers' dwelling, which was rotted and full of holes, with plywood to "provide a clean level surface for the needed equipment, tables, beds, chairs, etc." Missing iron handrails were replaced with rope. New davits were installed on the landing platform to off-load the 500-pound, five-kilowatt electrical generator, a fuel tank for the generator, and the heavy radar equipment. After the repairs and additions were completed, the working and living facilities were installed for the six Coast Guardsmen who were assigned to American Shoal Light from July through November 1980. Chief Holman described the project as having "great potential in our mission to protect lives and property and in the enforcement of federal laws."[19]

American Shoal and the other lights continued to operate automatically as lighted beacons, but in addition, they now served the ancient and traditional function as lookout towers. The Coast Guardsmen monitored the exodus of Cuban refugees to the United States and the "possible flow of vessels going to Cuba to pick up more people." (A number of private vessels from the Florida Keys did go to Cuba to carry back passengers.) The Coast Guardsmen also watched for and aided in the capture of any illegal contraband bound for the United States and evaluated a traffic-monitoring system in the Straits of Florida.

The men worked a rotation of two days on the tower and four days on shore. The schedule aboard the light, according to Holman, was not the usual four-hour shifts. During the day, two men were up and about sharing the watch responsibilities. One man at a time stood the nighttime watches, which each lasted six hours. The men on all three lighthouses remained in contact with their associated Coast Guard Station, a mobile unit, and with each other. This allowed the men on

American Shoal Lighthouse was automated in 1963, and it continues to serve as an important navigational aid. As a day mark and as a light, the lighthouse marks the reefs surrounding its submarine site and also the reefs in Looe Key Marine Sanctuary. As one of the Reef Lights, it not only saves ships from the reefs, but hopefully will save the reefs from the ships. (U.S. COAST GUARD OFFICIAL PHOTO)

watch "from one site to pass on information concerning sightings, and other operational info without undue delay." Each site had a battery backup in the event of power failure.[20]

At the completion of the project, Lieutenant R. C. Eccles reported: "There is no doubt in my mind that these lights can be effectively utilized to put another small dent in the tremendous flow of illegal maritime activity that transpires in and around the Keys."[21]

After the Mariel crisis was over, the lighthouses were once again emptied of human keepers, but there continues to be a great deal of activity in the waters around the American Shoal Light. The light serves as an important daymark for coastal shipping in the Florida Straits and marks the coral reefs for inshore fishing and diving boats.

Looe Key is also a popular spot for anglers and divers, where scientists have identified over two hundred kinds of reef fish, as well as amberjacks; hammerhead sharks; dolphins; pompanos; and king, cero, and Spanish mackerel. In 1981 the government designated Looe Key a Marine Sanctuary under Title III of the 1972 Marine Protection Research and Sanctuaries Act. The lighthouse, standing oceanside of Looe Key, should help prevent groundings in the area.

Unfortunately, the lighthouse does not always help prevent groundings in this dangerous area. In 1983 the eighty-nine foot shrimp boat *Cleo* struck the reef. One of the worst groundings occurred on August 11, 1994, when the University of Miami's research vessel *Columbus Iselin* crunched four major coral formations on Looe Key. The following year the university paid $200,000 in penalties to the National Oceanic and Atmospheric Administration (NOAA). NOAA uses the money collected from fines for coral rubble removal, reef rebuilding, reef markers, mooring buoys, and educational signs at boat ramps in the Keys.[22]

To further protect the only living coral reef system in the continental United States, Congress passed a bill in 1990 establishing the 3,500-square-mile Florida Keys National Marine Sanctuary. The sanctuary stretches from Biscayne National Park to the Dry Tortugas, including both the Atlantic and Gulf of Mexico sides. Now, when ships go aground, the fine collected by NOAA not only goes toward reef restoration but also to the Coast Guard, whose Aid to Navigation (ATON) personnel are using some of these funds to establish radar beacons (RACONS) on each of the six reef lights. RACONS, according to the Coast Guard, are "designed to produce a distinctive image on the screens of radar sets, thus enabling the mariner to determine his position with greater certainty than would be possible using a normal radar display alone." From atop the light towers, the RACONS will mark and identify the individual lighthouses on the reefs off the Florida Keys. RACONS, which should be visible to most commercial, shipboard radar systems six to twenty miles from the lighthouses, will prevent groundings and provide valuable protection for the living reef and the marine environment. Navigators of commercial vessels will easily recognize the American Shoal Lighthouse by its distinctive RACON Morse Code characters on their radar screens.[23]

To mariners in shallow-draft boats who sail past the light tower today, the tall structure may appear stark. Only the white paint on the central stair cylinder brightens the dark brown skeleton tower and house, and without the beautiful Fresnel lens, the modern optic and the stripped-down lantern room appear spartan. Yet, at night something magical happens. The tall tower blends with the darkness, and only the brilliant flashes can be seen. The light appears high above the reef and sea and a bit lower than the stars. Although a way of life on the tower has vanished, and new technology has taken over, American Shoal continues to show a familiar and reassuring guiding light.[24]

The notes for this chapter begin on page 290.

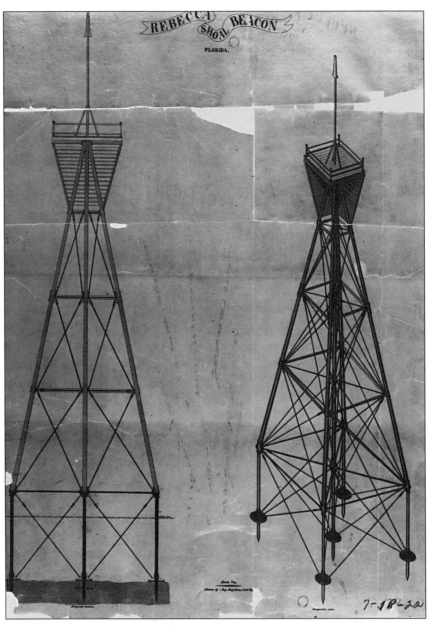

Drawing for a proposed day beacon on Rebecca Shoal. The first attempt at construction was made in 1854, but all efforts to establish a beacon failed until 1879. Lieutenant George Gordon Meade, in charge of the initial project, commented that no beacon of any kind had been erected, either in the United States or in Europe, in a position that was more exposed or offered greater obstacles. (NATIONAL ARCHIVES)

11. REBECCA SHOAL LIGHTHOUSE

FIRST LIGHTED 1886

The lighthouse on Rebecca Shoal was the last to be built in the Keys. Turbulent waters in the area of Rebecca Shoal, which lies in the Gulf of Mexico forty-three miles west of Key West, also made it the most difficult to erect. Surrounded by deep water, the bank itself lies about eleven feet deep. Other nearby reefs and hazardous areas, including Isaac Shoal, Halfmoon Shoal, and the Quicksands, create a pressing need for helpful markers and beacons. Here the current floods north in this section of the gulf at about one knot; it ebbs at a little less than a knot, but the strength of the current is greatly influenced by the wind.[1]

The waters of the Atlantic Ocean meet and mix with the waters of the Gulf of Mexico, making the ebb and flood tides unpredictable. Along the Atlantic coast, there are usually two high and two low tides during a twenty-four-hour period. Both the sun and the moon rule the ocean's tides, but the moon, because it is closer to earth, has about twice the influence. The moon's pull creates a bulge in the ocean directly beneath it and on both sides of the earth at the same time. Because the moon's orbit is predictable, the tides are predictable. For example, if a high tide at Miami, on the Atlantic, is at 12:00 P.M. on one day, on the next day, high tide will occur at 12:50 P.M.[2]

The tides in the Gulf of Mexico do not necessarily operate in the same manner. For example, Pensacola, Florida, on the northeast side of the gulf, has only one high and one low tide every twenty-four hours. The gulf is a natural ocean basin, though narrow and shallow compared to the Atlantic Ocean, where forces of the moon and sun keep a stationary wave moving at a certain speed. Because of the dimensions of the gulf, this wave does not always move back and forth through the basin twice a day.

The differences in tidal patterns between the Gulf of Mexico and the Atlantic Ocean contribute to the confusion of the two seas where their waters join. Another factor is the swift current of the Gulf Stream (also called the Florida Current as it flows north through the Florida Straits). Storms and high winds influence the tidal range as well as the direction and speed of local currents. The wind creates waves that run close and steep. The seas surrounding Rebecca Shoal are seldom calm; even on clear days with little wind the currents rush and collide in various directions and at various speeds, creating choppy water.[3]

There have been numerous shipwrecks and groundings due to these unpredictable sea conditions. Ships sailing this route sorely needed a lighted navigational aid at Rebecca Shoal. Plans were first made in 1847 to mark the shoal in some way; however, nothing came of them. In May 1852 the Light House Board sent Lieutenant George Gordon Meade, U.S. Army Corps of Topographical Engineers, to inspect the selected site. Having completed Carysfort Reef Lighthouse two months earlier, Meade examined the Rebecca Shoal and submitted a proposal for a beacon, accompanied by designs and estimates. Congress responded to the board's request for funding with an appropriation of $10,000. From Philadelphia, Meade reported to the board in 1854 that the wrought iron skeleton beacon was "manufactured, framed, and put together at this place, and shipped early in May to Key West." However, the appropriated money proved inadequate, and work could not continue until Congress granted an additional $5,000.[4]

Rebecca Shoal area is calmest during May, June, and July. Meade hoped to construct the beacon during this period, but the months passed without anything being accomplished. The appropriation was not the only factor that delayed construction; a local epidemic of yel-

low fever in the summer of 1854 prevented the workmen from pro-
curing the mangroves needed for the work platform pilings. As a result, Meade postponed the project until the next calm season.

When work resumed the following year, the engineer decided to
build the work platform on trestles instead of pilings. Workmen
quickly erected the platform and had nearly completed the wrought
iron skeleton beacon by May 17, 1855, when a violent gale compelled
the vessel with the workmen aboard to take refuge in Dry Tortugas
Harbor. When the storm eased three days later, the men returned to
the shoal. They found no trace of their previous labors; the sea had
carried away every part of the platform as well as the beacon. As soon
as new building materials could be supplied, the workmen renewed
their efforts, as Meade reported, "to gain a foot-hold on the shoal." But
in the middle of June, when the platform was near completion, heavy
seas rocked the trestles out of the sand and the platform collapsed.[5]

At the same time, Meade, having completed the Sand Key Lighthouse, began developing plans for the Sombrero Key Lighthouse. Although he remained in charge of the Rebecca Shoal project in 1855,
J. W. Jones of Philadelphia arrived to supervise the work with the help
of Captain Horatio G. Wright, the engineer in charge of building Fort
Jefferson in the Dry Tortugas. After massive waves destroyed the second platform at Rebecca Shoal, Jones determined that it would be impossible to build the platform on trestles, and that he would instead
use iron-shod mangrove pilings.

Jones set up a steam-driven pile driver on a shallow-draft vessel,
hoping to anchor the vessel on the shoal. For three weeks, workers
waited for the weather to clear, but there was not one day when it was
calm enough for work to resume. The eight-month contract with the
working party from Philadelphia expired, and the men, rejecting all
offers, could not be induced to stay. It also proved impossible to find
enough workers from Key West for the project. Jones sailed to
Philadelphia, organized another group of workmen, and returned to
Rebecca Shoal in August.

For six weeks the new workmen waited, but the weather never improved. After the appropriation ran out, Meade wrote the Light
House Board, "In reporting this failure, which no one can regret more
than myself, I feel it proper to observe . . . that no light-house structure

of any kind has been erected, either in this country or in Europe, at a position more exposed and offering greater obstacles than the Rebecca Shoal."[6]

In spite of the setbacks, Meade believed success was possible and sent another estimate to the board. Congress granted an additional $10,000 for a beacon on Rebecca Shoal, and work began again. Meade hoped to finish the beacon during the summer of 1857, but again the weather stymied every effort.

In March 1858, after completing the 142-foot screwpile lighthouse on Sombrero Key, Meade began to devote all of his time and energy to the Rebecca Shoal beacon. The Light House Board announced "The iron screw pile beacon on Rebecca Shoal will probably be completed during the coming winter." It was not to be. A violent storm in the fall of 1858 washed all evidence of the beacon away. The board, bested by nature for the time being, abandoned the project and instead marked the shoal with buoys.[7]

The Light House Board placed Meade in charge of both the Fourth and the Seventh Light House Districts. In 1860 he left the Florida Keys to direct the surveys of the Northern Lakes. At the outbreak of the Civil War, Meade requested military service and was assigned active duty with the Union Army. He was promoted to brigadier general of the Pennsylvania Volunteers on August 3, 1861, and on June 28, 1863, he was named commander of the Army of the Potomac. Seven months later he received recognition for his service and the thanks of Congress "for the skill and heroic valor [with] which, at Gettysburg [the Army of the Potomac] repelled, defeated, and drove back, broken and dispirited, beyond the Rappahannock, the veteran army of the Rebellion." Meade had defeated Robert E. Lee in the Civil War's crucial battle. He devoted his last service to his country as commissioner of Fairmont Park in Philadelphia. In a letter of tribute to Meade, one official wrote that "the plan and beautification [of Fairmont Park] . . . are ascribed to his energies more than to those of any other." Meade died November 6, 1872.[8]

The Carysfort Reef, Sand Key, and Sombrero Key lighthouses all attest to Meade's engineering skills. At Rebecca Shoal, the weather and seas defeated him, but new plans were in store for the site. In 1873 the board reported the completion of a series of iron day-beacons on the Florida reefs. The first series, distinguished by letters A to P, re-placed already established beacons. The second series, numbered from 1 to 8, marked previously unmarked areas. The Rebecca Shoal beacon, completed in May, was number 1. Five months later, a hurricane de-stroyed it. Rough weather during 1874 and 1875 made it impossible to replace the aid, but the Light House Board "proposed at an early day to erect a substantial structure" to mark this dangerous shoal. "De-signs have been completed for a new iron-pile beacon 75 feet high," re-ported the board in 1876. "It has not been possible to complete the work, but it will probably be erected during the ensuing year."[9]

The following year the board reported:

> . . . [that it had] submitted estimates for lights on American Shoal and Rebecca Shoal to illuminate the dark spaces between Sombrero Key and Sand Key, and Sand Key and Dry Tortugas lights on the Florida Reefs. The erection of these lights was contemplated in a plan adopted by the preliminary board of 1851, and their impor-tance has since been shown by the number of wrecks that have taken place on this portion of the Atlantic coast, which still remains unlighted. . . . A light upon this dangerous [Rebecca] shoal is much needed for the safety of a large commerce constantly passing in its vicinity. An estimate of $75,000 for commencing its construction is respectfully submitted."[10]

Workers assembled the beacon on land at Key West before taking it to the site on the shoal. In 1879 the board described the seventy-foot high beacon as ". . . a skeleton structure of iron and wood surmounted by a large cage of heavy timbers, and . . . a very good day mark. In clear weather it has been seen 13 miles distant." This beacon lasted longer than any other on the site and longer than most buoys that were often blown off-station. Nevertheless, the beacon was a day mark, and what mariners needed on this site was both a day mark and a lighted aid. Recognizing this, in 1884 the board proposed enlarging the struc-ture and converting it to a manned lighthouse.

The district engineer submitted plans for a "proper structure su-perimposed upon the 12-inch wrought-iron piles now upholding Rebecca Shoal day-beacon, with . . . other piles added." Congress

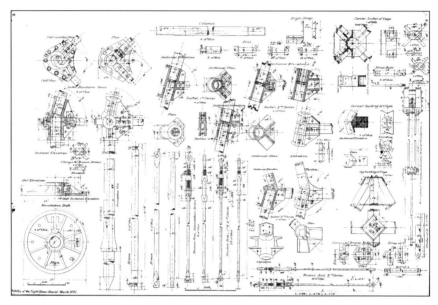

Detailed drawings for the 1876 Rebecca Shoal Day Beacon. Storms destroyed the four previous beacons; this one lasted longer than any of the others. In 1884 the enlarged foundation structure was used for the eventual erection of the Rebecca Shoal Lighthouse. (NATIONAL ARCHIVES)

appropriated $20,000 to implement the plan, but such plans were easier to fund than to accomplish at Rebecca Shoal. The board and the builders remained determined.[11]

All the materials needed for the lighthouse, including the ironwork, were delivered to a Key West warehouse by August 1885. In May 1886 work began. Workmen first built a working platform and then removed the seventy-five-foot beacon. The most challenging job was driving the iron screwpiles needed to support the lighthouse into the shoal through the iron disks. The Light House Board recorded: "There was much delay in getting the foundation in, on account of the exposed position and continuation of rough seas and bad weather; there was also much difficulty in putting in place the iron disks, as the bottom of the sea at this point is covered with large rocks, which have to be moved by a diver."[12]

Despite the unusual number of severe gales during the summer of 1886, the men completed the construction in six months. The light was first exhibited on November 1, 1886—an impressive accomplishment considering the history of failures at this site.[13]

The first keepers of the light were Mark Gage (Gaze), head keeper, a Floridian who had served on both Fowey Rocks and Carysfort Reef lighthouses; Francis McNulty, first assistant, an Englishman who transferred from American Shoal Lighthouse; and John F. Lowe, a second assistant from the West Indies who had not served on a light before. The keepers' home on Rebecca Shoal was a square, three-story wooden building designed for both displaying the light and as living quarters, with the lantern incorporated into the roof. The third-story keepers' quarters had four dormer windows, one on each side of the roof below the lantern. The general living area for the men was on the second floor. The keepers used the first floor for storage. The outside stairs on one side of the building led to a porch and to the main living area. Green shutters gave the house a homey look. The large over-hanging roof provided shade and added graceful lines to an otherwise boxlike building.

The house sat in the center of a large platform secured to the top series of iron piles. A gallery that ran around the house offered ample room for loading supplies aboard with davits. The keepers used a second set of davits to raise the lighthouse boat above the reach of waves. Two heavy-duty iron ladders led between the gallery and the landing deck, which lay just above sea level and was often awash.[14]

During the stormy weather of 1887, high seas badly damaged the iron deck plates. The keepers made several temporary repairs until new deck plates arrived the next year. At the same time, the superintendent of lights, J. V. Harris, assigned a larger boat to the station; in order to raise and lower it, the keepers attached winches to the davits.[15]

In 1889 Harris promoted McNulty to head keeper and Lowe to first assistant. Harris also appointed a new second assistant, George Richardson, a Key Wester who like Lowe had never served on a light before. Richardson soon experienced the most frightening aspect of lighthouse duty when a violent storm shook the lighthouse so severely that the tremors damaged the lens.

Although the Light House Board knew that the structure shook during heavy seas, inspectors had never been able to pinpoint the

A lighthouse was eventually established at Rebecca Shoal in 1886; the construction was more challenging and difficult than any of the other lighthouses in the Keys. The Coast Guard removed the house in 1953. (FLORIDA PHOTOGRAPHIC ARCHIVES)

cause. Engineers finally determined that heavy seas striking the two iron ladders, which led between the landing deck and the upper platform, caused the excessive motion. The designers had not anticipated that the wave action on these ladders could cause such extreme vibrations throughout the entire lighthouse. To remedy this, engineers replaced the heavy fixed ladders with lighter ladders, which the keepers raised out of the reach of the waves when not in use.

In 1893 the board made an important change in the light's characteristic. Originally, the light flashed alternately red and white. The board decided to introduce red sectors on the light to better warn mariners of the particularly dangerous shoals nearby. The placement of the red panels needed to be exact. Once in place, mariners could see only red flashes over the reefs, from west-southwest of the light and continuing counterclockwise to northwest.

From 1902 to 1903 the lighthouse was plagued by storms as well as a series of unfortunate incidents. In April, the district inspector,

F. Singer, reported that five of the prisms in the top row of the lens had cracked from the heat of the chimneys, which had melted. Singer believed the accident could have been prevented if the keeper on duty, George S. Wilson, had seen what was happening. "Wilson has defective vision," Singer reported, "and on testing . . . I found his eye sight with glasses was 7/20." Wilson, fifty years old at the time, was a former navy man who had served on Sombrero Key Light and then as first assistant keeper at Rebecca Shoal. In spite of the inspector's report, Wilson remained on duty at the light station; records do not indicate what, if anything, was done to improve his eyesight.[16]

On April 23, 1902, Wilson reported the following unfortunate event to the inspector of the Seventh Lighthouse District: "Sir: it is my painful duty to report that on Friday the 18th at 1:30 P.M. the Keeper Jas. R. Walker returned to this station in a very exhausted condition, and continued very nervous until Saturday the 19th about midnight, when he went out of his mind and continued in that condition all day Sunday and night, and on Monday morning about 4 A.M. he disappeared from the station, presumably fell or jumped overboard, his body has not been recovered."[17]

In June, Walker's widow, Maria, applied for and received the back pay due Walker. But the Lighthouse Service provided no death benefits for the spouses or families of keepers. (Congress did not enact retirement and disability benefits for lighthouse employees until 1918.) The misfortunes for those on the Rebecca Shoal Light did not end with Walker's death. The following year on June 25, 1903, George Wilson died while on duty. His family, too, was left without any death benefits.[18]

After Wilson died, the district superintendent of lights assigned Alfred A. Berghill as head keeper. Berghill had previously served on Rebecca Shoal Lighthouse as assistant keeper from 1897 to 1899. Berghill's assistants were John Peterson and Henry A. Keys.

In 1904 when the iron-pile foundation required scaling and painting, the keepers were assisted by men from the *Arbutus*, a lighthouse tender used for construction and repair work in the Seventh and Eighth Lighthouse districts. The 400-ton wooden vessel, built in 1876, measured 144.5 feet from bow to stem, with a beam of 25 feet. The *Arbutus* drew almost eleven feet, however, much too deep for maneuvering in shallow waters. The tender had to anchor off Rebecca Shoal, where small boats from the tender and the lighthouse brought in the needed men and supplies.[19]

Arbutus, the name of a genus of trees or shrubs of the heath family, seemed a strange name for a vessel serving in the semi-tropics. Traditionally all lighthouse vessels were named after a shrub, flower, or tree common to the vessel's district. But because many tenders moved from district to district their names were not always appropriate. Another tender serving in the Keys had an equally inappropriate name—*Ivy*.

In 1905 an inspector arrived on the *Ivy* to help keepers John Peterson and Thomas Kelly repair the malfunctioning revolving machinery at Rebecca Shoal. For several years, the keepers had found it difficult to keep the lens revolving smoothly. In 1903 a previous inspector reported that it "was so badly worn as to practically require renewal," and he urged replacing it at a cost of $550. The Light House Board approved the expenditure the following year, and the *Ivy* was enlisted to bring the new equipment to Rebecca Shoal.

A recent addition to the fleet, the steel, twin-screw steamer was twenty feet longer than the *Arbutus*, with a beam of thirty feet. The *Ivy* was better designed for shallow water, drawing between six feet, six inches and seven feet. It carried ballast and trimming tanks with enough capacity to bring the draft to about nine feet aft and about eight feet forward while on deep-sea duty. The optional shallow draft made it an ideal vessel for work in the Keys. The 550-ton vessel was built in 1904 and manned by five officers and a twenty-three-member crew. It serviced all the lights in the Keys for several years, delivering repair materials and crews, until the Light House Board transferred it to the Eighth District.[20]

The *Arbutus* brought Inspector J. Hood to the lighthouse in May 1907 for his semi-annual inspection. Shocked by the damage he discovered, he reported: "One of the braces on the main piling was carried away in a gale last September. A second brace was carried away in a very moderate blow during the past month." On close examination, he found the remaining foundation braces eroded and worn at every crossing point. He did not believe the tower would be safe in high winds and urgently recommended that repair work be undertaken before the hurricane season. The engineer overseeing the work wrote the Light House Board on August 9, 1907:

> The superintendent in charge of repairs to Rebecca Shoal light station . . . reported that four broken or weakened braces . . . have been replaced. This puts the station in good condition for the present. The remaining braces will be renewed as soon as the material can be obtained. Although this lighthouse has weathered a great many severe storms, notably one that was reported to blow 72 miles per hour, Oct. 17-18, 1906 . . . it has always shaken considerably, even in moderate weather. It is in a very exposed position, and I intend, as soon as I have the necessary data for an estimate, to recommend piling rip-rap about it as a further safeguard.[21]

After the hurricane season, Keeper John Peterson reported, "The recent heavy northwest storms did not damage the lighthouse. The storm seas were running half up the structure . . . . The new braces have made a great improvement as to the steadiness of the Light. The Lighthouse is as firm as a rock."[22]

In 1913 the Light House Board introduced illumination by means of the i.o.v. (incandescent oil vapor) system to all of the iron-pile lighthouses in the Florida Keys. The *Arbutus* arrived at Rebecca Shoal in 1914 with specially designed steel tanks for kerosene storage. While the men were suspending the tanks in the tower framework, the steamer *Veenbergen* ran aground on the shoal. The next year the same steamer again ran aground near the lighthouse! The keeper, Thomas M. Kelly, along with his assistants J. P. Roberts Jr., and T. L. Kelly, aided the *Arbutus* in working the steamer off. Not long after, the keepers and the *Arbutus* helped dislodge another steamer, the *Nordvahlen*, from the reef near the lighthouse and gave aid to the disabled American steamer *Standard*.[23]

The hurricane in September 1919 brought death as well as destruction. The storm smashed the glass panes in the lantern of the lighthouse and caused serious damage to the lens. The Spanish steamer, *Valbanera*, capsized nearby. According to lighthouse historian, Neil E. Hurley, "The sunken wreckage of the ship was found a few miles from the lighthouse after the storm. There were no survivors from the 488 passengers and crew."[24]

On July 28, 1925, *The Key West Citizen* reported a historic ending and a new beginning for the Rebecca Shoal Lighthouse: "The Lighthouse tender *Sundew*, left this morning for Rebecca Shoal light station, where machinists Harry Shaw and William Vassie will be taken for the purpose of changing the light from a vapor type light to an acetylene type. . . . Changing Rebecca Shoal light places this station in the same class as Key West . . . it eliminates the need for keepers from one of the most dangerous reef lights."

The automatic light began functioning on August 1, 1925. Two days later, the paper gave additional news: "There is now at the station gas sufficient to operate on for the period of one year. This type of apparatus is considered more reliable even than those where keepers are in attendance." The keepers transferred to other lighthouses in the Keys. Alonzo Baker, head keeper, according to *The Key West Citizen*, "will go on duty at Sand Key; C. Turner, first assistant, will transfer to Alligator Reef Light Station; and Robert J. Moore, second assistant, is assigned to Fowey Rocks."

Soon after automation, the Rebecca Shoal Lighthouse began to deteriorate. Once unmanned, the attractive keepers' house became too inviting. The house and the light were vandalized as people came aboard the lighthouse and defaced the structure, ripped off doors, knocked out windows, and removed whatever might be of value to them. In December 1944, C.W. Harwood, operations planning officer for the Seventh Coast Guard District, proposed the "reconstruction of the superstructure of the lighthouse" and recommended electrification of the light. "The installation of a small engine-generator unit (probably about 800-watt, air-cooled) would obviate the necessity of changing batteries every four months. Wind-driven generators have been used to a limited extent in the Service. If such installations have proved successful, it may be applied to Rebecca Shoal Light. The monthly average wind velocity at Key West has been approximately ten miles per hour over a period of seventy years."[25]

Once the Coast Guard Aid to Navigation branch (ATON) electrified the light, it was no longer cost-effective to maintain the empty dwelling. In 1953 the house was removed, to be replaced by a square skeleton tower. A small white structure was built on the brown pile platform for the acetylene equipment. The group flashing light was displayed sixty feet above sea level; the white light could be seen a distance of nine miles, and the red light a distance of six. This beacon withstood storms and waves for over thirty years, before the Aid to Navigation Team (ANT) replaced it in 1985. Three years later ATON changed the light's characteristic to show four flashes every fifteen seconds while increasing the range to thirteen miles for the white light and twelve miles for the red sectors.

In the 1990s personnel from ANT installed a solar-powered Amerace 190-millimeter rotating optic on the beacon. This optic did not perform well, however, as rough seas caused the sixty-six-foot skeleton tower to vibrate, affecting the light's rotation. The team later installed a fixed 250-millimeter optic that could withstand the vibrations. ATON also changed the light's characteristic to flashing six-second. Mariners can see the white light for nine miles and the light in the red sector, from 254° to 302°, for six miles. This modern solar-powered optic now marks Rebecca Shoal and warns mariners of the navigational hazards of Isaac Shoal, Halfmoon Shoal, and the Quicksands.[26]

Nevertheless, wrecks and groundings continue to occur. It is hard to imagine how vessels navigated this treacherous stretch of the Florida Straits before the Lighthouse Service built the first beacon. When the lighthouse was finally established, the plan adopted in 1851 by the preliminary Light House Board to illuminate the dark spaces between Cape Florida and the Dry Tortugas was finally realized.

If the importance of preserving historic structures had been as widely accepted in 1953 as it is today, perhaps there would be a different ending to the history of Rebecca Shoal Lighthouse. But the keepers' house is gone forever, and with it a part of Florida's historic lighthouse architecture and maritime heritage. Fortunately, the successful preservation and protection of the Key West and Cape Florida light stations bodes well for the iron pile reef lighthouses and the Dry Tortugas Light Station. The rising tide of public concern for preservation of historic beacons and light stations testifies to the worth of these structures beyond their past utilitarian value. Those involved with the preservation of America's lighthouses have become the new keepers of the lights.

The notes for this chapter begin on page 292.

The Rebecca Shoal Lighthouse was automated in 1925. In 1953 the building was removed from the iron pile foundation and an acetylene beacon was erected in its place. In 1985 the acetylene beacon was replaced with the beacon pictured. A solar-powered Amerace 190-millimeter rotating optic now marks the dangerous waters surrounding Rebecca Shoal. (U.S. COAST GUARD OFFICIAL PHOTO)

NOTES

ABBREVIATIONS USED IN THE NOTES:

MCPL/KW   Monroe County, May Hill Russell Public Library, Key West

MCPL/I   Monroe County Public Library, Helen Wadley Branch, Islamorada

NA   National Archives, Washington, D.C.

USDC   U.S. Department of Commerce

USDCL   U.S. Department of Commerce and Labor

INTRODUCTION

1. Theodore Leba Jr., "Structural Aspects of Lighthouse Design" (unpublished typescript, U.S. Coast Guard, Treasury Department, Washington, D.C., ca. 1940), pp. 1-2, NA; Paolo Curto, "The Pharos Lighthouse," *Oceans*, July 1981, pp. 8-9; John Naish, *Seamarks, Their History and Development* (London: Stanford Maritime Limited, 1985), p. 17.

2. Dudley Witney, *The Lighthouse* (Boston: New York Graphic Society, 1975), p. 14.

3. Kevin M. McCarthy, *Lighthouses of Ireland* (Sarasota, FL: Pineapple Press, Inc., 1997), pp. 25-26.

4. Elenor Loarie Schoen, "Beacons, Marks and Signs," *Sea Frontier,* May-June 1973, p. 156.

5. Francis Ross Holland Jr., *America's Lighthouses, Their Illustrated History Since 1776* (Brattleboro, VT: The Stephen Greene Press, 1972), pp. 6, 15-17, 26.

6. U.S. Statutes at Large, 1st Congress, 1st session, 1789, vol. 1, p. 53.

7. Schoen, "Beacons, Marks and Signs," pp. 159, 162; Holland, *America's Lighthouses,* p. 155.

8. Arnold Burgess Johnson, *The Modern Light-House Service* (Washington, D.C.: Government Printing Office, 1889), p. 25.

9. Douglas B. Hague and Rosemary Christie, *Lighthouses: Their Architecture, History and Archaeology* (Llandysul Dyfed, Wales: Gomer Press, 1975), pp. 136-137, 221.

10. "Light House Board," "Light House Papers," *Documents Relating to Light Houses* 1789-1871, Record Group 26, p. 472, NA; U.S. Congress House, 34th Congress, 1st session, 1856, H. Doc. 164, Serial 868.

11. U.S. Statutes at Large, 29th Congress, 2nd session, 1847, Vol. 9, p. 175; Leba, "Structural Aspects of Lighthouse Design," pp. 4-5.

12. Francis Ross Holland Jr., *Great American Lighthouses* (Washington, D.C.: The Preservation Press, 1989), p. 31.

13. U.S. Statutes at Large, 30th Congress, 2nd session, 1849, vol. 9, p. 367; U.S. Congress House, 32nd Congress, 1st session, 1851, Ex. Doc. 55, pp. 190-191, Serial 642.

14. U.S. Congress House, 32nd Congress, 1st session, 1851-1852, H. Exec. Doc. 55, pp. 190-191, 211-212, Serial 642; Betty Bruce, "Notes on U.S. Naval Records, July 1850" (unpublished) MCPL.

15. Woodberry Lowery, *The Lowery Collection: A Descriptive List of Maps of the Spanish Settlements Within the Present Limits of the United States. 1502-1820,* ed. Philip Lee Phillips, (Washington, D.C.: Government Printing Office, 1912), pp. 23, 440-441; Mendel L. Peterson, *The Last Cruise of the HMS Loo* (Washington, D.C.: Smithsonian Institution, 1955), p. 17.

16. Douglas Botting, ed., *The Pirates*, (Alexandria, VA: Time-Life Books, 1978), p. 143; Charles M. Brookfield and Oliver Griswold, *They Call It Tropical* (Coconut Grove, FL: The Data Press, 1960), p. 20. Bahamian and Florida newspapers reported sporadic pirate activity until 1829.

17. William Marvin, *A Treatise on the Law of Wreck and Salvage* (Boston: Little Brown and Company, 1858), pp. 4-5.

18. U.S. Statutes at Large, 15th Congress, 2nd session, 1819, vol. 3, p. 523; U.S. Congress House, 17th Congress, 2nd session, 1823, H. Doc. 29, Serial 78; John Watson Simonton, letter to Secretary of the Navy Smith Thompson, December 1821, MCPL.

19. Jefferson B. Browne, *Key West: The Old and the New* (Gainesville, FL: University of Florida Press, a facsimile reproduction of the 1912 edition, 1973), p. 7.

20. "Message from the President of the United States, Transmitting Information In Relation to the Fortifying of Thompson's Island, Usually Called Key West," *American State Papers* (Washington, D.C.: Gales and Seaton, 1823), vol. 6, pp. 5-6.

21. U.S. Statutes at Large, 17th Congress, 1st session, 1822, vol. 3, p. 720; U.S. Congress House, 13th Congress, 1st session, 1848, H. Doc. 189, Serial 524.

22. U.S. Statutes at Large, 17th Congress, 1st session, 1822, vol. 31, p. 684; U.S. Congress Senate, 18th Congress, 2nd session, 1825, S. Doc. 17, Serial 109.

23. Marvin, *A Treatise on the Law of Wreck and Salvage,* pp. 4-6; Edwin C. Bearss, *Fort Jefferson National Monument Florida Shipwreck Study: The Dry Tortugas* (Washington, D.C.: U.S. Department of the Interior, National Park Service, 1971), pp. 32-33.

24. U.S. Statutes at Large, 18th Congress, 1st session, 1824, vol. 4, p. 62; ibid., 2nd session, 1825, vol. 4, pp. 132-133.

25. Cape Florida, Key West, Sand Key, Dry Tortugas light stations, clipping files, Record Group 26, NA; George R. Putnam, *Lighthouses and Lightships of the United States* (Boston: Houghton Mifflin, 1933), p. 106.

26. Dorothy Dodd, "The Wrecking Business on the Florida Reef, 1822-1860" *Florida Historical Quarterly,* 22 (4): 182-183, 1944.

27. Ibid., pp. 184-185; U.S. Statutes at Large, 19th Congress, 1st session, 1826, vol. 4, p. 138; ibid., 29th Congress, 2nd session, 1847, vol. 9, pp. 131-132. The original court was abolished by the admission of Florida into the Union in 1845, and in 1847, a federal court for the Southern District of the United States was established in its place.

28. Marvin, *A Treatise on the Law of Wreck and Salvage,* p. 338.

29. Ibid., pp. 105; M.M. Cohen, *Admiralty Jurisdiction, Law, and Practice* (Boston: Soule and Bugbee Law Publishers, 1883), pp. 131-134.

30. U.S. Congress Senate, 30th Congress, 2nd session, 1849, S. Doc. 30, Serial 531.

31. U.S. Congress House, 31st Congress, 2nd session, 1851, H. Doc. 12, Serial 598; Leba, "Structural Aspects of Lighthouse Design," p. 5.

32. Johnson, *The Modern Light-House Service,* p. 8.

33. Holland, *America's Lighthouses,* pp. 106-108.

34. Ponce de León Inlet Light Station clipping file 1835-1887; Cape Canaveral Light Station clipping file, 1835, Record Group 26, NA.

35. Jupiter Inlet Light Station clipping file, 1850-1866, Record Group 26, NA.

36. Dodd, "The Wrecking Business on the Florida Reef," p. 199.

CHAPTER 1

1. Neil E. Hurley, *Keepers of Florida Lighthouses 1820-1939* (Alexandria, VA.: Historic Lighthouse Publishers, 1990), p. 21.

2. Stuart B. McIver, *Fort Lauderdale and Broward County* (Ft. Lauderdale: Windsor Publishers, n.d.), p. 15.

3. Ibid., pp.15-18; Hurley, *Keepers of Florida Lighthouses,* p. 21; Neil E. Hurley, *An Illustrated History of Cape Florida Lighthouse* (Camino, CA: Historic Lighthouse Publishers, 1989), pp. 15-16.

4. John W. B. Thompson, Charleston, South Carolina, letter to the Lighthouse Service, 1837, Record Group 26, NA.

5. Thomas J. Leib, Lieutenant, U.S. Navy letter to Alexander J. Dallas, Esqr., Commanding U.S. Naval Forces in the West Indies, August 17, 1836, Florida Collection, MCPL/I.

6. Ibid.

7. Ibid., John W. B. Thompson, Charleston, South Carolina, letter to the Lighthouse Service, 1837, Record Group 26, NA.

8. U.S. Statutes at Large, 17th Congress, 1st session, 1822, vol. 3, p. 698; ibid. 18th Congress, 1st session, 1824, vol. 4, p. 61; *Documents Relating to Lighthouses,* 1789-1871, p. 305, Record Group 26, NA.

9. *Documents Relating to Lighthouses,* 1789-1871, p. 305.

10. My correspondence with Becky Roper Matkov, Executive Director, Dade Heritage Trust, January 12, 1998. A limited supply of historic bricks removed from the light tower during restoration is available to collectors and preservationists.

11. Hurley, *Keepers of Florida Lighthouses,* p. 21; Saint Augustine Light Station clipping file, 1823, Key West Light Station clipping files, 1824-1825, Cape Florida Light Station clipping files, 1837, 1846, Record Group 26, NA. The Cape Florida clipping file contains a letter from "S. Pleasonton to John P. Kennedy, Chairman, &c., House of Representatives."

12. U.S. Statutes at Large, 24th Congress, 2nd session, 1837, vol. 5, p. 185; ibid. 29th Congress, 1st session, 1846, vol. 9, p. 94; *Documents Relating to Lighthouses,* 1789-1871, p. 305; Cape Florida Light Station clipping file, 1852.

13. "Nautical Intelligence," *Hunt's Merchants' Magazine and Commercial Review* (New York: George W. & John A. Wood, 1847), p. 205; U.S. Congress, 32nd Congress, 1st session, Ex. Doc. 55, pp. 210, 212, 235, Serial 642.

14. Lieutenant George G. Meade, "Report to the Light House Board, October 26, 1853," Record Group 26, NA; Cape Florida Light Station clipping file, 1855.

15. U.S. Statutes at Large, 33rd Congress, 1st session, 1854, vol. 10, p. 341; Cape Florida Light Station clipping file, 1855; William Marvin, *A Treatise on the Law of Wreck and Salvage* (Boston: Little, Brown and Co., 1858), pp. 215, 220.

16. Hurley, *An Illustrated History of Cape Florida Lighthouse,* pp. 26-27.

17. M. M. Cohen, *Admiralty Jurisdiction, Law, and Practice* (Boston: Soule and Bugbee Law Publishers, 1883), pp. 132-133; Cape Florida Light Station clipping files, 1861-1866.

18. Hurley, *Keepers of Florida Lighthouses,* p. 22.

19. Ibid., p. 61; Cape Florida Light Station clipping files, 1875-1878.

20. U.S. Department of Commerce, National Oceanic and Atmospheric Administration, National Ocean Service, *U.S. Atlantic Coast Pilot,* 1990 (Washington, D.C.: NOAA, 1990), vol. 5, p. 188.

21. U.S. Department of Transportation, U.S. Coast Guard, *U.S. Atlantic and Gulf Coast Light List,* 1990 (Washington, D.C.: Government Printing Office, 1990), vol. 3, p. 8; my correspondence with Captain R. D. Peterson, U.S. Coast Guard, Chief, Aids to Navigation Branch, Seventh Coast Guard District.

22. Geoffrey Tomb, "To the Lighthouse: Famed beacon will cast light on centennial," *Miami Herald,* July 27, 1996, Section B, p. 1.

23. My correspondence with Becky Roper Matkov, Executive Director, Dade Heritage Trust, January 12, 1998.

24. U.S. Department of Transportation, U.S. Coast Guard, *U.S. Atlantic and Gulf Coast Light List,* 1979 (Washington, D.C.: Government Printing Office, 1979), vol. 2, pp. viii, 78; my interview with Chief Richard "Beau" Lewis, Seventh Coast Guard District, Aids to Navigation, (ATON), Miami, January 7, 1998.

25. My correspondence with Becky Roper Matkov, Executive Director, Dade Heritage Trust, January 12, 1998.

CHAPTER 2

1. Jefferson B. Browne, *Key West: The Old and the New* (Gainesville: University of Florida Press, a facsimile reproduction of the 1912 edition, 1973), p. 199; Dorothy Dodd, "The Wrecking Business on the Florida Reef, 1822-1860" *Florida Historical Quarterly* 22(4): 175, 1944.

2. U.S. Congress House, 13th Congress, 1st session, 1813, H. Doc. 189, pp. 2, 8, 15, 22, Serial 524; U.S. Congress Senate, Executive Journal, vol. 111, 1823, pp. 312-313; U.S. Statutes at Large, 18th Congress, 2nd session, 1825, vol. 4, pp. 132-133.

3. *The Territorial Papers of the United States, The Territory of Florida*, 1821-1824, compiled and edited by Clarence E. Carter (Washington, D.C., 1956), vol. 22, pp. 385-387; U.S. Statutes at Large, 18th Congress, 1st session 1823, vol. 4, p. 61. In his March 28, 1822, letter to Thompson, Perry states that he named the island "Thompson's island," and he named the harbor "Port Rodgers" for Commander John Rodgers, president of the Board of Navy Commissioners.

4. U.S. Statutes at Large, 18th Congress, 1st session, 1823, vol. 4, p. 61.

5. U.S. Congress House, 18th Congress, 2nd session, 1825, H. Doc. 17, Serial 109.

6. *The Pensacola Gazette,* December 3, 1825, p. 3; U.S. Congress House, 19th Congress, 1st session., 1825, H. Doc., 19, Serial 131; Dodd, "The Wrecking Business on the Florida Reef," pp. 182-183.

7. U.S. Congress House, 19th Congress, 1st session, 1825, H. Doc. 19, Serial 131; Dodd, "The Wrecking Business on the Florida Reef," pp. 182-183; Betty Bruce, "Genealogical Notes" (unpublished), MCPL/KW; Neil E. Hurley, *Keepers of Florida Lighthouses* 1820-1939 (Alexandria, VA.: Historic Lighthouse Publishers, 1990), p. 71; U.S. Congress House, 25th Congress, 3rd session, 1838, H. Doc., 24, Serial 345.

8. Hurley, *Keepers of Florida Lighthouses,* p. 71; Ivan Tannehill, *Hurricanes: Their Nature and History* (CT: Greenwood Press, 1938), p. 152.

9. Petition, Key West, FL, to Samuel Pleasonton, fifth auditor of the Treasury, Washington, D.C., 1843, (NA), on file, Florida Collection, MCPL/KW.

10. Stephen R. Mallory, Key West, letter to secretary of the Treasury, Washington, D.C., October 20, 1846, MCPL; Tannehill, *Hurricanes: Their Nature and History*, p. 152.

11. Stephen R. Mallory, Key West, letter to Secretary of the Treasury, Washington, D.C., October 20, 1846, MCPL.

12. U.S. Congress House, 13th Congress, 1st session, 1848, H. Doc. 27, Serial 516.

13. "Key West Lighthouse Restoration Project," Research Papers (unpublished), Key West Lighthouse Museum; Key West Light Station clipping file, 1848.

14. Ibid.; Descriptions of Key West Light Station, 1848-1865, Record Group 26, NA.

15. Hurley, *Keepers of Florida Lighthouses 1820-1939*, p. 71; Key West Light Station clipping file, 1859, Record Group 26, NA.

16. *The War of the Rebellion: A Compilation of the Official Records of the Union and Confederate Armies* (Washington, D.C.: Government Printing Office, 1902), Series 1, vol. 1, pp. 342-343; Browne, *Key West: The Old and the New,* pp. 91-92, 179.

17. Bruce, "Genealogical Notes," MCPL/KW; Hurley, *Keepers of Florida Lighthouses,* pp. 71-72.

18. Key West Light Station clipping files, 1868, 1872, 1873, 1878-1886.

19. "Key West Lighthouse Restoration Project," Key West Lighthouse Museum; Key West Light Station clipping file, 1887.

20. Bruce, "Genealogical Notes," MCPL/KW; Hurley, *Keepers of Florida Lighthouses,* p. 72.

21. Key West Light Station clipping file, 1891.

22. Ibid., 1892-1895; Alden Solovy, *Solares Hill,* November 1984, p. 20.

23. Key West Light Station clipping files, 1892-1895, 1908; USDCL *Annual Report* 1910, p. 517.

24. *The Key West Citizen,* October 2, 1952.

25. USDCL, *Annual Report,* 1910, p. 526; Key West Light Station clipping file, 1910.

26. Hurley, *Keepers of Florida Lighthouses,* p. 72; USDC, *Annual Report*, 1915, p. 594.

27. H. G. Cutter, *History of Florida* 1513-1913 (Chicago: Lewis Publishing Co., 1923), vol. 2, p. 305; Bruce, "Genealogical Notes," MCPL/KW.

28. My interviews with Susan Olsen, 1989; "Old Lighthouse to Reopen," *The Miami Herald,* November 15, 1990, Section B, p. 1.

CHAPTER 3

1. Admiralty Records of the District Court of the United States, District of Florida, Silas Denison, et al. versus the bark, *Pacific,* New York to Mobile. These records are on file at the East Point, Georgia, repository of the National Archives, and microfilms of the records are available MCPL/KW, and at the Historic Florida Keys Preservation Board.

2. Ibid.

3. National Oceanic and Atmospheric Administration, National Ocean Service, Charts 11434, 11438; U.S. Department of Commerce, National Oceanic and Atmospheric Administration, National Ocean Service, *U.S. Atlantic Coast Pilot* (Washington, D.C.: NOAA, 1990), vol. 5, p. 102.

4. Edwin C. Bearss, *Fort Jefferson National Monument, Florida, Shipwreck Study—The Dry Tortugas* (Washington, D.C.: U.S. Department of the Interior, National Park Service, 1971), p. 1; my interview with Bill Gilmartin, National Marine Fisheries Service, August 23, 1991. The last time Caribbean Monk seals were seen was in the 1950s. They are now extinct.

5. Henry M. Stommel, *The Gulf Stream: A Physical and Dynamical Description* (Berkeley: University of California Press, 1965), pp. 68-69; Lippincott's *New Gazetteer* (Philadelphia: Lippincott, 1906), p. 776.

6. Bearss, *Shipwreck Study—The Dry Tortugas,* pp. 4-5; "A Plan of the Tortugas and Part of the Florida Keys, Surveyed by George Gauld, M.A., 1773, for the Right Honorable the Board of Admiralty," Library of Congress, Washington, D.C.

7. Clarence E. Carter, ed., *The Territorial Papers of the United States, The Territory of Florida,* 1821-1824, (Washington, D.C., 1956), vol. 22, pp. 387-388.

8. U.S. Statutes at Large, 16th Congress, 1st session, 1822, vol. 3, p. 698.

9. Ibid., 18th Congress, 1st session, 1824, vol. 4 , p. 61; Dorothy Dodd, "The Wrecking Business on the Florida Reef, 1822-1860," *Florida Historical Quarterly* 22 (4):182-183, 1944.

10. William Pinkney, Lighthouse Superintendent, Key West, letters to Stephen Pleasonton, fifth auditor, Treasury Department, Washington, D.C., March 9, 22, April 27, May 11, and July 1, 1826, Record Group 26, NA.

11. "Report of John Rodgers, July 3, 1829," U.S. Congress Senate, 21st Congress, 1st session, 1829, S. Doc. 1, Serial 192.

12. Bearss, *Shipwreck Study—The Dry Tortugas,* pp. 47-48.

13. Maria R. Audubon, *Audubon and His Journal* (New York: Dover Publications, an unabridged and unaltered republication of the first edition originally published in New York by Charles Scribner's Sons, 1897), vol. 2, pp. 346, 371-372.

14. Bearss, *Shipwreck Study—The Dry Tortugas,* p. 51.

15. Ibid., pp. 13-14.

16. Francis Ross Holland Jr., *Great American Lighthouses* (Washington, D.C.: The Preservation Press, 1989), pp. 29-31.

17. U.S. Congress Senate, Report from Secretary of the Treasury, January 26, 1838, *Public Documents Printed by Orders of the Senate of the United States,* 25th Congress, 2nd session, 1838, S. Doc. 93, p. 4, Serial 315.

18. U.S. Congress House, 25th Congress, 3rd session, 1838, H. Doc. 24, p. 4, Serial 345.

19. Holland, *Great American Lighthouses,* p. 31.

20. Bearss, *Shipwreck Study—The Dry Tortugas,* pp. 15, 18.

21. Ibid., p. 15; U.S. Congress House, 32nd Congress, 1st session, 1851, Ex. Doc. 55, p. 141, Serial 642.

22. U.S. Congress House, 32nd Congress, 1st session, 1851, Ex. Doc. 55, p. 24, Serial 642.

23. Ibid., pp. 214, 218.

24. U.S. Statutes at Large, 32nd Congress, 1st session, 1852, Vol. 10, p. 119.

25. Albert Manucy, *A Constructional History of Fort Jefferson*, 1846-1874 (Washington, D.C.: U.S. Department of the Interior, National Park Service, 1961), p. 65. The fort was designed by Colonel Joseph G. Totten, Chief Engineer, U.S. Army Corps of Engineers, from 1838 to 1864.

26. Dry Tortugas Light Station clipping file, Appendix no. 17, H. G. Wright, Captain of Engineers, Fort Jefferson, FL, letter to Lieutenant T. A. Jenkins, U.S.N., secretary, Light House Board, Washington, D.C., September 23, 1855, Record Group 26, NA.

27. Ibid.; Willard Bethurem Robinson, *American Forts: Architectural Form and Function* (Urbana: University of Illinois Press, 1977, Published for the Amon Carter Museum of Western Art, Fort Worth), p. 115.

28. Dry Tortugas Light Station clipping file, Appendix no. 17; Sharon Wells, *Forgotten Legacy: Blacks in Nineteenth Century Key West* (Key West, FL: Historic Key West Preservation Board, 1982), p. 17; 1840, 1850, 1860 Censuses, Key West, FL. In the 1840 census, there were ninety-six slaves. In 1850, the number had increased to 431, and in 1860, there were 451; many were hired out to the government to work on the construction of Fort Taylor and Fort Jefferson.

29. U.S. Statutes at Large, 34th Congress, 1st session, 1856, vol. II, p. 99; U.S. Department of the Interior, National Park Service, National Register of Historic Places Inventory, OMB no. 1024-0018, Section 7, Description, 1984; my own observations, January 1983, November 1990.

30. Dry Tortugas Light Station clipping file, 1858; "Nautical Intelligence," *Hunt's Merchants' Magazine and Commercial Review,* 38:613, 1858.

31. U.S. Department of the Interior, National Park Service, National Register of Historic Places Inventory, OMB no. 1024-0018, Section 7, Description, 1984.

32. Dry Tortugas Light Station clipping file, Appendix no. 17, Wright, letter to Jenkins.

33. Neil E. Hurley, *Keepers of Florida Lighthouses 1820-1939* (Alexandria, VA.: Historic Lighthouse Publishers, 1990), pp. 49, 51; Manucy, *A Constructional History of Fort Jefferson*, p. 66.

34. Dry Tortugas Light Station clipping file, 1861.

35. History of the 47th Regiment of Pennsylvania Veteran Volunteers, on file at Fort Jefferson National Monument, Dry Tortugas, Florida.

36. Dry Tortugas Light Station clipping file, 1866; Hurley, *Keepers of Florida Lighthouses 1820-1939*, pp. 49-52; History of the 47th Regiment of Pennsylvania Veteran Volunteers.

37. Dry Tortugas Light Station clipping files, 1866, 1871.

38. Ibid., 1874, 1875; U.S. Statutes at Large, 43rd Congress, 2nd session, 1875, vol. 18, p. 381.

39. Dry Tortugas Light Station clipping files, 1875, 1876.

40. Ibid., 1876; U.S. Statutes at Large, 43rd Congress, 2nd session, 1875, vol. 18, p. 381.

41. Dry Tortugas Light Station clipping files, 1880-1899.

42. Hurley, *Keepers of Florida Lighthouses,* pp. 1, 54, 75, 107, 117; USDCL, *Annual Report,* 1905, p. 190; U.S. Department of the Interior, National Park Service, National Register of Historic Places Inventory, OMB no., 1024-0018, Section 7, Description, 1984.

43. Dry Tortugas Light Station clipping file, 1894; USDCL, *Annual Report,* 1910, p. 534; USDC, *Annual Report,* 1913, pp. 353-354.

44. USDC, *Annual Report,* 1922, p. 191, 1923, p. 196; U.S. Department of the Interior, National Park Service, National Register of Historic Places Inventory, OMB no. 1024-0018, Section 7, Description, 1984.

45. USDC, *Annual Report,* 1921, p. 108; ibid., 1926, p. 180; U.S. Department of the Interior, National Park Service, National Register of Historic Places Inventory, OMB no. 1024-0018, Section 7, Description, 1984.

46. My correspondence with Captain R. D. Peterson, U.S. Coast Guard, Chief, Aids to Navigation Branch, Seventh Coast Guard District, July 30, 1991.

47. U.S. Department of Transportation, U.S. Coast Guard, *U.S. Atlantic and Gulf Coast Light List,* 1990 (Washington, D.C.: Government Publications Office, 1990), vol. 3, p. 10; 1997, vol. 3, p. 11. My interview with Lt. Christopher Shivery and Chief Richard Lewis, ATON, Miami, January 6, 1998.

48. U.S. Department of Transportation, U.S. Coast Guard, *U.S. Atlantic and Gulf Coast Light List,* 1997 (Washington, D.C.: Government Printing Office, 1997), vol. 3, p. 11. My interview with Chief Richard "Beau" Lewis, Seventh Coast Guard District, Aids to Navigation, Miami, January 8, 1998.

49. My own observations, January 1983 and November 1990; my interview with Chief Charlie Pantelakos, Seventh Coast Guard District, Aids to Navigation Team, Key West, January 9, 1998.

CHAPTER 4

1. J.W. None, *Piloting Directions for the Gulf of Florida, the Bahama Banks, and Islands* (London: J.W. Norie & Co., 1820), p. 11; U.S. Statutes at Large, 19th Congress, 1st session, vol. 4, p. 173; Sand Key Light Station clipping file, Record Group 26, NA. Although the clipping file for the light station consists mainly of excerpts from the annual reports of the Light House Board, it also contains a brief history of the first Sand Key Lighthouse.

2. U.S. Treasury Department, *Light List* (Florida), 1848 (Washington: U.S. Treasury Department, 1848), no. 200; Neil E. Hurley, *Keepers of Florida Lighthouses 1820-1939* (Alexandria, VA: Historic Lighthouse Publishers, 1990), pp. 49, 105.

3. Hurley, *Keepers of Florida Lighthouses,* p. 105; William Randolph Hackley, "Diary," furnished by Dr. R.L. Goulding, MCPL/KW.

4. My correspondence with Gladys E. Bolhouse, curator of manuscripts, Newport Historical Society, Newport, R.I., September 17, 1986.

5. Hopner vs. Appleby, Document File 129-5, Newport Historical Society, Newport, R.I.; my correspondence with Arthur H. Eddins Jr., Piedmont, CA, November 24, 1986. Eddins is Appleby's great, great, great grandson.

6. *The Territorial Papers of the United States, The Territory of Florida,* 1821-1824, compiled and edited by Clarence E. Carter (Washington, D.C., 1956), vol. 22, p. 723.

7. Letter from William Hunter, Newport, R.I., to Commodore David Porter, Key West, May 6, 1825, Document File 129-5, Newport Historical Society, Newport, R.I.; 1830 Census, Key West, MCPL/KW; Admiralty Record Book of the U.S. District Court of Florida (Key West), microfilm, MCPL/KW.

8. Dorothy Dodd, "The Wrecking Business on the Florida Reef, 1822-1860," *Florida Historical Quarterly*, 22(4): 184, 1944.

9. U.S. Congress House, 28th Congress, 1st session, 1843, H. Doc. 38, Serial 442.

10. Stephen Pleasonton, Washington, D.C., letters to Stephen R. Mallony, superintendent, Seventh district, Key West, July 7 and October 19, 1846, Sand Key Light Station clipping file.

11. *Mercury,* Newport, R.I., November 7, 1846, p. 3; Arthur H. Eddins Jr., Piedmont, CA, letter to Betty Bruce, Key West, November 24, 1986, MCPL/KW. Six people were lost at Sand Key. The identity of one person is unknown.

12. I.W.P. Lewis, "Screw Pile Lighthouses," *Appleton's Magazine*, December 1852; Marcus W. Price, director, General Records Division, NA, letter to Aime J. Forand, House of Representatives, Washington, D.C., January 25, 1949.

13. Sand Key Light Station clipping file, 1846; Willard Flint, *Lightships of the United States Government,* Reference Notes (Washington, D.C.: Coast Guard Historian's Office, USCG Headquarters, 1989) index 081.

14. U.S. Statutes at Large, 29th Congress, 1st session, 1845, vol. 9, p. 177; ibid., 30th Congress, 2nd session, 1848, vol. 9, p. 298.

15. Historic Key West Preservation Board, *Historic American Building Survey,* Key West, FL, August 1967, p. 16, MCPL/KW; Sand Key Light Station clipping file, 1848.

16. *Hunt's Merchants' Magazine,* January 1850, pp. 34-35; ibid., January 1852, p. 56.

17. Report by George Meade to Col. J.J. Albert, Topographical Engineer, August 27, 1853, Reports, Specifications, Etc., 1848-1855, Record Group 26, NA.

18. Ibid., Sand Key Light Station clipping file; *Gleason's Pictorial Magazine,* September 9, 1854, p. 152.

19. Report of William Shubrik, President of the Light House Board, January 8, 1852, Record Group 26, NA; Report by George Meade to Col. J.J. Albert.

20. Report by George Meade to Col. J.J. Albert; Hurley, *Keepers of Florida Lighthouses,* p. 105.

21. Old Lighthouse Records, no. 71, Abstracts of Contracts 1800-1855, NA; Records of Lighthouse Keepers and Salaries, 1852-1900, NA.

22. Report by George Meade to Col. J.J. Albert; Sand Key Light Station, Appropriations, p. 331, Record Group 26, NA. Total amount expended in constructing, finishing, and maintaining the lighthouse for three months: $101,520.39.

23. George G. Meade, letter to Captain S. F. DuPont, August 23, 1853, Item W9-6815, pp. 329-330, Eleutheran Mills Historical Library, Greenville, DE.

24. Sand Key Light Station clipping file, 1856.

25. Ibid., 1871-1874.

26. Ibid., 1875.

27. Ibid., 1886, 1891.

28. The Sand Key Weather Station Journals, 1910, pp. 9, 17-19, MCPL/KW.

29. Charles G. Johnson, Reports to William Dutcher, American Ornithological Union, 1902-1904, Audubon Research Center, Tavernier, Florida.

30. Charles G. Johnson, Reports to William Dutcher, 1903.

31. David L. Capra, *USCG Lighthouses and Lightships* (Washington, D.C.: Department of Transportation, 1976), p. 2.

32. My correspondence with U.S. Coast Guard, Aids to Navigation Branch, Seventh District, Miami, FL, February 7, 1980.

33. My correspondence with J.V. O'Shea, Lieutenant Commander, U.S. Coast Guard, Aids to Navigation Branch, Seventh District, Miami, FL, December 15, 1987.

34. Captain R.D. Peterson, U.S. Coast Guard, Aids to Navigation Branch, Seventh District, Miami, FL, to Wright Langley, Director, Historic Florida Keys Preservation Board, Key West, February 8, 1991.

35. Ibid.

36. U.S. Department of Transportation, U.S. Coast Guard, *U.S. Atlantic and Gulf Coast Light List,* 1997 (Washington, D.C.: Government Printing Office, 1997), vol. 3, p. 11; my interview with Chief Charlie Pantelakos, ANT, Key West, January 15, 1998, Islamorada, Florida.

37. Lt. Bob Garrott, "Live Reef Saves *Miss Beholden,*" *Coastline* (Miami: Seventh Coast Guard District), April 1993, p. 8.

38. PA1 Charles Smith, "Freighter Runs Aground," *Coastline,* March 1997, pp. 1-2.

39. My interview with Chief Richard "Beau" Lewis, Seventh Coast Guard District, Aids to Navigation, Miami, FL, January 8, 1998.

CHAPTER 5

1. Woodberry Lowery, *The Lowery Collection: A Descriptive List of Maps of the Spanish Possessions Within the Present Limits of the United States, 1502-1820*, ed. Phillip Lee Philips (Washington, D.C.: Government Printing Office, 1912), p. 377; Bureau of Topographical Engineers, *Florida Coast Survey,* 1846; U.S. Congress Senate, 30th Congress, 2nd session, 1848, S. Doc. 30, Serial 531.

2. William Marvin, *A Treatise on the Law of Wreck and Salvage* (Boston: Little, Brown and Co., 1858), p. 213.

3. Captain Howard Shansbury, report to Colonel J.J. Albert, February 21, 1848, Light House Board Reports, Specifications, etc., 1848-1855, Record Group 26, NA.

4. Charles M. Brookfield, "Key Largo Coral Reef: America's First Undersea Park," *National Geographic,* January 1962, p. 61; my interviews with Charles Brookfield, Coconut Grove and Islamorada, FL, 1979-1980; W.R. Bailey, "The Geography of Fevers," *Jamaica Historical Journal*, 1969, p. 28, copy on file MCPL/I.

5. U.S. Statutes at Large, 18th Congress, 1st session, 1824, vol. 4, pp. 61-62; ibid., 24th Congress, 2nd session, 1837, vol. 5, p. 185; ibid., 25th Congress, 2nd session, 1838, vol. 5, p. 292; ibid., 33rd Congress, 2nd session, 1855, vol. 10, p. 658. (During the next thirty years, Congress, in making appropriations for navigational aids on the reef, referred to it also as "Carry Force" and "Cary's Fort.")

6. "Captain John Whalton, Carysfort Lightship Keeper," Documents 1824-1834, collected by Sally Whalton (wife of Joseph C. Whalton, the great, great grandson of Captain John Whalton), MCPL/I.

7. George R. Putnam, *Lighthouses and Lightships of the United States* (Boston: Houghton Mifflin, 1933), p. 106; Willard Flint, *Lightships of the United States Government,* Reference Notes (Washington, D.C.: Coast Guard Historian's Office, USCG Headquarters, 1989), index 080.

8. "Captain John Whalton, Carysfort Lightship Keeper," Documents 1824-1834, MCPL/I.

9. Flint, *Lightships of the United States Government,* index 080; Documents Relating to Light Houses, 1789-1871, p. 308, Record Group 26, NA.

10. Ibid., U.S. Statutes at Large, 21st Congress, 1st session, 1830, vol. 4, p. 381; Jefferson Browne, *Key West: The Old and the New* (Gainesville, FL: University of Florida Press, a facsimile reproduction of the 1912 edition, 1973), p. 157.

11. Reprint of Edmund Smith's letter, 1836, Florida Collection, MCPL/KW.

12. Documents Relating to Light Houses, 1789-1871, p. 305.

13. Betty Bruce, "Genealogical Notes" (unpublished), Florida Collection, MCPL/KW. The families of both Michael Mabrity, Key West Lighthouse keeper, and his wife, Barbara Staccioli, who later became the lightkeeper after her husband's death, were also colonists of New Smyrna, FL. Feliciata was half sister to Michael Mabrity.

14. "Letter from Correspondent, July 1, 1837, from Indian Key," *Pensacola Gazette,* July 22, 1837, p. 3.

15. Clarence Edwin Carter, "Florida Territory, 1834-1839," *Territorial Papers of the United States* (Washington, D.C.: Government Printing Office, 1960), vol. 25, pp. 405-406.

16. John Lee Williams, *Territory of Florida* (New York: A. T. Goodrich, 1839), Reprint. (Gainesville, FL: University of Florida Press, Florida Facsimile Reprint Series, 1962), pp. 271-272.

17. U.S. Congress, 32nd Congress, 1st session, Ex. Doc. 55, pp. 232-233, Serial 642.

18. Ibid., pp. 213-214; Flint, *Lightships of the United States Government,* index 080.

19. U.S. Congress, 32nd Congress, 1st session, Ex. Doc. 55, p. 211, Serial 642; Documents Relating to Light Houses, 1789-1871, p. 740; Edward Dumas Malone, ed. *Dictionary of American Biography* (New York: Charles Scribner's Sons, 1935), vol. 15, pp. 85-86.

20. U.S. Congress, 32nd Congress, 1st session, 1851, Ex. Doc. 55, pp. 206-207, 211, Serial 642.

21. Francis Ross Holland Jr., *Great American Lighthouses* (Washington, D.C.: The Preservation Press, 1989), pp. 30, 45; Francis Ross Holland Jr., *America's Lighthouses: Their Illustrated History Since 1776* (Brattleboro, VT: The Stephen Greene Press, 1972), pp. 30-32.

22. Holland, *America's Lighthouses,* pp. 16, 21, 33.

23. Ibid., p. 52; U.S. Congress House, 34th Congress, 1st session, 1856, H. Doc. 164, Serial 868.

24. Carysfort Reef Light Station clipping file, 1849, Record Group 26, NA.

25. Ibid., 1851; Theodore Leba Jr., "Structural Aspects of Lighthouse Design" (Unpublished typescript, U.S. Coast Guard, Treasury Department, Washington, D.C., ca. 1940), p. 6, NA.

26. George Meade, *Life and Letters of George Gordon Meade* (New York: Charles Scribner and Sons, 1913), vol. 1, pp. 202-205; Malone, ed., *Dictionary of American Biography,* vol. 12, p. 474.

27. Richard Meade Bache, *Life of General George Gordon Meade* (Philadelphia: Coates and Co., 1897), p. 557.

28. "Extracts From Report of Lt. G.G. Meade to the Secretary of the Light House Board, July 31, 1852," p. 2, Carysfort Reef Light Station clipping file.

29. Ibid., p. 3; Secretary of the Treasury, Light House Board, *Annual Report,* 1894, p. 255. "While it is no part of the light-keeper's duty as such to look after wrecks, or to succor the distressed, many acts of heroism have been performed by keepers. . . . In those instances where, in doing so, they have endangered their own lives, they have received from the Secretary of the Treasury gold or silver medals in proportion to the danger incurred, not as compensation, but rather as marks of appreciation for their services."

30. Neil E. Hurley, *Keepers of Florida Lighthouses 1820-1939* (Alexandria, VA: Historic Lighthouse Publishers, 1990), p. 29; "Extracts From Report of Lt. G.G. Meade to the Secretary of the Lighthouse Board, July 31, 1852," p. 2, Carysfort Reef Light Station clipping files.

31. George W. Parson's Diary, 1873-1875, P.K. Yonge Library of Florida History, University of Florida, Gainesville, FL, microfilm copy Carysfort Reef File, MCPL/I.

32. Directions to Light-House Keepers, Sections VII, NA.

33. Carysfort Reef Light Station clipping file, 1859; "Nautical Intelligence," *Hunt's Merchants' Magazine and Commercial Review* (New York: George W. & John A. Wood, 1858), p. 614.

34. Journal of Light Station at Carysfort Reef, 1881, Civil Reference Branch, Suitland Section, NA; Hurley, *Keepers of Florida Lighthouses,* p. 33.

35. Journal of Light Station at Carysfort Reef, 1882, 1883, 1884.

36. Ibid., 1885; Carysfort Reef Light Station clipping file, 1886.

37. USDCL, *Annual Report,* 1894, pp. 226-237.

38. William Curry Harllee, *Kinfolks* (New Orleans: William Curry Harllee, 1935), vol. 2, p. 1690.

39. Carysfort Reef Light Station clipping file, 1892.

40. Records of Lighthouse Keepers and Salaries, 1852-1900, Record Group 26, NA; U.S. Bureau of the Census, *Historical Statistics of the United States, Colonial Times to 1957* (Washington, D.C.: Government Printing Office, 1960), p. 92.

41. My correspondence with Clement Brooks during 1980.

42. My interviews with Charles Brookfield, Coconut Grove and Islamorada, FL, 1979-1980.

43. Ibid., USDC, *Annual Report,* 1913, p. 353.

44. My interview with Captain J. Gillian, superintendent, John Pennekamp Coral Reef State Park, Key Largo, FL, 1980.

45. U.S. Department of Transportation, U.S. Coast Guard, *U.S. Atlantic and Gulf Coast Light List,* 1997 (Washington, D.C.: Government Printing Office, 1997), vol. 3, p. 9.

46. U.S. Congress, HR 5909, Public Law 101-605, November 16, 1990; Robert B. Halley, H.L. Vacher, and Eugene A. Shinn, *Geology and Hydrogeology of the Florida Keys* (Elsevier Science B.V., 1997), p. 244.

47. Ibid., pp. 243-244; 1880, "Report on the Florida Reefs," *Memoirs of the Museum of Comparative Zoology*; Harvard University, Vol. VII, pp. 1-61.

48. My interview with Alison Fahrer, President, Pennekamp Coral Reef Institute, Inc., December 22, 1997.

49. "Memorandum" to Alison Fahrer from Dr. Samuel Snedaker, *Proposed Carysfort Lighthouse Offshore Marine Research Facility,* MCPL/I.

CHAPTER 6

1. USDC, National Oceanic and Atmospheric Administration, National Ocean Service, *United States, Gulf Coast, Florida, Florida Keys, Sombrero Key to Sand Key* (Washington, D.C.: NOAA, 1990), 26th ed.

2. Edmund Blunt, *American Coast Pilot* (New York: E. & G.W. Blunt, 1842), p. 248.

3. U.S. Statutes at Large, 24th Congress, 1st session, 1837, vol. 5, p. 185.

4. George R. Putnam, *Lighthouses and Lightships of the United States* (Boston and New York: Houghton Mifflin Company, 1917), pp. 203, 206-207; Willard Flint, *Lightships of the United States Government,* Reference Notes (Washington, D.C.: Coast Guard Historian's Office, USCG Headquarters, 1989) index 082; Neil E. Hurley, *Keepers of Florida Lighthouses 1820-1939* (Alexandria, VA: Historic Lighthouse Publishers, 1990), p. 73.

5. Hurley, *Keepers of Florida Lighthouses,* p. 73; Francis Ross Holland Jr., *America's Lighthouses: Their Illustrated History Since 1716* (Brattleboro, VT: The Stephen Greene Press, 1971), pp. 27, 56-57. Jefferson B. Browne, *Key West: The Old and the New* (Gainesville, FL: University of Florida Press, a facsimile reproduction of the 1912 edition, 1973), pp. 12, 223; Flint, *Lightships of the United States Government,* U.S. Congress House, 25th Congress, 3rd session, 1838, H. Doc. 24, Serial 345.

6. Putnam, *Lighthouses and Lightships of the United States,* p. 209; Holland, *America's Lighthouses*, p. 56.

7. USDC, National Oceanic and Atmospheric Administration, National Ocean Service, *U.S. Atlantic Coast Pilot,* 1989 (Washington, D.C.: NOAA, 1989), vol. 4, p. 98.

8. U.S. Congress House, 28th Congress, 1st session, 1843, H. Doc. 38, Serial vol. 441.

9. Ivan Tannehill, *Hurricanes: Their Nature and History* (Connecticut: Greenwood Press, Inc., 1938), pp. 192-193; "Worst In the History of Man," *Martello* (Key West: Key West Art and Historical Society, 1972), 6: 20-21, 1972.

10. "Commercial Cities and Towns of the United States, Key West, Florida," *Hunt's Merchants' Magazine and Commercial Review* (New York: George W. & Jno. A. Wood, 1852), vol. 26, p. 56.

11. Northwest Passage Light Station clipping file, 1852, Record Group 26, NA.

12. Ibid. 1853.

13. Ibid.; Rebecca Shoal clipping file, 1854, Record Group 26, NA; E. Ashby Hammond, "Health and Medicine in Key West," *Journal of the Florida Medical Association,* 56(8): 637-639, 1969.

14. Northwest Passage Light Station clipping file, 1855.

15. Ibid.; Hurley, *Keepers of Florida Lighthouses,* p. 73.

16. Northwest Passage Light Station clipping files, 1860-1869.

17. Ibid., 1870-1879; U.S. Statutes at Large, 45th Congress, 3rd session, 1879, vol. 21, p. 381.

18. Northwest Passage Light Station clipping file, 1879.

19. Putnam, *Lighthouses and Lightships of the United States,* p. 186; Holland, *America's Lighthouses,* p. 56; Northwest Passage Light Station clipping files, 1885, 1892-1893.

20. Light House Board, Correspondence, 1901-1910, Box 11, File 52, Record Group 26, NA; Hurley, *Keepers of Florida Lighthouses,* p. 76.

21. Bureau of Lighthouses, Correspondence, 1911-1939, File 864, Record Group 26, NA.

22. Ibid.; USDCL, *Annual Report,* 1910, p. 517.

23. Bureau of Lighthouses, Correspondence, 1911-1939, File 864.

24. Ibid.

25. Ibid.

26. Ibid.

27. My correspondence with Betty Bruce, December 1990 and February 1991; Lighthouse file, Florida Collection, MCPL/KW.

28. USDC, National Oceanic and Atmospheric Administration, National Ocean Service, *Atlantic Coast Pilot,* 1997, vol. 4, p. 240.

CHAPTER 7

1. "Nautical Intelligence," *Hunt's Merchants' Magazine and Commercial Review* (New York: George W. & John A. Wood, 1857), pp. 487-488.

2. William Marvin, *A Treatise on the Law of Wreck and Salvage* (Boston: Little, Brown and Co., 1858), pp. 2-3.

3. Sombrero Light Station clipping file, George G. Meade, letter to the Light House Board, April 22, 1854, Record Group 26, NA.

4. National Park Service, U.S. Coast Guard, and Department of Defense, *Historic Lighthouse Preservation Handbook* (Washington, D.C. Government Printing Office) Part IV.B, p. 2.

5. Sombrero Light Station clipping file, George G. Meade, letter to the Light House Board, April 22, 1854, Record Group 26, NA.

6. Ibid.

7. Ibid.; my own examination of Coffins Patches and East and West Turtle Shoal.

8. Woodberry Lowery, *The Lowery Collection: A Descriptive List of Maps of the Spanish Settlements Within the Present Limits of the United States 1502-1820,* ed. Philip Lee Phillips, (Washington, D.C.: Government Printing Office, 1912), pp. 23, 440-441; P. Lee Phillips, *A List of Maps in the Library of Congress Preceded by a List of Works Relating to Cartography* (Washington, D.C.: Government Printing Office, 1901), p. 284.

9. "Nautical Intelligence," *Hunt's Merchants' Magazine* (1850), p. 116; ibid., 1852, p. 126-127; U.S. Statutes at Large, 33rd Congress, 2nd session, 1855, vol. 10, p. 658; USDCL *Annual Reports,* 1857 through 1880. By 1868 the light was referred to as "Dry Bank, Sombrero Key." After 1880 the lighthouse was called "Sombrero Key" or "Sombrero Shoal."

10. George G. Meade, letter to the Light House Board, April 22, 1854.

11. Sombrero Key Light Station clipping file, 1856; U.S. Statutes at Large, 34th Congress, 1st session, 1856, vol. 11, p. 658; U.S. Congress House, 34th Congress, 1st session, 1856, H. Doc. 127; Serial 867; "Nautical Intelligence," *Hunt's Merchants' Magazine* 1857, p. 617.

12. Sombrero Key Light Station clipping file, 1857.

13. USDCL *Annual Report,* 1894, p. 233.

14. Sombrero Key Light Station clipping file, Appropriations: August 31, 1852, $35,000; March 3, 1855, $65,000; August 18, 1856, $24,105; March 3, 1857, $29,053.81.

15. "Nautical Intelligence," *Hunt's Merchants' Magazine* 1858, p. 233.

16. Neil E. Hurley, *Keepers of Florida Lighthouses 1820-1939* (Alexandria, VA: Historic Lighthouse Publishers, 1990), pp. 49, 115; Sombrero Key Light Station clipping file, 1866.

17. Hurley, *Keepers of Florida Lighthouses,* p. 117; Journal of Light Station at Sombrero Key, 1872, Civil Reference Branch, Suitland Section, NA.

18. Journal of Light Station at Sombrero Key, 1873. "Turtlers" or "spongers" refer to boats used in hunting turtles or gathering sponges.

19. Hurley, *Keepers of Florida Lighthouses,* pp. 49, 106, 118; "Extracts From Report of Lt. G.G. Meade to Secretary of the Light House Board, July 31, 1852, p. 2, Carysfort Reef Light Station clipping files, Record Group 26, NA.

20. Journal of Light Station at Sombrero Key, 1879.

21. Hurley, *Keepers of Florida Lighthouses,* p. 118.

22. Ibid., p. 120; Lighthouse File, MCPL/KW.

23. Lighthouse File, MCPL/KW; Journal of Light Station at Sombrero Key, 1879.

24. Hurley, *Keepers of Florida Lighthouses,* pp. 1, 34, 119.

25. USDC, Bureau of Lighthouses, *Annual Report,* 1913, p. 359; Journal of Light Station at Sombrero Key, 1912.

26. Journal of Light Station at Sombrero Key, 1912.

27. John Watts, "Fatality Marred Sombrero's Record," *Florida Keys Keynoter,* March 31, 1960, sec. B, p. 6.

28. My interview with Jack Steffney, charter boat captain, Marathon, FL, 1979.

29. My correspondence with Lieutenant Commander J.V. O'Shea, U.S. Coast Guard, Seventh District, December 1, 1987.

30. My interview with Chief Richard "Beau" Lewis, U.S. Coast Guard, ATON, Miami, January 5, 1998.

31. My interview with Chief Charlie Pantelaos, ANT, Key West, January 9, 1998.

32. U.S. Department of Transportation, U.S. Coast Guard, *U.S. Atlantic and Gulf Coast Light List,* 1997 (Washington, D.C.: Government Printing Office, 1997), vol. 3, p. 10.

CHAPTER 8

1. "Testimony of Mr. Peyton Henley, Court of Inquiry into the Loss of the U.S. Schooner *Alligator*; Held on board the U.S. Frigate *Guerriere* at Norfolk, VA, Dec. 13, 1822," microfilm, "U.S. Navy Court Martials and Courts of Inquiry," NA 273 15, collected by John Viele and on file at the MCPL/I.

2. J. M. Dale, Norfolk, VA, letter to Arthur Sinclair, Navy Department, Washington, D.C., December 3, 1822, NA.

3. "Testimony of Mr. Peyton Henley," on file MCPL/I.

4. J. M. Dale, Norfolk, VA, letter to Arthur Sinclair, Navy Department, Washington, D.C., December 3, 1822, NA.

5. *Directory of American Fighting Ships* (Washington, D.C.: Government Printing Office, 1959), vol. 1, s.v. "USS Alligator."

6. *Log of the USS Alligator,* NA; Francis B. C. Bradlee, *Piracy in the West Indies and its Suppression* (Salem, MA: The Essex Institute, 1923), pp. 30-31; Alice Russell and Annis K. Olsen, "U.S. Naval Log Books," Records of the Bureau of Naval Personnel, Record Group 24, NA. Dates involving naval engagements can sometimes differ because logbook entries used "sea time," and the day was calculated from noon on one day to noon the next. Begin-

ning in 1848 the day was calculated in logbooks according to "civil time," from midnight to midnight of each calendar day.

7. *Directory of American Fighting Ships,* vol. 1, s.v. "USS Alligator"; J. M. Dale, letter to Arthur Sinclair, December 3, 1822.

8. U.S. Statutes at Large, 17th Congress, 1st session, 1822, vol. 13, p. 720.

9. "Nautical Intelligence," *Hunt's Merchants' Magazine and Commercial Review* (New York: George W. & John A. Wood, 1852), 27: 126-127, July 1852; ibid., 37:617, July 1857; Terance H. Nolan et. al., *Cultural Resource Survey of Key West* (Tallahassee, FL: Department of State, Division of Archives History and Records Management, Miscellaneous Project Report Series no. 48, 1979), p. 31.

10. Alligator Reef Light Station clipping file, 1857, Record Group 26, NA.

11. Ibid., 1869; ibid., 1869.

12. Ibid., 1870.

13. Ibid.

14. *Colonial Records of Spanish Florida*, 1570-1577, Publications of the Florida State Historical Society, No. 5 (Deland, FL, 1925) vol. 1, pp. 31-53; Bernard Romans, *A Concise History of East and West Florida* (New York: n.p., 1775); Reprint Floridiana Facsimile and Reprint Series (Gainesville: University of Florida Press, 1962), p. 292.

15. Peter Richard Jutro, "Lignumvitae Key" (Ph. D. dissertation, Cornell University, 1975), pp. 292-295, 321-322.

16. Ibid., pp. 105-106.

17. "Indian Key," prepared by Long Key State Recreation Area (Tallahassee: Florida Department of Natural Resources, Division of Recreation and Parks, 1984), pp. 58-64.

18. Jutro, "Lignumvitae Key," p. 138.

19. Alligator Reef Light Station clipping file, 1872.

20. Ibid., 1873.

21. Ibid.; Dorothy Dodd, "Wreck Ashore," *The Florida Handbook* (Tallahassee, FL: Peninsular Publishing Company, 1975-1976), p. 1.

22. Neil E. Hurley, *Keepers of Florida Lighthouses 1820-1939* (Alexandria, VA: Historic Lighthouse Publishers, 1990), p. 1; Journal of Light Station at Alligator Reef, 1874, Civil Reference Branch, Suitland Section, NA.

23. Journal of Light Station at Alligator Reef, 1876.

24. Ibid.

25. USDCL, *Annual Report,* 1894, pp. 240, 244.

26. Ibid, p. 222; ibid., 1906, pp. 167-168; ibid., 1907, p. 555; ibid., 1909, p. 645; USDC, *Annual Report,* 1913, p. 353; ibid., 1919, p. 749.

27. Journal of Light Station at Alligator Reef, 1935; Lighthouse File, MCPL/KW.

28. Francis Ross Holland Jr., *Great American Lighthouses* (Washington, D.C.: The Preservation Press, 1989), pp. 53-54.

29. USDC, *Annual Report,* 1939, p. 115; my interview with Dick Gooravin, Islamorada, FL, 1980.

30. Ibid.

31. Lighthouse File, MCPL/KW.

32. My interview with Chief Richard "Beau" Lewis, Seventh Coast Guard District, Aids to Navigation, Miami, Florida, January 6, 1998.

33. U.S. Department of Transportation, *U.S. Coast Guard, U.S. Atlantic and Gulf Coast Light List,* 1997 (Washington, D.C.: Government Printing Office, 1997), vol. 3, p. 11.

CHAPTER 9

1. Cape Florida Light Station clipping file, 1875, Record Group 26, NA; Betty Bruce, "Historical Notes Compiled from Lloyds of London, no. 2368" (unpublished) MCPL/KW; Lighthouse Records, Deeds on File, Record Group 26, NA.

2. "Abstract of Contract of Pusey Jones & Company for Fowey Rocks," Abstract of Lighthouse Contracts, vol. 2, 1877-1897, p. 1, Record Group 26, NA.

3. Fowey Rocks Light Station clipping file, 1876.

4. Ibid., 1877; Frederick A. Talbot, *Lightships and Lighthouses* (Philadelphia: J. B. Lippincott Co., 1913), pp. 202-203.

5. Ralph Middleton Munroe and Vincent Gilpin, *The Commodore's Story* (New York: Ives Washburn, 1930), p. 78.

6. Ibid., p. 79; Fowey Rocks Light Station clipping file, 1877.

7. Fowey Rocks Light Station clipping file, 1877; USDC, "Decription of Fowey Rocks Light Station, March 31, 1913," Record Group 26, NA.

8. Fowey Rocks Light Station clipping file, 1877, 1878; U.S. Statutes at Large, 44th Congress, 1st session, 1876, vol. 19, p. 3.

9. SDCL *Annual Report,* 1894, pp. 236, 240.

10. Journal of Light Station at Fowey Rocks, 1878, Civil Reference Branch, Suitland Section, NA.

11. Jefferson B. Browne, *Key West: The Old and the New* (Gainesville: University of Florida Press, a facsimile reproduction of the 1912 edition, 1973), p. xix.

12. Neil E. Hurley, *Keepers of Florida Lighthouses 1820-1939* (Alexandria, VA: Historic Lighthouse Publishers, 1990), pp. 22, 61-62, 137-142.

13. Thelma Peters, *Lemon City* (Miami: Banyan Books, 1976), pp. 118-119.

14. Irving R. Eyster, Islamorada, FL, letter to Wright Langley, director, Historic Florida Keys Preservation Board, Key West, April 4, 1991.

15. USDC *Annual Report*, 1913, p. 353; ibid., 1914, p. 535; ibid., 1915, p. 621; ibid., 1916, p. 681; ibid., 1920, p. 715.

16. My correspondence with Lieutenant Commander J.V. O'Shea, Assistant Chief, Aids to Navigation, Seventh Coast Guard District, Miami, FL, December 15, 1987.

17. PA2 Toni Long, "ATON Teams Tame Treacherous Waters," *Coastline* (Seventh Coast Guard District, Miami), August/September 1992, p. 6A.

18. Taylor Engineering, Inc., "Inspection and Site Investigation," September 1994. Report available at U.S. Coast Guard Aid to Navigation, Seventh District, Miami.

19. U.S. Department of Transportation, U.S. Coast Guard, *U.S. Atlantic and Gulf Coast Light List,* 1997, (Washington, D.C.: Government Printing Office, 1997), vol. 3, p. 9; my interview with Chief Richard "Beau" Lewis, Aids to Navigation Branch, Seventh Coast Guard District, January 6, 1998; Neil Hurley, Florida Lighthouse Web site: http://www.erols.com/lthouse/home.htm.

CHAPTER 10

1. American Shoal Light Station clipping file 1874, Record Group 26, NA.

2. John C. Holt, Key West, letter to the Atlantic Mutual Insurance Co., New York, February 17, 1845, Historical Association of South Florida Library, Miami, FL.

3. Mendel L. Peterson, *The Last Cruise of the HMS Loo* (Washington, D.C.: Smithsonian Institution, 1955), pp. 4, 13-14.

4. Ibid., pp. 23-27.

5. William Marvin, *A Treatise on the Law of Wreck and Salvage* (Boston: Little, Brown and Co., 1859), p. 215.

6. A. D. Bache, Superintendent, U.S. Coast Survey, Washington, D.C., report to W.M. Meredith, Secretary of the Treasury, Washington, D.C., May 16, 1850, Record Group 26, NA; "Nautical Intelligence," *Hunt's Merchants' Magazine and Commercial Review* (New York: George W. & John A. Wood, 1850), p. 116; ibid., 1852, pp. 126-127; ibid., 1857, p. 615.

7. Marvin, *A Treatise on the Law of Wreck and Salvage,* p. 218.

8. American Shoal Light Station clipping files, 1874, 1875, 1876.

9. U.S. Statutes at Large, 45th Congress, 2nd session, 1878, vol. 20, p. 214; "Abstract of Contract of Phoenix Iron Company for American Shoal Light," Abstract of Lighthouse Contracts, vol. 2, 1877-1897, p. 31, Record Group 26, NA.

10. American Shoals Light Station clipping files, 1878-1881; U.S. Statutes at Large, 45th Congress, 2nd session, 1879, vol. 20, p. 381.

11. USDC, *Description of American Shoal Light Station,* March 31, 1913, pp. 4-5, Record Group 26, NA.

12. Ibid., pp. 2-5; "The Lantern Room," *The Keeper's Log,* 1(1):15-17, 1984.

13. Neil E. Hurley, *Keepers of Florida Lighthouses 1820-1939* (Alexandria, VA: Historic Lighthouse Publishers, 1990), p. 11.

14. USDCL, Directions to Lightkeepers, Showing Them How to Perform Their Duties (Washington, D.C.: USDCL); "The Lantern Room," pp. 15-17.

15. USDCL *Annual Report*, 1911, p. 517; USDC *Annual Report,* 1913, p. 353; ibid., 1914, pp. 525, 562; ibid., 1915, p. 561; USDC, *Description of American Shoals Light Station,* March 31, 1913, pp. 5-6.

16. *Encyclopaedia Britannica* (Chicago, London, Toronto: Encyclopaedia Britannica, Inc., 1955), vol. 18, p. 905b; *Key West Citizen*, December 8, 1931, p. 2.

17. Patti Altland, "Wealth of History Is Found in Florida's Lighthouses," *The Key West Citizen,* May 26, 1964, Lighthouse File, MCPL/KW.

18. "U.S. Coast Guard, Off-shore Radar/Sight Evaluation," U.S. Coast Guard Key West Station, Key West.

19. My interview with Chief Warrant Officer Gregory Holman, U.S. Coast Guard, Key West, May 1982.

20. Ibid.

21. Lieutenant (j.g.) R.C. Eccles, report on file, U.S. Coast Guard, Key West.

22. Clipping File, "Coral Reefs and Islands—Florida," MCPL/I; "UM Begins Penance with $200,000," *Miami Herald,* August 20, 1994, Section B, p. 1; USDC, National Oceanic and Atmospheric Administration, *United States Coast Pilot* (Washington, D.C.: Government Printing Office, 1996), vol. 4, p. 239.

23. Department of Transportation, United States Coast Guard, 1997, *Special Notice to Mariners* (Miami: United States Coast Guard Seventh District), p. 18.

24. Department of Transportation, *U.S. Coast Guard, U.S. Atlantic and Gulf Coast Light List,* 1990 (Washington, D.C.: Government Printing Office, 1990), vol. 3, p. 9. The American Shoal Light flashes three times every fifteen seconds.

CHAPTER 11

1. The ship *Rebecca* wrecked on the shoal in 1856, but this may be a coincidence as the first documented mention of the name "Rebecca" Shoal appears in U.S. Statutes at Large, 29th Congress, 2nd session, 1847, vol. 9, p. 177. The shoal is also called "Rebecca" in U.S. Congress House, 30th Congress, 2nd session, 1848, House Executive Document 27, Serial 516; USDC, National Oceanic and Atmospheric Administration, *U.S. Atlantic Coast Pilot* (Washington, D.C.: NOAA, 1990), Vol. 5, p. 101.

2. National Oceanic and Atmospheric Administration, National Ocean Service, *U.S. Tide Tables, Atlantic Coast* (Washington, D.C.: NOAA, 1990), pp. 105-113.

3. Henry M. Stommel, *The Gulf Stream: A Physical and Dynamical Description* (Berkeley: University of California Press, 1965), pp. 68-69; Hans Leip, *The River in the Sea* (New York: Putnam, 1957), pp. 202, 209-210: "The amount of water normally flowing through the Straits of Florida between Havana and Key West would fill a hundred million baths every second . . . certain months the volume rises."

4. U.S. Statutes at Large, 29th Congress, 2nd session, 1847, vol. 9, p. 177; ibid., 32nd Congress, 2nd session, 1852, vol. 10, p. 117; ibid., 33rd Congress, 1st session, 1854, vol. 10, p. 341; Rebecca Shoal Light Station clipping file, 1854, Record Group 26, NA.

5. Rebecca Shoal Light Station clipping file, 1855.

6. Ibid.

7. U.S. Statutes at Large, 34th Congress, 1st session, 1856, vol. 11, p. 99; Rebecca Shoal Light Station clipping files, 1857, 1858.

8. George Meade, *Life and Letters of George Gordon Meade* (New York: Charles Scribner and Sons, 1913), vol. 1, p. 289.

9. Rebecca Shoal Light Station clipping files, 1873.

10. Ibid., 1874-1878.

11. Ibid.; U.S. Statutes at Large, 48th Congress, 1st session, 1884, vol. 23, p. 197.

12. Rebecca Shoal Light Station clipping files, 1877-1886.

13. Ibid., 1877-1886.

14. Ibid., 1887-1888; Neil E. Hurley, *Keepers of Florida Lighthouses 1820-1939* (Alexandria, VA: Historic Lighthouse Publishers, 1990), p. 91.

15. Rebecca Shoal Light Station clipping file, 1888; Hurley, *Keepers of Florida Lighthouses,* pp. 91-92.

16. Ibid.

17. Light House Board, Correspondence, 1901-1910, Record Group 26, NA.

18. Ibid., USDC, *Annual Report,* 1918, p. 682.

19. Hurley, *Keepers of Florida Lighthouses,* p. 92-93; USDCL, *Annual Report,* 1904, pp. 222-225.

20. USDCL, *Annual Report,* 1904, p. 223; ibid., 1905, p. 193; ibid., 1908, p. 633.

21. Light House Board, Correspondence, 1901-1910.

22. Ibid.

23. Superintendent of Documents, number c 9.38/1:19; USDC, *Annual Report,* 1914, p. 535; ibid., 1915, p. 621.

24. Neil E. Hurley, Web site: http://www.erols.com/lthouse/home.htm.

25. Memorandum from C.W. Harwood, Operations Planning Officer, December 1, 1944, no. 5750, USCG, Washington, D.C.

26. Department of Transportation, U.S. Coast Guard, *U.S. Atlantic and Gulf Coast Light List*, 1985 (Washington, D.C.: Government Printing Office, 1985), vol. 2, p. 12; 1988, vol. 3, p. 13; 1991, vol. 3, p. 10; 1997, vol. 3, p. 11; *U.S. Atlantic Coast Pilot,* 1989, vol. 5, p. 101; 1997, vol. 5, p. 141; my correspondence with Captain R.D. Peterson, Chief, Aids to Navigation Branch, Seventh Coast Guard District, July 1991. My interview with Chief Charlie Pantelaos, ANT, Key West, January 8 and 12, 1998.

INDEX

Acetylene, 62, 63, 65, 93, 175, 177, 266, 268
Admiralty Court, Key West, 25, 26, 31, 41, 72,
   107, 129 (*see also* U.S. District Court,
   Southern District of Florida)
Agassiz, Louis, 157
Aids to Navigation (ATON), 99, 100, 123–24, 125,
   154, 199, 219, 232, 233, 235, 252–53, 266–67
   (*see also* U.S. Coast Guard)
Aids to Navigation Team (ANT), 98, 99, 100, 121,
   124–25, 154, 196, 198, 199, 219, 233, 249, 267
   (*see also* U.S. Coast Guard)
Ajax Reef, Miami, Florida, 41 (*see also* Vessels)
Akin, Lemuel S., Captain, 79
Alemán, José, 44
Alibama, 34
Allen, William Howard, Lieutenant, U.S. Navy,
   203–5
Allentown (Key West, Florida), 205 (*see also*
   Allen, William Howard; Vessels, *Alligator*)
Alligator Reef, 205, 206, 207, 210, 219, 241 (*see also*
   Lighthouses; Vessels)
American Coast Pilot, 80, 166 (*see also Atlantic Coast
   Pilot*)
America(n), 15, 22 (*see also* United States)
   colonies, 15, 16
   Revolution, 16
American Shoal, Florida Reefs, 238, 239, 240, 242,
   249 (*see also* Lighthouses)
American Revolution, 16, 30
Appleby, Eliza, 106, 108 (*see also* Lighthouse
   keepers: Appleby, Joshua)
Argand, Ami, 116 (*see also* Argand lamp)
Argand lamp, 79, 116 (*see also* Lewis, Winslow)
Army of the Potomac, 258 (*see also* Meade, George
   Gordon)
Association of the American Institute of
   Architects, 165
Atland, Patti, 249 (*see also Key West Citizen*)
Atlantic, 13, 31
   coast, 256

Ocean, 49, 74, 155, 252, 255, 256
Atlantic Coast Pilot, 179, 180
Atwater-Kent (*see* Radio)
Audubon, John James, 78
Automation, 63, 66, 121, 153, 154, 178, 198, 219,
   232, 234, 249, 251, 266, 268

Babcock, (?), Chief Engineer, Light House
   Department, 193
Bache, Hartmann, Major, U.S. Corps of
   Topographical Engineers, 20 (*see also*
   Lighthouses: Brandywine Shoal)
Bache, Richard, 140 (*see also* Meade, George
   Gordon)
Baggs, Bill, 44
Bahamas, 21, 22, 25, 127, 135, 189, 238, 244
   channel, 21
   Nassau, 49
   New Providence, 22, 23, 24, 49
Baker, Charles S., Captain, 148
Baker, George, Captain, 82 (*see also* Lighthouses:
   Garden Key)
Baldwin, John T., Superintendent of Lights
   (1853–1861), 172
Beacon, 25, 174, 206, 211, 215, 237, 239, 240, 259
   (*see also* Radio beacon)
   radar (RACONS), 125, 253
   Rebecca Shoal day beacon, **254**, 256, 257–58,
      259, **260**, 267
   rotating beacon, 199, 267 (*see also* Directional
      Code Beacon, DCB; Vega Rotating Beacon,
      VRB)
   temporary, **123**, 124
Bethel, William H., Captain (wife, Mary), 211 (*see
   also* Indian Key)
Bicentennial Lighthouse Fund (1989), 65
Big Pine Key, Florida, 210 (*see also* Looe Key)
Bill Baggs Cape Florida State Recreational Park,
   44, 47 (*see also* Baggs, Bill; Lighthouses: Cape
   Florida)

Biscayne Bay, Florida, 47, 131, 133, 155, 210
Biscayne National Park, 44, 252
"Black List," **242** (*see also* Wreckers; Wrecking, license; Vessels)
Blunt, Edmund M. (*see American Coast Pilot*)
Blunt, G. W. (*see American Coast Pilot*)
Boston, Massachusetts, 40, 51, 111 (*see also* Lighthouses: Boston; Minot's Ledge)
  harbor, 15–16, 19
Brannan, James M., Captain, U.S. Army, 56–57 (*see also* Civil War)
Brick construction, 272n; Cape Florida, 38, 39, 44, 221; Fort Jefferson, 82; Garden Key, 77, 83; Key West, 51, 52, 64–65; Loggerhead Key, 84, 85, 91, 92, 95, 96, 102; Sand Key, 103–4
Britain (*see* Great Britain)
Brookfield, Charles, 129–31, 151–53, 158
Browne, Jefferson B., Superintendent of Lights (1893–1897), 56, 57, **228**, 229 (*see also* Lighthouse keepers)
Budd, Thomas S., Captain, 82
Bureau of Lighthouses, 44, 63, 68, 175, 178, 232, 245
  Annual Report, 215
Burns, Haydon, Governor, 44
Bush, George, President of the United States, 155

Calusa Indians, 207, 209, 210
Cape Canaveral, Florida, 30 (*see also* Lighthouses)
Cape Florida, Florida, 24, 25, 34, 49, 50, 76–77, 129, 237, 267 (*see also* Lighthouses)
Cape Hatteras, North Carolina, 136
Cape Sable, Florida, 24, 31, 134, 237
Carnegie Institute, 93
  biological laboratories, 102
Caribbean, 20, 24
  Monk Seal, 74
Carysfort Marine Laboratory (CML), 161–62
Carysfort Reef (Carysford), Key Largo, Florida, 21, 25, 29, 127, 129, **130**, 131, 132, 135–36, 138, 139, 150, 153, 155, 201, 210, 213 (*see also* Lighthouses; Vessels: *Winchester*, TMS)
Catoptric apparatus, 141 (*see also* Fresnel lens; Reflectors)
Cayo Hueso (*see* Key West)
Cayo Sombrero (*see* Sombrero Key)
Characteristic (*see* Lighthouse characteristic; Revolving light)
Charleston, South Carolina, 135, 136
Charlotte Bay, Florida, 24
Chase, Wiliam H., Captain, U.S. Army Corps of Engineers, 80
Cipra, David L., Chief Boatswain Mate, USCG, 120–21
Cistern, 44, 55, 59, 85–86, 94, 105
Civil War, 42, 56, 87, 189–90, 207, 258
Coffin's Patches, 185–86, 187 (*see also* Lighthouses: Sombrero Reef)
Cohasset, Massachuetts, 19 (*see also* Lighthouses: Minot's Ledge)

Collector of customs, 29, 51, 52 (*see also* Superintendents of Lights)
Combs, Bob, Deputy Sheriff, 217
Commerce Department (*see* U.S. Department of Commerce)
Confederate soldiers, 30–31 (*see also* Civil War)
Confederacy, 56, 57 (*see also* Civil War)
Congress (*see* U.S. Congress)
Cohasset, Massachuetts, 19 (*see also* Minot's Ledge)
Conrad, Mary, 230–31
Cooley, William, 33–34, 133 (*see also* Lighthouse keepers)
Cook, Maggi, 46 (*see also* Dade Heritage Trust)
Coontihatchee, 33–34 (*see also* New River; Cooley, William)
Coral reefs, 13, 21, 24, 77, 78, 83, 107, 110, 155, 157, 199, 211, 212, 241, 252 (*see also* Reefs)
Cottrell, Jeremiah, Captain, Northwest Passage Lightship, 167–68
Crawl Key, Florida Reefs, 186 (*see also* Lighthouses: Sombrero Key)
Crocker Reef, Florida reefs (*see* Lighthouses: Alligator Reef)
Cuba, 21, 49, 74, 76, 77, 135, 167, 169 (*see also* Lighthouses: Morro)
  Havana, 13, 22, 108, 135, 230, 238
  Mariel, 250, 252
  Matanzas, 201, 203
Cudjoe Key, Florida Keys, 249 (*see also* Lighthouses: American Shoal)
Custom house (*see* Lighthouse Depot)

Dade County, 47, 210 (*see also* Indian Key)
Dade, Francis L., Captain, U.S. Army, 210
Dade Heritage Trust, 45, 46
Dale, John M., Lieutenant, U.S. Navy, 201, 203, 205 (*see also* Vessels: *Alligator*, USS)
Dallas, Alexander J., Esq., Commander, U.S. Navy, 37 (*see also* Lighthouses: Cape Florida)
Dearborn, (?), Collector of Customs, Boston, Massachusetts, 38
De Boer, Jennie, 63 (*see also* Lighthouses: Key West; Lighthouse keepers: Bethel, Mary Elizabeth, and Bethel, William A.)
de León, Ponce, 21, 74
Demeritt, William W., 63–64, **66**, 177, 179
Denison, Silas, 71, 72, 73
Dennison, William C., 111 (*see also* Lighthouses: Sand Key)
Dibrell, W. C., lighthouse inspector, 174, 175, 178
Directional Code Beacon (DCB, rotating optic), 98, 99, 100
Directions to Lightkeepers, 244–45 (*see also* Keepers' duties)
Disk-pile, 186, 212, 223, 260 (*see also* Iron pile lighthouse; Lighthouses: Alligator Reef, Carysfort Reef, Fowey Rocks, Rebecca Shoal, Sombrero Key)
Doharty, C. J., 118–19 (*see also* Sand Key Weather Station)

Douglass, Samuel J., Superintendent of Lights (1849–1853), 170, 171
Drake, Francis William, Captain, 221 (*see also* Vessels: *Fowey*, HMS)
Dry Bank, Florida Reefs, 186 (*see also* Sombrero Key)
Dry Tortugas, Florida Keys, 24, 25, 29, 31, 50, 71, 74, 76, 77, 78, 82, 93, 99, 129, 155, 167, 189, 237, 252, 257, 259, 267 (*see also* Lighthouses: Dry Tortugas Harbor Light, Garden Key; Loggerhead Key)
    islands of, Bird Key, 75; Bush Key, 75, 88; East Key, 71, 74, 75; Garden Key, 75, 77, 78, 79, 80, 82, 88, 90, 91, 93, 99; Hospital Key (Sand Key), 75; Loggerhead Key, 75, 79, 82, 88, 93, 99, 102; Long Key, 75, 80; Middle Key, 75; North Key, 75; Northeast Key, 75; Southwest Key, 75, 76
    map, **72**
    National Park, 95, 99, 101 (*see also* Lighthouses: Loggerhead)
Duck Key, Florida Keys, 187, 218
Dutcher, William, 119–20
Dutton, George, Captain, U.S. Army Corps of Engineers, 80

Easby, George Gordon Meade, **162**
East Florida Herald, 25
Eccles, R. C., Lieutenant, USCG, 252
Ecclesiastical Lights, 15
Edison, Thomas, 64
Eighth Lighthouse District, 263, 264 (*see also* U.S. Coast Guard)
Electricity, 62, 94, 232, 266 (*see also* Solar power)
Elliot Key, 209, 230 (*see also* Biscayne Bay)
Emancipation Proclamation, 84 (*see also* Slaves)
England, 15, 17, 20, 22, 185, 244 (*see also* Trinity House; Great Britain)
English, 15 (*see also* England)
Europe, 16, 19, 21, 137, 238, 254, 258
Fahrer, Alison, 157–58
Fairmont Park, Philadelphia, 258 (*see also* Meade, George Gordon)
Fiveash, John W., 107 (*see also* Lighthouse keepers: Appleby, Joshua)
Flash tube array, 121, 199, 232, 233
Florida Current (*see* Gulf Stream)
Florida Department of Environmental Protection, Division of Recreation and Parks, 47
Florida Herald, The, Saint Augustine, 105, 206
Florida Keys, 13, 17, 18, 20–22, 23, 31, 74, 157, 237, 240, 244, 250, 253, 258, 265
Florida Keys National Marine Sanctuary, 125, 155, 252
Florida Legislative Council, 24–25
Florida Lighthouse Association, Inc. (*see* Hurley, Neil)
Florida reefs, 39, 49, 88, 107, 129, 140, 156, 184, 185, 201, 221, 236, 237, 239, 258
Florida Supreme Court, 149, 229
Florida State Parks Department, 45

Florida Straits, 22, 23, 49, 50, 73, 82, 109, 135, 156, 189, 238, 250, 256, 267, 292n
Florida Territorial Legislature, 50, 210
Floridian, Pensacola, The, 106–7
Forrester, Mary, 106 (*see also* Lighthouse keepers: Appleby, Joshua)
Fort Jefferson, Garden Key, Dry Tortugas, Florida, 82, 83, 84, 87, 88, 90, **93**, 101, 257
    National Monument, 72, 100
Fort Zachary Taylor, Key West, Florida, 56, 65
47th Regiment of Pennsylvania Veteran Volunteers, 88 (*see also* Fort Jefferson)
Fowey Rocks, Florida reefs, 29, 42, 225, 230, 237, 241 (*see also* Lighthouses; Miami, Florida)
France, 137, 185
Freeman, (?), Captain, U.S. Marines, 204
French Reef, Florida Reefs, 215
Fresnel, Augustine Jean, 20, 137
Fresnel lens, 20, 79, 80, 81, 82, 136, 137, 138, 244, **246**; Alligator Reef, 214, 215; American Shoal, 241, 243, 253; Cape Florida, 39, 40, 44, 56; Carysfort Reef, 141–42, 145, 152, 154, **162**; Fowey Rocks, 227, **231**, 232–33; Garden Key, 84; Loggerhead Key, 84, 85, 92, 94–95, 98, **99**; Northwest Passage, 172, 173, **176**, **178**; Sand Key, 112, **113**, 114, 115, 121; Sombrero Key, 188, **192**, 196, 198, 199 (*see also* catoptric apparatus)
Fuller, (?), Captain, 230–31

Gallatin, Albert, Secretary of the Treasury, 68, 136
Garden Cove, 133–34 (*see also* Lighthouses: Carysfort Reef; Whalton, John)
Garden Key, 25, 82, 83 (*see also* Lighthouses: Dry Tortugas)
Gardner, Charles E., Captain, *Pacific*, 71, 73, 74
Gardner, J. H., 59 (*see also* Lighthouses: Key West)
Gauld, George, 75, 103, 186
Gedney, (?), Lieutenant, U.S. Navy, 80
Gettysburg, Virginia, 258
GPS (Global Positioning System), 155
Gordon, Adam, Superintendent of Lights (1838–1845), 80, 108, 168, 169
Great Britain, 15, 16, 184 (*see also* England)
Gulf of Mexico, 23, 71, 74, 76, 82, 155, 166, 205, 252, 255–56
Gulf Stream, 13, 21, 22, 23, 74, 143, 198, 199, 206, 211, 217, 239

Hackley, William Randolph, 105
Half Moon Shoal, Florida Reefs, 255, 267 (*see also* Rebecca Shoal)
Haiti, 131
Halley, Robert, 155–56, 159, 161
Halley's comet, 118–19 (*see also* Sand Key Weather Station)
Hamilton, Alexander, Secretary of the Treasury, 17, 68
Hartsterne, H. J., Lieutenant, 40

Harbor, 15, 16, 17, 19, 23, 24, 30, 39, 50, 52, 53, 66, 77, 78, 80, 83, 87, 91, 103, 109

Harris, J. V., Superintendent of Lights (1885–1889), 261

Harris, Mary Ann Perry, 108

Harwood, C. W., 266

Haskins, Henry B., lighthouse inspector, 174

Hawk Channel, Florida Keys, 150, 190, 215

Heler, Thomas J., Captain, 40

Hemingway, Ernest, 166

Henley, Peyton, 201, 203

Henry Lepaute, Paris, France, 92, 143, 188, 192, 227, 241 (*see also* Fresnel lens)

Hillsboro Inlet, Florida, 34

Historical Association of Southern Florida Museum, Miami, Florida, 154

Holman, Gregory, Chief Warrant Officer, USCG, 250

Homestead, Florida, 198, 218

Hood, J., lighthouse inspector, 264–65

Hopner, Charles, 107 (*see also* Lighthouse keepers: Appleby, Joshua)

Horr, John F., Superintendent of Lights (1889–1893), 61

House of Representatives' executive documents, 54–55

Housman, Jacob, 209–11 (*see also* Indian Key)

Howe, Charles, Superintendent of Lights (1861–1869), 42, 172

Hoyt, John C., 110–11, 237–38 (*see also* Insurance)

Hubbard, John, 149

Humphries, Noah, 38–39

Hunt's Merchant Magazine, 85, 170, 189, 239–40

Hurley, Neil E., 235, 265

Hurricanes, 169; 1835: 53–54; 1841: 53, 108; 1842: 53, 80, 108, 109; 1844: 108, 109, 169; 1846: 29, 53, 81, 108–9, 170; 1856: 113, 187; 1865: 113, 172; 1870: 114; 1873: 89, 96, 258; 1875: 91; 1878: 227–28; 1906: 265; 1909: 62, 118, 174; 1910: 63, 119; 1927: 245; 1935: 153, 215, 218; 1960: 198, 218–19; 1965: 219; 1992: 45, 47, 233

Hutcheson, (?), Sergeant (*see* 47th Regiment of Pennsylvania Veteran Volunteers)

Hydraulic lamp (*see* Lamps)

I. P. Morris and Company, Philadelphia, 187 (*see also* Iron pile lighthouses; Lighthouses: Sombrero Key)

Incandescent oil vapor (i.o.v.), 62, 92, 93, 94, 152, 174, 178, 195, 197, 215, 232, 245, 265

Indian Key, Florida, 33, 34, 133, 134–35, 207, 209, 210, 211, 213

Indian River, Florida, 30

Indians, 33–34, 35, 35–37, 133, 134, 207, 210 (*see also* Culusa Indians; Seminole War)

Insurance, 137, 237–38 (*see also* Holt, John)

Iron pile lighthouse, 17, 18, 19–20, 42, 110, 111, 122, 126, 127, 128, 138, 144, 184–85, 187, 206, 212, 221, 223, 240, 244, 249, 260, 263, 265, 268 (*see also* Beacon: Rebecca Shoal day beacon; Lighthouses: Alligator Reef, American

Shoal, Carysfort Reef, Fowey Rocks, Minot Ledge, Sand Key, Sombrero Key; Screwpile lighthouse)

Isaac Shoal, Florida Reefs, 255, 267 (*see also* Rebecca Shoal)

Isaac Well & Company, 131–32 (*see also* Lightships, *Caesar*)

Islamorada, Florida Keys, 217, 218 (*see also* Matecumbe Key)

Islas de los Martires (Martyr Islands) (*see* Florida Keys)

J. V. Merrick and Son, 110 (*see also* Lantern: Sand Key)

Jones, J. W., 257 (*see also* Beacon: Rebecca Shoal day beacon)

James, James W., 111 (*see also* Lighthouses: Sand Key)

Jenkins, T. A., Lieutenant, U.S. Navy, 83 (*see also* Light House Board)

Jacksonville, Florida, 30 (*see also* Lighthouses)

Jamaica, 77, 213

Jefferys, Thomas, 127 (*see also* Carysfort Reef)

John F. Riley Iron Works, 110 (*see also* Iron pile lighthouse; Lighthouses: Sand Key)

John Pennekamp Coral Reef State Park, 155

Johnson, Charles, Captain, 25

Jupiter Inlet, Florida, 134 (*see also* Lighthouses)

Keepers' duties, 56, 190, 218, 244, 247, 283n

Keepers' house/quarters, Alligator Reef, 215, 217; American Shoal, 236, 241, 249–50; Cape Florida, 43, 44, 45, 46; Carysfort, 126; Fowey Rocks, 222, 225, 226, 228; Garden Key, 82, 83, 89, 93, 98; Key West, 51, 55, 59, 63–64, 66; Loggerhead Key, 85, 86, 92, 94, 100; Minot's Ledge, 17, 19; Northwest Passage, 171, 172–73; Rebecca Shoal, 261; Sand Key, 105, 108, 109, 111, 114, 115–16, 117, 121, 122, 125, 126; Sombrero Key, 187–88

Keepers' salaries, 39, 55, 87, 112, 150–51, 174, 227, 244

Kennedy, (?), Captain, 193

Kerosene (mineral oil), 61, 62, 118, 148, 152, 173, 245 (*see also* Incandescent oil vapor)

Key Biscayne (*see* Biscayne Bay)

Key Largo, Florida, 20, 76, 127, 129, 133, 149, 163, 209 (*see also* Lighthouses: Carysfort Reef)

Key Vaca (Vaca Key), Florida, 106, 107 (*see also* Lighthouse keepers: Appleby, Joshua; Lighthouses: Sombrero)

Key West, Florida, 20, 22, 23–24, 25, 29, 33, 34, 38, 41, 42, 49, 50, 51, 52, 54, 71, 76, 77, 78, 81, 84, 87–88, 103, 105, 106, 107, 108, 110, 114, 117, 118, 129, 131, 133, 134, 135, 149, 150, 152, 165, 166–67, 171, 183, 185, 189, 190, 194, 205, 206, 208, 209, 210, 219, 230, 239, 240, 243, 255, 256, 259, 266 (*see also* Lighthouse Depot)
harbor, 23, 24, 103
Art and Historical Society, 64

Key West, Florida (*cont.*)
  Lighthouse Museum, 65, 192, 196, 198 (*see also*
    Lighthouses: Key West)
  Key West Citizen, 62, 249, 266
  Key West Inquirer, 34, 79
  Key West Journal, The, 118
Kitchen (building),
  Cape Florida, 35, 44, 46; Key West, 55, 59, 61;
    Loggerhead, 83, 85–86, 88, **92**, 94, 100, 108

L. Sautter & Company, Paris, France, 85 (*see also*
    Fresnel lens; Lighthouses: Loggerhead Key)
Lamps, 40, 52, 55, 77, 80, 81, 105, **116**, 148, 152,
    228; carcel, 112; hydraulic, 112, **113**, 114, 145;
    French, 112; solar powered, 124, 199; spider,
    136; whale oil, 17 (*see also* Flash tube array;
    Reflectors)
Lantern, 19, 31, 36, 244, **247**, **248**; Alligator Reef,
    214, 218; American Shoal, 243, 253; Cape
    Florida, 45; Carysfort, 141, 146; Fowey
    Rocks, **226**, 226–27, 228, 233; Garden Key,
    80, 81, 83, 84, 89; Key West, 52, 55, 59, 61–62;
    Loggerhead Key, 85, **90**, 91; Northwest
    Passage, 171, 172, 173; Rebecca Shoal, 261;
    Sand Key, 105, 108, 111–12, **113**, 118, **191**
Leba, Theodore, Jr., 29
Lee, Robert E., General, 258
Leib, Thomas J., Lieutenant, U.S. Navy, 37–38
    (*see also* Lighthouses: Cape Florida)
Lewis, I. W. P., 110, 123, 126, 138, 144
Lewis, Richard "Beau," Chief Warrant Officer,
    ATON, 199, 219
Lewis, Winslow, 79, 136, 137–38, 144
Light House Board, 29, 30–31, 39–40, 41, 42, 44,
    56, 57, 59, 61, 62, 64, 68, 82, 83, 84, 85, 87, 88,
    90, 91, 92, 93, 94, 110, 111, 112, 114, 115, 118,
    138, 140, 141–42, 143, 144, 146, 149, 166, 170,
    171, 172, 173, 184, 185, 187, 188, 189, 190,
    195, 202, 206, 207, 211, 212, 214, 221, 222,
    227, 237, 240, 241, 244, 256, 257, 259, 261,
    262, 264, 265
  Annual Report, 212, 278n
Light List, 138
Light stations (*see* Lighthouses)
  journals, 146, 147, 148, 150, 195, 197, 213, 214,
    215, **216**, 217, 227–28
  watch records, 146, 159
Light tower, **248**; Boston, 16; Cape Florida, 36, 38,
    39, 44, 45, **46**, 221; Fowey Rocks, **222**, 225–26;
    Jupiter Inlet, 30; Key West, 51, 52, 55, 61, 64;
    Garden Key, 71, 77, 80, 82, 83, 84, 90, 91;
    Loggerhead Key, 88, 89, 90–91, **95**; Sand
    Key, 105, 107, 115, 116; Sombrero Key, 188
    (*see also* Lighthouses)
Lightboats (*see* Lightships)
Lighthouse characteristic, 17; Alligator Reef, 212,
    219–20; American Shoal, 241, 245, 291n;
    Carysfort Reef, 142, 145, 149–50, 153, 154;
    Fowey Rocks, 235; Key West, 55, 63;
    Loggerhead Key, 85, 92, 98, 100; Northwest
    Passage, 173, 174, 175, 179; Rebecca Shoal,

262, 266–67; Sand Key, 105, 112, 118, 124;
    Sombrero Key, 188, 199 (*see also* Beacon;
    Optics; Revolving light)
Lighthouse Depot, 23, 24, 50
  Key West, Florida, 63, 240
  Staten Island, New York, 44, 87, 118, 141, 148
Lighthouse illumination (*see* Directional Code
    Beacon, DCB, rotating optic; electricity;
    Flash tube array; incandescent oil vapor
    (i.o.v.); kerosene (mineral oil); lamps;
    reflectors; Vega Rotating Beacon; whale oil)
Lighthouse keepers, 142, 247 (including U.S.
    Coast Guardsmen)
  Anderson, Frederick, Key West, 57
  Appleby, Joshua, Sand Key, 106–9
  Archer, William, Fowey Rocks, 230
  Archer, William, Jr., American Shoal, 230
  Baker, Alonzo, Rebecca Shoal, 266
  Baldwin, Harry, Carysfort Reef, 152
  Bates, William, American Shoal, 244; Garden
    Key, 193, 244; Sand Key, 193, 244; Sombrero
    Key, 193, 244
  Bell, Edward, Carysfort Reef, 142, 143, 145–48;
    Key West, 146; Sand Key, 146; Sombrero
    Key, 146
  Berghill, Alfred A., Rebecca Shoal, 263
  Berry, Charles B., Sand Key, 112
  Bethel, Joseph, Garden Key (wife, Nicolosa, née
    Mabrity), 57; Sombrero Key, 57, 60, 189, 190,
    194
  Bethel, Mary Elizabeth, Key West, 57, 59–60,
    62, 63, **65**
  Bethel, Merril A., Key West, 63
  Bethel, William A. (wife, Mary Elizabeth, née
    Mabrity), **60**; Alligator Reef, 59, 213; Dry
    Tortugas, 59; Key West, 57, 59–60, 61, 62–63
    (*see also* Whalton, Stephen F.); Pensacola, 59;
    Northwest Passage, 59
  Billberry (Billborg), George R., Jr. (wife,
    Sarrah), Alligator Reef, 92, 213–14;
    Loggerhead Key, 92; Northwest Passage, 92;
    Sand Key, 92; Sombrero Key, 92
  Bowman, Charles, Sand Key, 112
  Brightman, Latham, Sand Key, 112
  Brooks, Clement, Carysfort Reef, 151–52, **156**
  Brost, F. A., Alligator Reef, 148; Carysfort
    Reef, 148
  Browne, Jefferson B., Fowey Rocks, 228–29
  Butts, Joseph, Sombrero Key, 194
  Carey, Oratio C., Northwest Passage, 174
  Carroll, John J., Key West (wife, Mary
    Armanda, née Mabrity), 57, 59
  Carroll, Mary Armanda Fletcher, Key West,
    57, 59
  Carter, Aaron, Cape Florida, 33, 35–36, 37
  Cassidy, Thomas, Sombrero Key, 194
  Cooley, William, Cape Florida, 34–35
  DeCourcy, Fredrick, Sombrero Key, 194
  Dubose, John, Cape Florida, 33, 35
  Duke, Reason, Cape Florida, 39
  Eickhoff, Michael, Sombrero Key, 195

Fabal, Miguel, Sombrero Key, 195
Flaherty, John R., Garden Key, 77; Sand Key, 105
Flaherty, Rebecca, Garden Key, 77; Sand Key, 105–6
Franklin, Thomas A., Alligator Reef, 213
Frow, John W. (wife, Adelaida), Cape Florida, 42, 227, 229; Fowey Rocks, 44, 227, 229
Frow, Joseph, Cape Florida, 42, 229
Frow, Simeon, Cape Florida, 42; Fowey Rocks, 44, 229
Gage (Gaze), Mark, Carysfort Reef, 261; Fowey Rocks, 261; Rebecca Shoal, 261
Gibson, George H., Northwest Passage, 174
Glover, Edward, Garden Key, 78
Gooravin, Dick, USCG, Alligator Reef, 217, 218
Hall, (?), Carysfort Reef, **158**
Halseman, Edwin, Key West, 56
Harris, William Hunt, Carysfort Reef, 149; Northwest Passage, 149
Himmenez, Joseph, Garden Key, 105; Sand Key, 105
Hudson, Edward, Sand Key, 112
Jefferson, (?), Sombrero Key, 194
Jenks, "Captain," Carysfort Reef, 152, 153, **158**
Johnson, Charles G., Sand Key, 119–20
Johnson, Charles M., Carysfort Reef, 141, 153, 163
Johnson, Henry, American Shoal, 244; Sombrero, 244
Kelly, T. L., Rebecca Shoal, 265
Kelly, Thomas M. (wife, Kathleen), Rebecca Shoal, 265; Sand Key, 120
Kerr, Benjamin (wife, Henriette), Garden Key, 87; Loggerhead Key, 87
Keys, Henry A., Rebecca Shoal, 263
Lightbourn, James P., Loggerhead Key, 87
Lopez, John M., Northwest Passage, 178
Lowe, John E., Rebecca Shoal, 261
Lowe, Samuel, Sombrero Key, 194–95
Mabrity, Barbara Traccioli, Key West, 52–53, 54, 55, 57, 189, 282n
Mabrity, Michael, Key West, 52, 57, 189, 282n
Magill, Harry Warner, Carysfort Reef, 147–48; Garden Key, 148
Magill, Harry, Mrs., Carysfort Reef, 147–48; Garden Key, 148
McNutley, Francis, American Shoal, 150; Carysfort Reef, 150; Rebecca Shoal, 150, 261
Moore, Robert J., Fowey Rocks, 266; Rebecca Shoal, 266
Palmer, Richard, Fowey Rocks, 232
Parker, Willis, USCG, Sombrero Key, 197–98
Pervis, Jones A., Alligator Reef, 215
Peterson, John, 232; Northwest Passage, 177, 178; Rebecca Shoal, 263, 265
Pierce, "Captain," Carysfort Reef, 151
Reike, Rudolph, Carysfort Reef, 194; Sombrero Key, 194–95
Richards, Richard C., Alligator Reef, 215

Richardson, Dudley, Alligator Reef, 244; American Shoal, 244
Richardson, George, Rebecca Shoal, 261
Richardson, William, Key West, 56; Northwest Passage, 172
Roberts, J. P., Jr., Rebecca Shoal, 265
Russell, Charles, Cape Florida, 42
Salas, Charles E., Cape Florida, 42
Saunders, Robert H., Sombrero Key, 190
Seymour, Adolphus, Sombrero Key, 190, 194
Seymour, Hiram S., Sombrero Key, 190
Shanahan, Henry, Key West, 60, 63
Solomon, William, Garden Key, 87
Thompson, John W., Cape Florida, 33, 35–38; Garden Key, 79
Thompson, Robert H. (wife, Julia), Fowey Rocks, 229
Turner, C., Alligator Reef, 266; Rebecca Shoal, 266
Walker, James R., (wife, Maria), Rebecca Shoal, 263
Watkins, John, Sombrero, 197
Warner, L. C., Carysfort Reef, 146–47
Weatherford, Henry P., Fowey Rocks, 230, 232
Weatherford, Martin, Alligator Reef, 195; Carysfort Reef, 148–49; Sombrero Key, 195
White, Richard, Sombrero Key, 190, 193
Williamson, Furman, USCG, Sombrero Key, 197–98
Wilson, George S., Rebecca Shoal, 263; Sombrero Key, 195, 263
Lighthouse libraries, 149, **154**, 246
Lighthouse Service, 19, 55–56, 64, 81, 82, 84, 94, 110, 120, 150, 167, 229, 246, 263, 267 (*see also* Light House Board; U.S. Coast Guard)
history, **68**
Lighthouse tenders
Activa, 87; *Alice*, 147; *Arbutus*, 214–15, 263–64, 265; *Fern*, 118; *Hudson*, 124; *Ivy*, 246, 264; *Magnolia*, 177; *Mangrove*, 215; *Sundew*, 266; "Supply Boat to Sand Key Lighthouse," **106**
Lighthouses, 133 (*see also* Light towers)
Alligator Reef (off Upper Matecumbe Key, Florida), **cp 5**, 31, **202**, 206, 208, 210, 211–12, 214, 215, 217, 219, 246, 250
American Shoal (off Big Pine Key, Florida), **cp 7, cp 12**, 31, **236**, 237, 241, 243–44, 245, 246, 249, 250, **251**, 252, 253, 259, 291n
Bell Rock (Scotland), 184
Boston (Little Brewster Island, Massachusetts), 15, **16**
Brandywine Shoal (Delaware Bay), 20
Cape Canaveral (Florida), 30, 31
Cape Florida (Biscayne Bay, Florida), **cp 2, cp 3**, 31, **32**, 33–35, **35**, 38–47, **43**, 45, **46**, 57, 76, 105, 133, 141, 189, 206, 221, 267
Carysfort Reef (off Key Largo, Florida Keys), **cp 4**, 20, 31, 57, 88, 111, **126**, 127, **128**, 140–42, **144**, 146, 149, 152, 153, 155, 157, **159, 160**, 161, **162**, 184, 185, 186, 188, 189, 193, 206, 214, 219, 241, 246, 256, 258, 281n

Charleston (Morris Island, South Carolina), 30
Coffins Patches (*see* Lighthouses: Sombrero Key)
Dry Bank (*see* Lighthouses: Sombrero Key)
Dry Tortugas (*see* Lighthouses: Garden Key,
    Dry Tortugas Harbor Light, and
    Loggerhead Key)
Dry Tortugas Harbor Light, 93–94, **97**, **98**, **100**
    (*see also* Lighthouses: Garden Key)
Fowey Rocks (off Miami, Florida), **cp 1**, 31, 44,
    148, 161, 153, 219, 221, **222**, **224**, 227, 228,
    233, **234**, 235, 237, 240
Garden Key (Dry Tortugas, Florida Keys), **cp**
    9, 38, 57, 73, 78, 80, 81, 82, 83, 91, 105, 109,
    189, 193
Hooks Point Lighthouse, Waterford, Ireland,
    15
Jupiter Inlet (Florida), 30–31, 206
Key West (Florida), 31, 39, **48**, 52–57, **58**, 59,
    60–67, **69**, **70**, 105, 109, 161, 189, 267
Loggerhead Key (Loggerhead Key, Dry
    Tortugas, Florida Keys), **cp 10**, 31, 57, 72, 81,
    84, **86**, 88, 90–92, **92**, 93, 94, **95**, **96**, 99, **100**,
    161, 186, 189, 206, 267
Maplin Sands Lighthouse (Thames Estuary,
    England), 19 (*see also* Mitchell, Alexander)
Minot Ledge (Cohasset, Massachusetts), **18**, 19
Morro (Havana, Cuba), 76, 136
Northwest Passage (off Key West, Florida
    Keys), **164**, 165, 171–74, **175**, **176**, 179, **180**
Pharos of Alexandria (Egypt), 13, **14**, 15
Ponce de León (Mosquito Inlet, Florida), 30
Rebecca Shoal (off Dry Tortugas, Florida
    Keys), 72, 189, 255, 259–60, **262**, 266, 267, **268**
    (*see also* Beacon: Rebecca Shoal day beacon)
Saint Johns River (Jacksonville, Florida), 30
Sand Key (off Key West, Florida Keys), **cp 8**,
    cp 11, 31, 53, 57, 76, 88, 103, **104**, 109, **115**,
    117, 118, 121, **122**, **123**, 124–25, **126**, 170, 184,
    185, 188, 189, 190, 193, 241, 257, 258, 278n
Sea Girt (New Jersey), 94
Skerryvore Rocks (Scotland), 184, 189
Sombrero Key (off Key Vaca, Florida Keys), **cp**
    6, 31, 57, 85, 88, 181, **182**, 183, 184, 189, 193,
    196, 197, 199, 206, 241, 246, 250, 257, 258,
    286n
South Stack, Holyhead, England, 138
St. Augustine (Florida), 30, 39
Thames estuary light (England) (*see* Maplin
    Sands Lighthouse)
Twin Lights (Navesink, New Jersey), 80
Tybee (Savannah, Georgia), 30
Lightships, 77, 131, 138, **166**
    Caesar, 131–32; *Florida* (also referred to as the
    "Carysfort Lightship"), 132–33, 135–36, 138,
    141; *Honey*, 109, 110; Northwest Passage
    (also referred to as the Key West Lightboat),
    166, 167, 168–69, 170
Lincoln, Samuel B., 38, 51
Linnard, Thomas B., Major, U.S. Army Corps of
    Topographical Engineers, 139

Little Conch Reef, Florida Keys, 213 (*see also*
    Alligator Reef)
Log (*see* Light stations, journals; watch records)
Loggerhead Key, Dry Tortugas, Florida Keys, 75,
    81, 82, 84, 85, 86, 88, 89, 91, 93, 94, 99 (*see also*
    Lighthouses)
Long Key, Florida Keys, 215, 217
Looe (Loo) Key, Florida Reefs, 237, 238, 239, 252
    (*see also* Vessels)
    Marine Sanctuary, 251, 252
LORAN (Long Range Navigation), 155
Louisiana Territory, 22, 75
Lucernes, 145

Mallory, Stephen, Superintendent of Lights
    (1845–1849), 29, 53–54, 109, 170
Mantanas (Mantana) (*see* Indian Key, Florida)
Marine Protection Research and Sanctuary Act,
    252 (*see also* Looe Key)
Marrero, J. F., 190
Marvin, William, Judge, **26**, 28, 41, 73, 74, 183, 239
    (*see also* Admiralty Court)
Maryland, 34
Massachusetts Bay Colony, 15, 16 (*see also*
    Lighthouses: Boston)
Matecumbe, 21 (*see also* Islamorada, Florida;
    Lighthouses: Alligator Reef)
    Lower, 207
    reef, 203
    Upper, 217
Matkov, Becky Roper, 47 (*see also* Dade Heritage
    Trust)
Mayer, Alfred, 102
Meade, George Gordon, Lieutenant, U.S. Army
    Corps of Topographical Engineers, 32, 40,
    111, 114, 139–42, 182, 184–89, 193, 200, 254,
    256–58; Captain, **188**; Major General, 258;
    Commander of the Army of the Potomac, 258
Meade, Richard Worsam (*see* Meade, George
    Gordon)
Mercury, 94, 98
Meuer, W. H., 59 (*see also* Lighthouses: Key West)
Miami, Florida, 33, 45, 46, 47, 198, 231, 233, 234,
    235, 245, 249, 255 (*see also* Lighthouses: Cape
    Florida; Fowey Rocks)
Miami Herald, 120
Miami News, 44
Mineral oil (*see* Kerosene)
Mini Laurel, Inc., 155
Mississippi River, 29, 76, 77, 136
Mitchell, Alexander, 17, 19, 20, 128, 138
Monroe County, 211 (*see also* Indian Key)
Monroe, James, President of the United States, 23,
    50, 107, 205
Morris Island, South Carolina (*see* Lighthouses:
    Charleston)
Mosquito Inlet (*see* Lighthouses: Ponce de León;
    Ponce de León Inlet, Florida)
Mosquito Patrol, 206 (*see also* West Indies
    Squadron)

National Park Service, 99, 102

National Register of Historic Places, 44, 67, 121

National Marine Sanctuary (*see* Florida Keys National Marine Sanctuary)

National Oceanographic and Atmospheric Agency (NOAA), 124, 125, 157, 252

Neill, Fredrick, 105 (*see also* Lighthouse keepers: Rebecca Flaherty)

New England, 22

New Jersey, 49

New Orleans, Louisiana, 22, 82, 136

New Providence (*see* Bahamas)

New River, Florida, 33, 34, 133

New Smyrna, Florida, 133

New York, New York, 22, 87, 109, 114, 131, 203, 213

New York Herald, 81

Newport, Rhode Island, 107, 108 (*see also* Lighthouse keepers: Appleby, Joshua)

Norfolk, Virginia, 107, 201

Northwest Passage, Key West, Florida, 167, 170–71, 174 (*see also* Lighthouses; Lightships)

"Notice to Mariners," 85, 106, 138

O'Brien, John, 168

Optics (*see* Fresnel lens; Directional Code Beacon, DCB; Vega, VRB)
 rotating, 121, 124, 199, 233, 268

O'Shea, J. V., Lieutenant Commander, ATON, 233

Pacific Reef Light, Florida Reefs, 233

Pantelakos, Charlie, Chief Warrant Officer, ANT, 199

Paris, France, 56

Parsons, George W., 142–43, 145–46

Patterson, Alexander L., Captain, Northwest Passage Lightship, 169–70

Paulding & Kemble, Cold Spring, New York, 211, 221 (*see also* Lighthouses: Alligator Reef, Fowey Rocks)

Pearson, R., Captain, 195

Pease, William C., Lieutenant, U.S. Navy, 53–54

Pennekamp Coral Reef Institute, Inc., 157

Pensacola Gazette, 25, 50, 51, 134, 209

Pensacola, Florida, 50, 256

Perry, Madison Starke, 41–42

Perry, Matthew C., Lieutenant Commander, U.S. Navy, 50, 76, 273n

Philadelphia, Pennsylvania, 111, 138, 139, 171, 185, 187, 256
 1876 Centennial, 227

Phillips, G., 87

Phoenix Iron Company, Trenton, New Jersey, 240 (*see also* Lighthouses: American Shoal)

Pinkney, William, Superintendent of Lights (1824–1829), 52, 77, 132

Piracy, 20, 22, 23, 24, 76, 133, 201, 203–5, 206 (*see also* Porter, David, Commodore, U.S. Navy)

Pirates (*see* Piracy)

Pleasonton, Stephen, fifth auditor of the U.S. Treasury Department, 38, 39, 51, 53, 55, 68, 77, 79, 80, 81, 109, 131–32, 137–38, 168, 170

Ponce de León (*see* de León, Ponce)

Ponce de León Inlet, Florida, 30 (*see also* Lighthouses)

Porpoise Island (*see* Sand Key, Florida)

Port Rodgers, 273n (*see also* Key West; Rodgers, John, Commodore, U.S. Navy)

Porter, David, Commodore, U.S. Navy, **20**, 24, 50, 52, 107, 135, 205

Porter, David Dixon, Lieutenant, U.S. Navy, 20, 40, 135, 136

Presidential Reorganization Act (1939), 64, 68, 217

Pusey, Jones & Company, Wilmington, Delaware, 221, 223 (*see also* Lighthouses: Fowey Rocks)

Putnam, George R., Commissioner of Lighthouses, 68

Quicksands, Florida Reefs, 255, 267 (*see also* Rebecca Shoal)

Radar, 250 (*see also* Beacon: radar, RACONS)

Radio, 245–46

Radio beacon, 94, 100, 232, 233, **234**

Rappahannock River, 258

Rebecca Shoal, Florida Reefs, 29, 255, 256, 257, 259 (*see also* Lighthouses)

Reef Lights, 29, 125, 199, 219, 233, 240, 251, 266

Reef(s), 21, 22, 24, 29, 39, 40, 41, 42, 44, 49, 50, 53, 71, 73, 74, 75, 76, 77, 79, 80, 81, 82, 92, 102, 107, 118, 125, 127, 131, 147, 156, 185, 223, 238, 239, 240, 251

Reflector(s), 17, 40, 55, 77, 80, 81, 105, 108, 141, 142

Revolving light, 17, 80, 94, 98, 105, 111, 112, 142, 145, 188
 machinery, 148, 152–53, 154, 214, 243, **246**

Ricker, M. D., Captain, 134–35

Rock Key Channel, 109 (*see also* Key West; Sand Key)

Rodgers, John, Commodore, U.S. Navy, 77, 78, 273n

Rodgers, Woodes, 22 (*see also* Bahamas)

Rollins, W., Captain, 135, 239

Roman Empire
 Lighthouses, 15

Romans, Bernard, 207, 209

Roosevelt, Franklin D., President of the United States, 64
 Reorganization Order No. 11, 64

Rosenstiel School of Marine and Atmospheric Science, 162–63

Rotating optics (*see* Optic)

Rules of wrecking (*see* Salvage law)

Saint Augustine, Florida, 50, 51, 52, 133, 209

Salas, Juan P., 49

Salvage, 23, 24, 25, 28, 34, 49, 107, 183 (*see also* Wrecking; Wrecking license)

Salvage (*cont.*)
award, 25, 26, 28, 72, 74, 78, 132
law, 24, 26, 28–29, 72
Salvagers (*see* Wreckers)
Sambo Keys, Florida Reefs, 25, 50, 51, 52 (*see also*
Lighthouses: Key West)
Sand Key, Florida Reefs, 29, 103, 109, 110–11, 114,
118, 120–21, 169, 170, 237, 259 (*see also* Key
West; Lighthouses)
Sand Key Weather Station, Florida, **115**, 118 (*see
also* Doharty, C. J.)
Sergeant, Margaretta, 140 (*see also* Meade, George
Gordon)
Savannah, Georgia, 136
Sayer, Robert (*see* Jefferys, Thomas)
Screwpile lighthouse, 13, 17, 19, 20, 110, 111, 112,
127, **128**, 138–39, 140, 184, 237, 258, 260 (*see
also* Lighthouses: American Shoal,
Brandywine Shoal, Carysfort Reef, Minot's
Ledge, Rebecca Shoal, Sand Key, Sombrero
Key)
Sea Air Land Technologies, Inc. (SALT),
Marathon, Florida Keys, 219
Seminole War (Second), 30, 33, 133, 139, 210
Seventh Lighthouse District, 64, 235, 263, 266 (*see
also* U.S. Coast Guard)
Shansbury, Howard, Captain, 129
Shaw, Harry, 266
Shinn, Eugene, 155–56
Simonton, John Watson, 22, 23, 49–50
Singer, F., lighthouse inspector, 262–63
Slaves, 84, 88, 277n (*see also* Lighthouses:
Loggerhead Key; Fort Jefferson)
Smith, Ann, 120 (*see also Miami Herald*)
Smith, Edmund, 133
Smith, Keeney, and Halloday, 55 (*see also*
Lighthouses: Key West)
Snedaker, Samuel, Dr., 163
Solar power, 100, 121, 199, 219, 232, 233, 235, 267,
268 (*see also* Flash tube array; Vega Rotating
Beacon, VRB)
panels, 121, 124
Soldier Key, Florida, 223 (*see also* Lighthouses:
Fowey Rocks)
Sombrero Key, Florida Reefs, 21, 183, 184, 189,
237, 259 (*see also* Lighthouses)
South Carolina, 110, 238
Charleston, 23, 38, 107
Southwest Channel, Key West, Florida, 109 (*see
also* Key West; Sand Key)
Spain, 21, 22, 23, 195
Spanish (sailors, ships), 22, 74, 135, 238, 241
Florida, 131
Sperm oil (*see* Whale oil)
Stansbury, Howard, Captain, U.S. Army Corps of
Topographical Engineers, 139
Stevenson, Alan, 188–89
Straits of Florida (*see* Florida Straits)
Sun valve, 175

Swift, William H., Captain, U.S. Corps of
Topographical Engineers, 19 (*see also* Minot's
Ledge Lighthouse)

Tallahassee, Florida, 56
Tavernier, Key Largo, Florida Keys, 217
Territory of Florida, 24
Thompson, Smith, Secretary of the U.S. Navy, 23,
49, 107, 273n
Thompson's Island, 24, 273n (*see also* Key West)
Tortugas (*see* Dry Tortugas)
Totten, James, Lieutenant, U.S. Army Coast
Survey, 206, 239
Totten, Joseph G., Colonel, Chief Engineer, U.S.
Army Corps of Engineers, 276n
Triumph Reef Light, Florida Reefs, 233
Trinity House, 15, 17
Turtle Shoal (East and West) Florida Reefs, 186
(*see also* Lighthouses: Sombrero Key)

U.S. Army, 90 (*see also* Fort Jefferson)
U.S. Army Corps of Topographical Engineers, 19,
84, 127
U.S. Bureau of Alcohol, Tobacco, and Firearms,
121 (*see also* Lighthouses: Sand Key)
U.S. Coast Guard, 31, 45, 64, 66, 94, 100, 102, 121,
123, 125, 153, 159, 179, 196, 197, 198, 199,
217, 234, 249, 250, 253, 262 (*see also* Aids to
Navigation, ATON; Aids to Navigation
Team, ANT)
Auxiliary, 99
Civil Engineering Branch, 121
history, **68**
National Aids to Navigation School,
Yorktown, Virginia, 98, 99, 231, 233
U.S. Congress, 16–17, 19, 20, 23, 24, 25, 29, 38, 39,
44, 50, 51, 54, 61, 76, 81, 82, 84, 87, 89, 90,
103, 107, 109, 115, 131, 132, 136, 170, 172,
186–87, 205, 206, 212, 237, 240, 241, 252, 256,
257, 263
U.S. Corps of Topographical Engineers (*see* U.S.
Army Corps of Topographical Engineers)
U.S. Department of Commerce, 68, 146
Lighthouse Service Building, **67**
U.S. Department of Commerce and Labor, 68, 82
(*see also* Light House Board)
U.S. Department of the Interior
Fish and Wildlife Service, 121
U.S. Department of the Treasury, 17, 68
U.S. Department of Transportation, 68
U.S. District Court, Southern District of Florida,
27, 71, 271n
U.S. Lighthouse Service, 64
U.S. Navy, 203, 205, 249
"sea time," 287n
U.S. Treasury Department, 17 (*see also*
Pleasanton, Stephen; Hamilton, Alexander)
U.S. War Department, 90 (*see also* Fort Jefferson)
Union, 56, 72, 87
Army, 258 (*see also* Meade, George Gordon)

United States, 17, 19, 21, 22, 23, 24, 25, 27, 28, 29, 30, 250, 252, 254
Utting, Ashby, Captain, 238 (*see also* Vessels, *Loo*, HMS)

Vaca Key, Florida Keys, 190 (*see also* Lighthouses: Sombrero Key)
Vacher, H. L., 155–56
Vassie, William, 266
Vega Industries Limited, Porirua, New Zealand (*see* Vega Rotating Beacon)
Vega Rotating Beacon (VRB), 99–100, 154, 199, 219, **220**, 235
Vessels (*see also* Wrecking Vessels)
 Ajax, 210; *Alec Owen Maitland*, 155; *Alicia*, **230**, 230–32; *Alice B. Philips*, 232; *Alligator*, USS, 201, 203–5, **204**; *America* (*see* Akin, Lemuel S., Captain); *Ann Maria*, 201, 203; *Antaeus*, 215; *Arakanapka*, 225; *Benwood*, 153; *Billander Betty*, 238; *Brewster*, 41; *Carondelet*, 225; *Carysfort*, HMS, 127; *Champion* (*see* Pearson, R., Captain); *City of New York*, SS., 143; *Cleo*, 252; *Clyde* (*see* Kennedy, Captain); *Columbus Iselin*, 252; *Concord*, 78; *Contship Houston*, 125; *Crown*, 41; *Ellen Hood*, 40–41; *Eliza Mallory*, 41; *Elpis*, 155; *Esmeralda*, 135; *Eugene*, 148; *F. A. Everett*, 240; *Florence*, 78; *Florence Rodgers*, 213; *Fowey*, HMS, 221; *George Stodder*, 51; *Georgia*, U.S. Mail Steamer (*see* Porter, David D., U.S. Navy); *Gil Blas*, 34; *Igo*, 215; *Guerriere*, U.S. Frigate, 201; *Illinois*, U.S. Mail Steamer (*see* Hartsterne, H. J., Lieutenant); *Inwood*, 232; *Isabel* (*see* Rollins, W., Captain); *John Hoven* (*see* Ricker, M. D., Captain); *Isabel*, 135; *La Centella* (*see* Hopner, Charles); *Loo*, HMS, 238–39; *Marion*, U.S. Revenue Cutter, 78; *Mary Ann*, 107; *May Belle*, 232; *Miss Beholden*, 125; *Mississippi*, 239; *Moonstone*, 150; *Morris*, U.S. Navy (*see* Pease, William C., Lieutenant); *Moto*, U.S. Navy, 37; *Nana*, 129; *Nordvahlen*, 265; *Ocean Star*, 41; *Olivette*, 174; *Pacific*, 71, 75; *Rapid*, 190, 241 (*see also* Baker, Charles S., Captain); *Revenge*, 209; *Seagull*, U.S. Navy, 205; *Shark*, U.S. Navy (*see* Perry, Matthew C., Lieutenant Commander); *Shirley* (*see* Heler, Thomas J., Captain); *Standard*, 265; *Stranger*, U.S. Mail Steamer, 206; *Union*, U.S. Mail Steamer (*see* Budd, Thomas S., Captain); *Valbanera*, 265; *Veenbergen*, 265; *Venice* (*see* Young, John, Captain); *Wellwood*, 155; *William*, 81; *Winchester*, TMS, 129, 130, 131; *Yucatan*, 41
Viall, Sara, 106 (*see also* Lighthouse keepers: Appleby, Joshua)

Washington, D.C., 139
Watch room, 42, 61, 66, 84, 91–92, 98, 110, 111–12, **226**, 243
Webb, James, Judge, 78
Wellington, (?), Captain, 141 (*see also* Lightships: *Florida*)
West Indies, 20, 22, 107, 205, 261 (*see also* Porter, David, Commodore)
 Squadron, 20, 24, 50, 205
 Station, 23
Whale oil (sperm oil), 36, 52, 112, 142
Whalton, Felicita Isabela Bucciani (*see* Whalton, John, Captain)
Whalton, John, Captain, 131, 132, 133–34
Whalton, Stephen F., 61–62 (*see also* Lighthouses: Key West)
Whitehead's Point, Key West, Florida, 52, 53 (*see also* Lighthouses: Key West)
Wicker, Frank A., Superintendent of Lights (1873–1883), 172
Wilderness Preservation System, 121 (*see also* Sand Key)
Williams, John Lee, 127 (*see also* Carysfort Reef)
Windmill generator, 232, 266 (*see also* Electricity; Solar power)
Woodbury, Daniel P., Captain, U.S. Army Corps of Topographical Engineers, 84–85, 87, 89, 90 (*see also* Fort Jefferson; Lighthouses: Loggerhead Key)
Woodbury, Levi, Secretary of the Treasury, 80
World War II, 153, 197
World's Columbian Exposition, Chicago, 214, 227 (*see also* Lighthouses: Alligator Reef)
Wrecker(s), 22–23, 24, 25, **28**, 72, 73, 77, 78, 79, 129, 131, 134, 136, 183, **208**, 210, 213, 214, **230**, 232, 239, 240 (*see also* Denison, Silas; Housman, Jacob; Johnson, Charles; Wrecking vessels)
Wrecking, 22, 24, 26
 law, 25
 license, 26, **27**, 72, 107, 210
 register, 31
 Rule of wrecking, 26
Wrecking vessels, 29, 239, 240
 Brilliant, 134; *Champion*, 73; *Ehsha Beckworth*, 73; *Mary Ann*, 107 (*see also* Joshua Appleby); *Pee Dee*, 134; *Plume*, 71; *Sarah Isabella*, 210; *Shepard*, 73; *William Henry*, 209 (*see also* Housman, Jacob)
Wright, Horatio Governeur, Captain, U.S. Army Corps of Engineers, 82, 83–85 (*see also* Fort Jefferson; Beacon: Rebecca Shoal day beacon)
Wrought iron pile lighthouse (*see* Iron pile lighthouse)

Young, John, Captain, 82 (*see also* Lighthouses: Garden Key)

If you enjoyed reading this book, here are some other books from Pineapple Press on related topics. For a complete catalog, write to: Pineapple Press, P.O. Box 3899, Sarasota, FL 34240 or call 1-800-PINEAPL (746-3275).

Georgia's Lighthouses and Historic Coastal Sites by Kevin M. McCarthy with paintings by William L. Trotter. ISBN: 1-56164-143-X (PB)

Guardians of the Lights by Elinor De Wire. Stories of the men and women of the U.S. Lighthouse Service. ISBN: 1-56164-077-8 (HB); 1-56164-119-7 (PB)

Guide to Florida Lighthouses by Elinor De Wire. ISBN: 0-910923-74-4 (PB)

The Florida Keys: A History of the Pioneers by John Viele. ISBN: 1-56164-101-4 (HB)

Key Biscayne: A History of Miami's Tropical Island and the Cape Florida Lighthouse by Joan Gill Blank. ISBN: 1-56164-096-4 (HB); 1-56164-103-0 (PB)

Legendary Islands of the Ocean Sea by Robert H. Fuson. From the diaries and charts of early explorers, the story of the real and imagined islands of what we know as the Atlantic and Pacific Oceans.ISBN: 1-56164-078-6 (HB)

Lighthouses of Ireland by Kevin M. McCarthy with illustrations by William L. Trotter. ISBN: 1-56164-131-6 (HB)

Lighthouses of the Carolinas by Terrance Zepke. ISBN: 1-56164-148-0 (PB)

Search for the Great Turtle Mother by Jack Rudloe with illustrations by Marty Capron. Intrigued by turtle legends from many cultures, Rudloe travels the globe observing the silent rituals of sea turtles. ISBN: 1-56164-072-7 (HB)

Shipwrecks of Florida: A Comprehensive Listing (second edition) by Steven D. Singer. 2,100 wrecks off the Florida coast from the sixteenth century to the present. ISBN: 1-56164-163-4 (PB)

The Spanish Treasure Fleets by Timothy R. Walton. The story of how the struggle to control precious metals from Spain's colonies in Latin America helped to shape the modern world. ISBN: 1-56164-049-2 (HB)

Thirty Florida Shipwrecks by Kevin M. McCarthy with paintings by William L. Trotter. ISBN: 1-56164-007-7 (PB)